Week

WRITERS AND THEIR

EDITH WHARTON

EDITH WHARTON

EDITH
WHARTON

JANET BEER

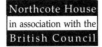
Northcote House
in association with the
British Council

© Copyright 2002 by Janet Beer

First published in 2002 by Northcote House Publishers Ltd, Horndon, Tavistock, Devon, PL19 9NQ, United Kingdom.
Tel: +44 (01822) 810066 Fax: +44 (01822) 810034.

British Library Cataloguing in Publication Data
A catalogue record for this book is available from the British Library

ISBN 0-7463-0898-1

Typeset by PDQ Typesetting, Newcastle-under-Lyme
Printed and bound in Great Britain by
The Baskerville Press, Salisbury, Wiltshire, SP2 7QB

Contents

Biographical Outline

* indicates short story collection.

1862	Edith Newbold Jones born on 24 January, third child of Lucretia and George Jones of New York.
1866–72	Travels in Europe with her family: visits England, France, Italy, Germany, and Spain.
1872	Returns to New York, where her family reside in winter. The summers are spent in Newport, Rhode Island.
1878	A volume of her poetry, *Verses*, is printed privately by her mother.
1879	She makes her debut in New York society.
1880	The family returns to Europe, owing to the ill health of George Jones.
1882	George Jones dies in Cannes. Edith returns to Newport with her mother and is briefly engaged to be married to Harry Stevens.
1883	Meets Walter Berry at Bar Harbor.
1885	Marries Edward Robbins Wharton and makes homes for herself and her husband in New York and Newport as well as travelling in Europe.
1888	Inherits a substantial amount from a cousin and takes an extended Mediterranean cruise.
1889	Poems published in *Harper's*, *Century*, and *Scribner's* magazines.
1891	First published story, 'Mrs Manstey's View', in *Scribner's Magazine*.
1893	Buys her own home, Land's End, in Newport.
1893–5	Period of ill health, suffering from nervous disorders.
1897	Publication of *The Decoration of Houses*, co-written with the architect Ogden Codman Junior.

1899	First volume of short stories, *The Greater Inclination,** published.
1900	First novella, *The Touchstone*, published.
1901	*Crucial Instances** published. Lucretia Jones dies in Paris. The Mount in Lenox, Massachusetts, designed and built.
1902	First novel, *The Valley of Decision*, published.
1903	*Sanctuary* published.
1904	Develops substantially her friendship with Henry James. *Italian Villas and their Gardens* and *The Descent of Man and Other Stories** published.
1905	*Italian Backgrounds* and *The House of Mirth* published.
1907	*The Fruit of the Tree* and *Madame de Treymes* published. Meets W. Morton Fullerton, the American journalist with whom she had an affair. Divides her year between Lenox in the summer and Paris in the winter.
1908	*The Hermit and the Wild Woman** and *A Motor-Flight through France* published.
1909	*Artemis to Actaeon and Other Verses* published.
1910	*Tales of Men and Ghosts** published. Affair with Fullerton comes to an end.
1911	*Ethan Frome* published. Separates from Edward Wharton and sells the Mount.
1912	Living in France. *The Reef* published.
1913	Her divorce is finalized. Publishes *The Custom of the Country*.
1914	Travels in North Africa. Settles in Paris for the duration of the war.
1915	*Fighting France: From Dunkerque to Belfort* published.
1916	*Xingu and Other Stories** published. Given the honour of the Chevalier of the Legion of Honour in recognition of her war work in France.
1917	*Summer* published. Visits Morocco.
1918	*The Marne* published. Buys a house to the north of Paris called Pavillon Colombe.
1919	*French Ways and their Meaning* published.
1920	*The Age of Innocence* and *In Morocco* published. Establishes a winter home in Hyères in the south of France.
1921	Pulitzer prize for *The Age of Innocence*.
1922	*The Glimpses of the Moon* published.

1923	Makes her final visit to America to receive honorary doctorate from Yale University. Publishes *A Son at the Front*.
1924	*Old New York* published.
1925	*The Mother's Recompense* and *The Writing of Fiction* published.
1926	*Here and Beyond** and *Twelve Poems* published.
1927	*Twilight Sleep* published. Death of Walter Berry.
1928	*The Children* published. Death of Edward Wharton.
1929	*Hudson River Bracketed* published.
1930	*Certain People** published.
1932	*The Gods Arrive* published.
1933	*Human Nature** published.
1934	*A Backward Glance* published.
1936	*The World Over** published.
1937	Dies on 11 August in Paris; buried in Versailles. Posthumous publication of *Ghosts*.*
1938	Posthumous publication of *The Buccaneers*.

Abbreviations

AI	*The Age of Innocence* (New York: D. Appleton & Co., 1920)
B.	*The Buccaneers* (New York: D. Appleton-Century Co., 1938)
BG	*A Backward Glance* (London: Constable & Co., 1972)
C.	*The Children* (New York: D. Appleton & Co., 1928)
CC	*The Custom of the Country* (New York: Charles Scribner's Sons, 1913)
EF	*Ethan Frome* (London: Constable, 1976)
FF	*Fighting France: From Dunkerque to Belfort* (New York: Charles Scribner's Sons, 1915)
FT	*The Fruit of the Tree* (New York: Charles Scribner's Sons, 1907)
FWM	*French Ways and their Meanings* (New York: D. Appleton & Co., 1919)
GAM	'The Great American Novel', *Yale Review*, NS 16 (July 1927)
GM	*The Glimpses of the Moon* (New York: D. Appleton & Co., 1922)
GS	*The Ghost Stories of Edith Wharton* (New York: Charles Scribner's Sons, 1973)
HM	*The House of Mirth* (London: Oxford University Press, 1936)
HRB	*Hudson River Bracketed* (New York: D. Appleton & Co., 1929)
IA	'Italy Again', unpublished manuscript, Beinecke Library, Yale University
IB	*Italian Backgrounds* (New York: Charles Scribner's Sons, 1905)
IM	*In Morocco* (New York: Charles Scribner's Sons, 1920)
IVG	*Italian Villas and their Gardens* (New York: da Capo Press Inc., 1988)

L.   *The Letters of Edith Wharton*, ed. R. W. B. Lewis and Nancy Lewis (London: Simon & Schuster Ltd, 1988)

L&I   'Life and I', unpublished manuscript, Beinecke Library, Yale University

Lit.   'Literature', unpublished manuscript, Beinecke Library, Yale University

MFF   *A Motor-Flight through France* (New York: Charles Scribner's Sons, 1908)

MR   *The Mother's Recompense* (New York: D. Appleton & Co., 1925)

Notes   Notes toward an Essay on Walt Whitman, unpublished manuscript, Beinecke Library, Yale University

NYD   *New Year's Day* (New York: D. Appleton & Co., 1924)

OM   *The Old Maid* (New York: D. Appleton & Co., 1924)

QDS   'Quaderno della studente', manuscript notebook, Beinecke Library, Yale University

R.   *The Reef* (New York: D. Appleton & Co., 1912)

ROS   *The Reckoning and Other Stories*, ed. Janet Beer (London: Phoenix Paperbacks, 1999)

S.   *Summer* (London: Constable, 1976)

SF   *A Son at the Front* (New York: Charles Scribner's Sons, 1923)

SHRB   Summary of *Hudson River Bracketed*, unpublished manuscript, Beinecke Library, Yale University

SN   'Subjects and Notes 1918–1923', manuscript notebook, Beinecke Library, Yale University

Sp.   *The Spark* (New York: D. Appleton & Co., 1924)

TS   *Twilight Sleep* (New York: D. Appleton & Co., 1927)

UCW   *Edith Wharton: The Uncollected Critical Writings*, ed. Frederick Wegener (Princeton: Princeton University Press, 1996)

VD   *The Valley of Decision* (New York: Charles Scribner's Sons, 1902)

WF   *The Writing of Fiction* (London: Charles Scribner's Sons, 1925)

Introduction

During her lifetime, and after, Edith Wharton could never escape the attentions of those who wished to label her as a writer whose art was of secondary importance to the other facts of her life. She was often described by a literary establishment wishing to put her and her enormous popularity in a smaller, less eminent place as a *grande dame*, detached from the real business of American letters, or as a pale imitator of her friend, Henry James. For many of her contemporaries and for succeeding generations, her work often seems to have been considered as secondary to the interest generated by her life and, indeed, her lifestyle. Even where her art is the matter under consideration, the critics have had difficulty in focusing on the work alone. She was berated in her early work for exposing the secrets of old New York to the attentions of the general public and criticized again in her later life for writing about an America that her long residence in France supposedly disqualified her from understanding. She was admonished for writing about working-class Americans, especially in her New England novellas *Ethan Frome* (1911) and *Summer* (1917), but also for writing about the leisure-class Americans of the Jazz Age and the manner in which they conducted their lives in the fashionable resorts of both America and Europe. To a certain extent this atmosphere of disapprobation was a central plank of the relationship she built up with the reading public as well as the critical establishment, although it was never one that she was comfortable with; for example, she instructed her publisher, Scribner's, to remove the words 'for the first time the veil has been lifted from New York society' from the jacket of her novel *The House of Mirth* (1905),[1] as she found the claim sensationalist and vulgar.

Edith Wharton could be said to have had a literary life, but this was a life she struggled to achieve for herself: turning her back on the leisure-class New York of her youth and making friends among many of the most cultured men and women of her generation in both Europe and America, keeping up her writing through the most difficult personal and cultural upheavals, and entering with gusto into the magazine and publishing house marketplace. She earned an enormous amount of money from her fiction, and had, as a result of the combination of these earnings and her inherited wealth, an extremely glamorous and affluent lifestyle. That she would have seen herself as impoverished in particular areas of personal fulfilment – her lack of a formal education, for instance, or her failure to sustain a romantic relationship with a man she could both love and respect intellectually – does not detract from the simple fact that her life was conducted at a high pitch of luxury and privilege. She married, but did not have children; she carried huge responsibilities for dependent relations and employees and, in the war years in France, for significant numbers of refugees; she had many friends but always felt herself deprived of familial and romantic love. These might seem like small complaints to make of a life that saw massive fame and public recognition, financial as well as aesthetic success, but it was an abiding source of unhappiness to Edith Wharton that she never found a soulmate to share the life of the mind as well as the body and her fiction is a constant testament to this disappointment. A passage marked in Wharton's copy of the collected *Essays* of George Eliot poignantly expresses her sense of that which a woman could bring to a relationship, here in the context of a discussion of Madame de Sablé: 'In this consideration consisted her pre-eminent charm: she was not a genius, not a heroine, but *a woman whom men could more than love* – whom they could make their friend, confidante and counsellor; the sharer, not of their joys and sorrows only, but of their ideas and aims' (emphasis in original).[2] Edith Wharton could count some of the most eminent men and women of the age amongst her friends; the dedications in the books in her library bear ample witness to her personal and professional importance to individuals ranging between Theodore Roosevelt, who wrote in the copy of *America and the World War* that he gave

2

her 'To Edith Wharton from an American-American! Theodore Roosevelt Feb 6th 1915', and Henry James, who sent her a copy of *The Golden Bowl* inscribed 'in sympathy'![3]

Edith Wharton's career has been susceptible to division by critics old and new into periods of high artistic achievement and periods of lower, potboiling journeywork, categories that actually have little coherence in a writing life that spanned forty years and a multiplicity of different genres. Wharton's most highly rated works – *The House of Mirth, Ethan Frome, The Custom of the Country, The Age of Innocence* – date between 1905 and 1920 and have had enduring popularity with a wide range of readers. Some of the works dismissed by the critics on publication in the 1920s and 1930s, however, found new audiences later in the century, with novels like *The Mother's Recompense* (1925) and *Twilight Sleep* (1927) attracting substantial critical interest.

In this book I will be looking at fiction and non-fiction from the whole of Wharton's writing life – from 1899 until her death in 1937 – talking about generic and thematic links between texts and discussing her critical, travel, and autobiographical writing in tandem with her life. I want to begin, however, with an overview of recent critical and biographical approaches to Edith Wharton and her work, detailing the range of responses since the resurgence of interest in Wharton's writing, which dates from the 1970s and the opening of the Wharton archives at the Beinecke Library, Yale University.

The first major account of the writer to be published after the archive material became accessible was R. W. B. Lewis's *Edith Wharton* (1975),[4] a detailed biography, which was closely followed by Cynthia Griffin Wolff's *A Feast of Words: The Triumph of Edith Wharton* (1977), a more critical study, which offers insights derived from psychoanalysis. Both these critics have been extremely influential in Wharton studies and, whilst others have followed, most recently Shari Benstock in her biography, *No Gifts from Chance: A Biography of Edith Wharton* (1994), their work provided the foundation for the large numbers of critical discussions of the writer that have been published subsequently. Lewis's biography was the first to benefit from full access to her personal papers, placed in the Beinecke Library at Yale University on Wharton's instruction, and he provides an overview of the cultural context of her life in both Europe and America, whilst Wolff's study explicates the works with insights derived from details of the life.

In other studies of the writer, the dominant mode is clearly feminist, as is to be expected in a critical climate that has been one of retrieval, rescuing Wharton the artist from her pigeon hole as 'friend of Henry James' or genteel 'lady writer', and placing her, fleshing her out, in the literary, social, and intellectual context of her age. Critics of Wharton have been much concerned with questions of genre, as Wharton wrote in so many different modes: short story, novella, novel, autobiography, literary criticism, art history, travel book, interior design, and cultural criticism being amongst the most obvious; but her life has continued to attract a good deal of attention and the vast majority of her critics also take account of the details of her personal life. Recently Frederick Wegener has edited and introduced *Edith Wharton: The Uncollected Critical Writings* (1996), and so the majority of her known work is now available in published form, accessible to scholars all over the world for whom she is a mainstream – not peripheral – figure in early twentieth-century American literature. The work of two other Wharton scholars has also been of great significance in the last few years, both in the fields of bibliography. The first, Sarah Bird Wright, has produced three important books: an edited edition of Wharton's travel writings, *Edith Wharton Abroad: Selected Travel Writings, 1888–1920* (1995), a critical analysis of *Edith Wharton's Travel Writing* (1997), and the *Edith Wharton A to Z* (1998), an invaluable guide to all aspects of Wharton's life and works. The work of the final scholar I wish to mention, however, is likely to be as instrumental in facilitating Wharton scholarship in the twenty-first century as the opening of the Yale archive was in the twentieth. The bookseller George Ramsden has spent sixteen years reassembling the surviving books from Edith Wharton's library into a collection that number approximately 2,600 volumes. The books corroborate and flesh out the nature and extent of Wharton's appetite for philosophy, literature, religion, science, and social science that is visible in her writing and, of course, her ease and familiarity with a numbers of different European languages. The annotations in her books are in English, French, and German and the precocity of her understanding of foreign languages and of complex intellectual issues is evident from the annotations in the books she was reading with her friend Emelyn Washburn when she was a teenager. The books in Edith Wharton's library provide an invaluable and inspiring resource and I would like to record my thanks and gratitude here to George Ramsden, whose long labour of love has retrieved and restored the integrity of her book collection.

1

Travel Broadens the Mind

Edith Wharton, née Jones, was first taken to Europe at the age of 4. Her parents were endeavouring to escape the deleterious effects a slump in property values was having upon their income and it was felt that the family could live more comfortably in Europe. So, in November 1866, the family set sail for England, later moving on to France, but also spending substantial portions of time in Italy, Spain, and Germany. Six formative years in Europe were sufficient to induce what the adult Edith Wharton would describe as her lack of affection for either the rural or the urban American landscape. On her return to Lenox, Massachusetts, site of the Mount, the American home to which she was most committed, she described her feelings in a letter to a friend, Sara (Sally) Norton of 5 June 1903:

> My first few weeks in America are always miserable, because the tastes I am cursed with are all of a kind that cannot be gratified here, & I am not enough in sympathy with our 'gros public' to make up for the lack on the aesthetic side. One's friends are delightful; but we are none of us Americans, we don't think or feel as the Americans do, we are the wretched exotics produced in a European glass-house, the most déplacé & useless class on earth! All of which outburst is due to my first sight of American streets, my first hearing of American voices, & the wild, dishevelled backwoods look of everything when one first comes home! You see in my heart of hearts, a heart never unbosomed, I feel in America as you say you do in England – out of sympathy with everything. And in England I like it *all* – institutions, traditions, mannerisms, conservatisms, everything but the women's clothes, & the having to go to church every Sunday. (L. 84)

The course of Edith Wharton's life and work can, in many ways, be understood with reference to the two passions that fuelled this outburst to Sara Norton. One, her profound aesthetic sense, nurtured in European scenes and kept alive by her regular foreign travels – exposure to the 'great inheritance of the past' (*VD* 107), as she would describe it – and the other, the ability to comprehend, as only the outsider can comprehend, something of the substance that humanizes a landscape, something of the interconnectedness of people and place that gives meaning to the individual and the collective life of a culture. That Edith Wharton felt herself out of sympathy with her native land did not mean that she did not understand it: her discomfort was perhaps one of the chief sources of inspiration for her work as writer both of fiction and of cultural criticism. Throughout her writing life she sought to communicate her sense of the importance of place, of literal terrain, but also the landscape of the imagination, her own powers of invention and expression being most freely exercised in the Old but on the subject of the New world.[1]

Edith Jones married Edward Robbins Wharton, a Bostonian in his middle thirties, in 1885; she had been engaged before, but that relationship had come to grief, and her mother, responsive to the social view that said that girls should be married young or risk the fate of the old maid, was eager to see her daughter settled. The marriage, though not really a love match, was in many ways liberating for Wharton, as from this point on she was free, much freer than other women of her era because of her independent wealth, to choose the lifestyle she wanted. At first she moved in familiar grooves: dividing her time in the United States between New York and Newport, Rhode Island, and travelling for a substantial portion of each year in Europe. During the early years of her marriage Wharton followed substantially the predictable pattern of activities for a woman of her class, but her literary tastes and her discontent with the absence of intellectual pursuits or stimulation led her to make friends with those whose interests went beyond the social whirl of leisure-class New York. One of these friends was the architect Ogden Codman Junior and it was in collaboration with Codman that Wharton co-wrote her first book, *The Decoration of Houses* (1897), a treatise on interior design. This project was significant for many reasons but chiefly because it was during the composition of this book that Wharton, as she later said in her autobiography, *A Backward Glance* (1934), learnt 'whatever I know about the writing of clear concise English' (*BG* 108), a facility that she attributed in part to the constructive criticism of one of her closest friends, the international lawyer Walter Berry. The influence of Berry and other friends, like Egerton Winthrop, a New Yorker of taste with the leisure time in which to exercise it, was crucial to her intellectual development at this time in her life. As she had not received anything like a formal education, she felt in need of guidance, which, as she says, Winthrop was able to provide:

> It was too late for me to acquire the mental discipline I had missed in the schoolroom, but my new friend directed and systematized my reading, and filled some of the worst gaps in my education. Through him I first came to know the great French novelists and the French historians and literary critics of the day: but his chief gift was to introduce me to the wonder-world of nineteenth century science. He it was who gave me Wallace's 'Darwin and Darwinism', and 'The Origin of Species', and made known to me Huxley, Herbert Spencer, Romanes, Haeckel, Westermarck, and the various popular exponents of the great evolutionary movement. (*BG* 94)

The result of this introduction to the social and natural scientists was one of the most important intellectual breakthroughs for Edith Wharton. The language and imagery of Darwinism permeate her fiction, most obviously in *The House of Mirth*, where it finds expression in the naturalistic thrust of events towards Lily Bart's destruction; Lily is depicted as a creature without the survival skills necessary to sustain life in the competitive world of the twentieth century. *The Age of Innocence* (1920), Wharton's Pulitzer prize-winning novel, also makes extensive use of insights gained from the social and natural scientists, as she commemorates a generation of New Yorkers expiring in 'the airless atmosphere of a perfectly irreproachable existence' (*AI* 50), entombed even before they become extinct.

Whilst her husband, known universally as Teddy, shared some of Wharton's interests, most notably travel and the keeping of small dogs, he was not an astute or stimulating companion and so Wharton's friendships with men like Berry and Winthrop in the early years, and Henry James, Bernard Berenson, and Geoffrey Scott later, were of crucial importance to her. It was not, however, until the early years of the twentieth century that the marriage came to seem more of a mental and physical incarceration than a bearable misalignment of interests, and, again, a thematic strain that is carried through the body of Wharton's work concerns relationships in which one partner feels entrapped and restricted by the limitations of the other. Wharton's biographer, R. W. B. Lewis, tells a story in which Teddy, walking with a friend 'a few paces behind Edith... pointed ahead and said: "Look at that waist! No one would ever guess that she had written a line of poetry in her life."'[2] The kind of attitude to art and artists revealed by this comic but sad little incident was finally to wear on Wharton's nerves and produce strains in the marriage that resulted in negative physical and mental reactions in both partners. When one was well the other was sick, when one happy in a particular place the other would be restive, eager for a change of scene; but the disparity between their respective interests and desires turned from the endurable to the intolerable only after Teddy's mental disturbance became more than Wharton could handle. She published her first full-length work of fiction, *The Valley of Decision*, in 1902 and was never again without a writing project, going from strength to strength – in terms of both achievement and public recognition – as a writer of both fiction and non-fiction. Also in 1902 Teddy suffered his first serious mental collapse and, with brief periods of remission, he was never really well again and the marriage ended in divorce in 1913.

In the early years of their marriage, however, the Whartons had travelled regularly to Italy, which was the setting for her first novel and the source of inspiration for her first two travel books: *Italian Villas and their Gardens* (1904) and *Italian Backgrounds* (1905). Herein Wharton was able to put to good use the skills she had acquired in the research and writing for the two prior books, *The Decoration of Houses* and *The Valley of Decision*. *The Valley of Decision* is a historical novel set in eighteenth-century Italy and was Wharton's first venture into the writing of the full-length novel, a great leap forward in terms of the fact that her previous work had been mainly in the short story, but a leap that was attended by both professional and personal uncertainties, some of which she overcame by extensive research in the period. The publication of the novel marked, in many ways, Wharton's final commitment to writing as a career, and, with the treatise on architecture and the novel that spoke of her immersion in the Italian scene already under her belt, she was the natural choice for the *Century* magazine when they commissioned a series of articles on the subject of *Italian Villas and their Gardens*. The essays that make up the book, which was illustrated by Maxfield Parrish, describe the villas that are distinctive to different regions of Italy; Wharton also included brief biographical details of the architects and landscape gardeners whose work she discusses in the text.

This book not only shows Wharton to be a discerning and sensitive interpreter of the Italian landscape; it also provides significant insights into some of the guiding principles of her art. In transmission of the principles of the relationship between house, garden, and landscape she talks of 'the secret to be learned from the villas of Italy' (*IVG* 13) – which is for all artists, writers, architects, and horticulturists alike – to learn how to produce 'a garden as well adapted to its surroundings as were the models which inspired it' (*IVG* 12). This is an aesthetic that is elaborated in her subsequent book, *Italian Backgrounds*, a less specifically focused collection of essays and impressions, which incorporated work from the previous ten years, including an explication of the imbrication of art, architecture, landscape, and the sense of history that she saw reflected in the Italian scene:

> It is because Italian art so interpenetrated Italian life, because the humblest stone-mason followed in some sort the lines of the great architects, and the modeller of village Madonnas the composition of the great sculptors, that the monumental foreground and the unregarded distances behind it so continually interpret and expound each other. Italy, to her real lovers, is like a great illuminated book, with here and there a glorious full-page picture, and between these, page after page of delicately pencilled margins, wherein every detail of her daily life may be traced. And the pictures and the margins are by the same hand. (*IB* 178–9)

This textual metaphor, a frequent device in Wharton's expression of both a life and an art that were given shape and expounded through the printed page and the bound volume, communicates her sense of the interrelatedness of content and form, of style and setting, and of aesthetic coherence.

The lessons learned in her Italian travels and writings were carried further in the books that treated the French landscape, in peace and in war. The features of the French way of life she would offer as the model of civilized living to a – largely indifferent – American audience in her 1919 study, *French Ways and their Meaning*, are enumerated in a series of books, beginning with the volume that has become her best-known travel guide, *A Motor-Flight through France* (1908), which opens, in celebratory tones that would not shame Mr. Toad: 'The motor-car has restored the romance of travel' (*MFF* 1). Again, written to be published as individual essays, this time in the *Atlantic Monthly*, the pieces that make up this collection do not only celebrate the French landscape; they also serve as a form of covert apologia for Wharton's imminent removal to France. Although officially resident in America until 1911, Wharton was well into the process of expatriation at the time of writing and much of her praise for French culture in all its forms is at the expense of America and most particularly the values that are communicated by national architectural priorities:

> the great castle of Philip Augustus... to come on this vigorous bit of mediaeval arrogance, with the little houses of Dourdan still ducking their humble roofs to it in an obsequious circle – well! to taste the full flavour of such sensations, it is worth while to be of a country where the last new grain-elevator or office building is the only monument that receives homage from the surrounding architecture. (*MFF* 32)

This book is replete with the joy of the sensate traveller, but it is also a didactic text brimful of the kind of object lesson that invariably finds the French model to be superior in conception and execution to the American. Wharton writes as 'we', referring to Americans as 'our self-sufficient millions', a people, by implication, resistant to the always 'salutory and surprising example' of French 'municipal pride' (*MFF* 51). National attitudes to the civic are very much at issue here, with America being chastised for its failure to understand the importance of coherence between the public and the private, both morally and architecturally. The tone of the book is often admonitory and the irony is rather too sour to suggest that she has much affection for her compatriots, who are consistently the targets of her mockery as she notes: 'but perhaps only the eye subdued to tin house-tops and iron chimney-pots can feel the full poetry of old roofs' (*MFF* 79).

11

To reflect on Wharton's didactic intent is not, however, to say that the book does not fulfil its expressed intention of communicating a sense of her wonder at the beauty of the French towns and countryside that she and her travelling companions passed through on their 'motor-flight'; there is clear and unforced admiration for the newly revealed stretches of country that had been invisible to travellers formerly limited by 'the approach to each town through the area of ugliness and desolation created by the railway' (*MFF* 1). Wharton undertook some of these travels in the company of her husband and her brother, Harry Jones, others with Teddy and Henry James. She was still moving back and forth across the Atlantic between her home, the Mount, in Lenox, Massachusetts, and a rented apartment in Paris at this time and her sense of the distinctions between American and French landscapes and cultures as she shaped them into the essays published in the *Atlantic Monthly* inevitably contributed to her decision to move on a permanent basis to Paris, a move that was made final by the sale of the Mount in 1911.

Wharton's appreciation and, indeed, love for the French landscape is nowhere more elegiacally recorded than in her book *Fighting France: From Dunkerque to Belfort*, published in 1915. Wharton's purpose here – to convert an American audience to an understanding of the nature of what is at stake in the war and why it is worth fighting for – is transparent. It is also evident throughout the volume that in the war work she undertook Wharton found both personal fulfilment and real engagement with a local, national and international community. The essays tell of her travels through war-torn France; they are informed by her work with refugees, her commitment to the cause, and her determination to witness the horrors of the front line. In a letter to Henry James written at the end of February 1915 she lets him know that she was the first woman to be allowed into the battle zone at Verdun, but also that she had an international audience for her work: 'First they said it was impossible – but the Captain had read one of my books, so he told the Colonel it was alright' (*L.* 348). This letter describes the scene in a church in the village of Blercourt where those soldiers too badly wounded to be transported away from the front were lying in rows in the nave whilst the curé – going about his business – intoned the Canticle of the Sacred Heart: 'Sauvez, sauvez la France, Ne l'abandonnez pas!' – a vignette that finds its way directly into *Fighting France*.

Her unwavering conviction that the whole of Western civilization was threatened by the German onslaught and her active engagement in the war effort were, however, not only expressed through her writing. As refugees poured into Paris, so she set up an organization called the American Hostels for Refugees, which housed, fed, clothed, and also found work for them; she organized the committees that managed this enterprise and established a network in America responsible for fund-raising. She arranged for a stunning array of literary, visual, and other artists – including Thomas Hardy, W. B. Yeats, John Singer Sargent, Henry James, Jean Cocteau, and Claude Monet – to donate prose, poetry, paintings, even musical scores, to a book that was published under the title *The Book of the Homeless* in 1915 – a fund-raising endeavour that, again, was aimed at a primarily American audience.[3]

The six essays in *Fighting France* – the first describing the look and feel of Paris at the beginning of the war, the next four giving accounts of visits to different parts of the front line, and the final essay attempting to encapsulate 'The Tone of France' – have the same educative intent as her earlier travel books, but they are, unsurprisingly, more centrally concerned with the effects wrought by the destruction of the carefully tended and nurtured villages and countryside of France. The tragedy of war for Wharton is expressed in terms that would inform her sense of the relationship between people and landscape throughout her writing career. Her emphasis, as she witnessed the scenes of devastation, is upon the loss of continuity in French life. War not only dislocates people; it also causes havoc with material and territorial identity, so that the annihilation 'of the long murmur of human effort, the rhythm of oft-repeated tasks' (*FF* 4) is, for her, the most terrible feature of the war-torn countryside. Wharton commemorates the fact that the most mundane local knowledge has been lost in the areas that saw the heaviest fighting, and when she describes the ruined settlements she saw 'In Argonne' she seems to be describing the removal of history itself from the landscape, as signposts had been torn down, village names removed, and even the sentinels seemed unaware of the name of the places they were guarding. She testifies to the beauty of everyday life as she details the scenes that so poignantly signify its loss:

> the vision of all the separate terrors, anguishes, uprootings and rendings apart involved in the destruction of the obscurest of human communities. The photographs on the walls, the twigs of withered box above the crucifixes, the old wedding-dresses in brass-clamped trunks, the bundles of letters laboriously written and as painfully deciphered, all the thousand and one bits of the past that give meaning and continuity to the present of all that accumulated warmth nothing was left but a brick-heap and some twisted stove-pipes! (FF 58)

As Kristin Lauer acknowledges in her essay on American attitudes to Edith Wharton – in particular to the work that came out of the war but was published later – 'To see the war in terms of the salvation of French culture was, in the twenties, to be old-fashioned, even reactionary',[4] but Wharton could see the war in no other way – she described what she saw and felt. The necessity to preserve and foster the understanding of French civilization underpins the majority of her writing in peace and in war, even when her ostensible subject is America.

Her final guide to *French Ways and their Meaning*, published in 1919, can be seen to mark a definitive moment in the relationship between Wharton and her reviewers, indeed, between Wharton and her American audience. Although Wharton never became a French citizen – Henry James's adoption of British citizenship in 1915 had not met with her approval – she did act as an apologist and proselytizer for the French way of life as superior to the American and in this book she is straightforward and unashamed of her preferences. Whilst she has some interesting things to say about the role of the French woman in society in contrast to the American woman, who, she says, 'is still in the kindergarten' (FWM 101), the book is, in common with her prior travel books, a teaching text, designed to demonstrate that 'the most profitable way of trying to interpret French ways and their meaning is to see how this long inheritance may benefit a people which is still, intellectually and artistically, in search of itself' (FWM, p. xi).

The impressions that form Wharton's last travel book *In Morocco*, published in 1920, were gained on her trip to North

Africa in 1917. Just as the Italian books had opened up to their readers a set of aesthetic possibilities that Wharton herself was still in the process of assimilating, this text contains much of interest as it probes – albeit gently – a culture so distinct and divergent from western Europe and America that her declaration 'There is no guide-book to Morocco' (*IM* 3) evidences her being forced back into a more genuinely exploratory mode, especially in the chapter that deals with 'Harems and Ceremonies'. However, there is still a large portion of the book that, as the *Nation* reviewer noted, 'accepts without question the general theory of imperialism'[5] and in particular French intervention in North Africa. Her chapter on 'General Lyautey's Work in Morocco' includes a list of works effected by the French Protectorate, which is merely catalogued, not glossed in any way at all; as with all things French, the superiority of the Gallic way at home and abroad is taken, by Wharton, for granted.

The works of non-fiction that follow the books centrally or tangentially concerned with French culture – *The Writing of Fiction* (1925) and *A Backward Glance* (1934) – leave the mission to demonstrate French cultural pre-eminence substantially behind, even though the latter, her autobiography, bears witness to her passion for her adopted country. *The Writing of Fiction* has a line from Thomas Traherne as its epigraph: 'Order the beauty even of Beauty is' – a quotation that also appears in one of Wharton's manuscript notebooks as her personal 'Motto' (QDS). Order was a first principle in life and art for Wharton and her brief discussions of writers and the craft of writing in this book reflect both her prejudices, as she dismisses 'stream of consciousness' and other contemporary trends – 'in certain schools formlessness is now regarded as the first condition of form' (*WF* 14) – and her preferences. She celebrates a number of writers in chapters entitled 'Telling a Short Story', 'Constructing a Novel', and 'Character and Situation in the Novel', chief amongst them James, Eliot, Austen, Balzac, Stendhal, Meredith, Trollope, and Tolstoy; American writers apart from James are hardly mentioned. She does, however, dedicate a whole chapter to an artist less established than the canonical authors who serve as her exemplars in the art of fiction: she ends the book with a discussion of the writing of Marcel Proust, who died in 1922. She admired Proust immensely, and read her own handsomely bound edition of *À la recherche du temps perdu* with a pencil in her hand to correct the printer's errors as well as to mark significant passages. In *The Writing of Fiction* she uses his work to illustrate the selfsame artistic tenets as had been enumerated in her travel books, particularly those treating Italy: she describes him as an artist in the 'great line of classic tradition', because he worked not as an 'unintelligible innovator' but as a 'renovator'. He combines, according to Wharton, a full understanding of the traditions within which he wrote, specifically Racine and Saint-Simon, but, in addition, 'With a general knowledge of letters extending far beyond the usual limits of French culture he combined a vision peculiarly his own; and he was thus exceptionally fitted to take the next step forward in a developing art without disowning its past, or wasting the inherited wealth of experience'(*WF* 153–4). This is the great informing logic of Edith Wharton's work in both fiction and non-fiction, in autobiography as much as in literary criticism or travel writing, and it is amply illustrated in *The Writing of Fiction*. She wanted to exegeticize the manner in which tradition could be built upon, adapted to new surroundings or new purposes in art, in culture, and in the business of living; to repeat the phrase from *Italian Villas and their Gardens*, both her creed and her educative mission were founded on the practical aesthetics of producing 'a garden as well adapted to its surroundings as were the models which inspired it' (*IVG* 12).

In all sorts of ways the impetus for telling the story of her own life follows the same pattern as the momentum behind the writing of her previous works of non-fiction: the desire to explain the aesthetic effect, whether it is the effect of a culture, a landscape, or, as in the case of the autobiography, a writer. In her unpublished and published autobiographies Wharton was seeking to account for the phenomenon of Edith Wharton: her emphasis is on her exceptionalism, on the extraordinary fact of a writer being produced from what was a largely philistine and certainly reactionary social background. *A Backward Glance* has always been considered as something of a disappointment as an autobiography because of its reticence but also for its reluctance to contend with the structural and linguistic complexities of the retrospective view. However, it can be made to yield a different kind of interest if considered in relation to her earlier attempts to write versions of her own life and, in particular, her interest in tracing her own development as a creative artist.[6] *A Backward Glance* is, therefore, of most interest not as the story of a life told in full and intimate detail but for its account of that which the 70-year-old writer wished to memorialize about the society from which she came and which she subsequently adapted to her own purposes. It is possible to gain insight into the interpretations she wished to put upon various of the features of her New York upbringing by examining, briefly, her account of the influence of her mother, Lucretia Jones, and the excision of both her husband, Teddy Wharton, and her lover, Morton Fullerton, from her memoir, and the substitution of her friendship with Walter Berry as the central defining relationship of her life.

Wharton made a number of attempts to tell her own story through the medium of both fiction and autobiography. Around 1913 she was working on a novel to be called 'Literature', into which are incorporated some of the formative experiences of her own childhood but here translated into the life story of a fictional character called Richard Thaxter. There are eight fully written chapters as well as a detailed plan of the whole novel in the Wharton archives at Yale University, but the manuscript breaks off at the point where the artist passes from child to manhood. Similarly Wharton's first attempt to set down her own story in a straightforward way, 'Life and I', probably written around 1922, does not proceed much beyond the end of girlhood and again remained unpublished in her lifetime. It seems likely that she did not get very far with this version because it is more candid about her mother and the ill effects of Lucretia Jones's narrow and somewhat arbitrary domestic regime than Wharton actually thought it prudent to be – at least in public. For instance, in the telling of a story about the day before her wedding when she asked her mother 'What being married was like' she leaves the reader in no doubt about her feelings when her mother refused to give her any real help, simply reminding her in the coldest of manners that 'men are made differently from women'. Wharton's verdict on this encounter, as retold in 'Life and I', is unequivocal:

> The dreaded moment was over, & the only result was that I had been convicted of stupidity for not knowing what I had been expressly forbidden to ask about or even think of!...I record this brief

conversation because the training of which it was the beautiful and logical conclusion did more than anything else to falsify & misdirect my whole life'. (L&I, ellipsis in original)

The tragic effects wrought in Wharton's emotional life by her mother's narrow edicts and frigid demeanour, in particular, Lucretia Jones's failure to communicate with her daughter on any but the most distant level, are candidly explored in the early autobiographical fragment. However, in *A Backward Glance*, Wharton describes one of Lucretia's many arbitrary rules – that her daughter was forbidden to read novels – as having conferred many benefits:

> In a day when youthful innocence was rated so high my mother may be thought to have chosen a singular way of preserving mine when she deprived me of the Victorian novel but made me free of the Old Testament and the Elizabethans. Her plan was certainly not premeditated; but had it been, she could not have shown more insight. Those great pages, those high themes, purged my imagination; and I cannot recall ever trying to puzzle out allusions which in tamer garb might have roused my curiosity'. (*BG* 72)

In the formal autobiography the impetus behind the writing is to locate the role of her mother in an account of the accomplished fact of the mature, successful artist, not to revisit the pain of the young woman approaching significant events in her life. Wharton gives her mother credit for as much as she possibly can in *A Backward Glance*; she talks about the difference that her age has made to her appreciation of the manner of her upbringing: 'I used to say that I had been taught only two things in my childhood: the modern languages and good manners. Now that I have lived to see both these branches of culture dispensed with, I perceive that there are worse systems of education' (*BG* 48). Thus the closed mind of Lucretia Jones is seen to have been wise and worthy after all. Similarly, in the relentless urge towards the positive in her published autobiography, Wharton celebrates her relationship with her lifelong friend, Walter Berry, as one that need not be attended by the difficulties of dealing with the decline of her relationship with her husband or of giving away the secret of her affair with the American journalist, Morton Fullerton, with whom she was involved between 1908 and 1910.

18

Teddy Wharton receives only brief direct mention in *A Backward Glance*, once at the point of their marriage and again when she describes his illness, 'the creeping darkness of neurasthenia' (*BG* 326), as one of the reasons behind her decision to sell her American home, the Mount. Walter Berry, however, whom she had known since 1883, was not only a friend but an adviser; she could satisfy what would otherwise be a lacuna in her story by making him the person with whom she had the most significant relationship of her life, even though most of their friends and contemporaries believed that Wharton would have liked the relationship to have been even more intimate than it was. Although Berry never seems to have found Edith Wharton physically attractive – his tastes in women were for younger, prettier, less intellectual companions – he did bring together the personal and the professional sides of her existence by answering the call of friend as well as mentor, and she forgets any disappointment in the terms of their relationship in order to pay fulsome tribute to him in her autobiography: 'I cannot picture what the life of the spirit would have been to me without him. He found me when my mind and soul were hungry and thirsty, and he fed them till our last hour together. It is such comradeships, made of seeing and dreaming, and thinking and laughing together, that make one feel that for those who have shared them there can be no parting' (*BG* 119). And, indeed, there was no parting, as she was buried in a plot she had bought, adjacent to Berry's, in the Cimetière des Gonards in Versailles in August 1937. She could be unequivocal in her praise of Berry – ironically enough – because he was not husband, lover, or fellow artist. The other most significant relationships with men in her life were with Teddy Wharton, Morton Fullerton, and Henry James, and all were difficult in one way or another; the complexities could not be smoothed over in the same way that Wharton manages in the version of the role of Walter Berry in her creative as well as emotional life in the autobiography.

In *A Backward Glance* Wharton's declared intent is to give an insight into the New York world in which she had her beginnings before it finally disappears, to retrieve the old order that exists only in her memory 'as much a vanished city as Atlantis or the lowest layer of Schliemann's Troy' (*BG* 55) as well as to document her own part in it, not the least of which is the leaving of it. The same sort of conservative world view that set the tone for her wartime writings about France is on display here in her last-minute tribute to her native land and for very many of the same reasons. Just as Wharton had feared that France as she knew it would be swept away by German force – both ideological and literal – in the 1930s, so, from a distance of 3,000 miles and twenty-five years, she also feared that her America, specifically 'the tight little citadel of New York' (*AI* 28) as she called it in her 1920 novel, *The Age of Innocence*, had vanished beyond the power of most people's recall; it would be her aim, in this book, to commemorate it.

A Backward Glance was published in 1934, three years before her death, and although it is obviously not without interest, representing, as it does, the coming-together and rewriting of many earlier attempts to explore some of the formative experiences of her life, it is rather too polite and restrained a text to communicate a real sense of process. At the last Wharton was torn between her wish to portray the society of her birth as a place of settled and established standards and customs and the desire to point out the extraordinary fact that such a society had produced the artist, Edith Wharton. She says, 'I had to fight my way to expression through a thick fog of indifference' (*BG* 122), and the most remarkable thing about the autobiography is the manner in which she constructs the text so as to make a virtue of such indifference. However, earlier in her career, Wharton was less celebratory in her treatment of New York: the first novel she wrote to be set in her own time and place takes a very critical look at the closed world of the leisure classes in the city as it documents the tragic fate of one woman who falls outside the charmed circle of *The House of Mirth* but has none of the resources of an Edith Wharton to prevent her from going under.

2

Writing New York – Old and New

Many of Edith Wharton's novels and stories are set in and around New York and in this chapter I want to focus on three of the best known and most accomplished of these. The texts: *The House of Mirth*, published in 1905, *The Custom of the Country*, published in 1913, and *The Age of Innocence*, published in 1920, represent her work in three periods of distinct creative activity and show to good effect her command of a range of genres. *The House of Mirth* can be said to work broadly within the perameters of American naturalism, *The Custom of the Country*, described by Wharton herself as a 'chronicle-novel' (*BG* 183), follows the traditional pattern of the realist novel of manners, and *The Age of Innocence* is an historical novel, looking back over fifty years to the New York of her girlhood. All three novels have in common their setting, which was Wharton's own, as she describes it in *A Backward Glance*, 'fashionable New York...There it was before me, in all its flatness and futility, asking to be dealt with as the theme most available to my hand, since I had been steeped in it from infancy, and should not have to get it up out of note-books and encyclopaedias' (*BG* 207).

All three novels, in different ways, incorporate a view of leisure-class New York that gives credit to what Wharton would have seen as its virtues whilst also laying bare its failings. She does this not in a sensationalist manner but by weaving the conflicts generated by the clashes between the old and the new in terms of manners, mores, and the people who espouse them. Life in nineteenth-century America, in the upper reaches of society, as she says, again in her autobiography, was in some ways indistinguishable from life in western Europe: 'my French and English friends told me, on reading *The Age of Innocence*, that they had no idea New York life in the ''seventies had been so like that of the English cathedral town, or the French *"ville de province"*, of the same date' (*BG* 175). Things were about to change, however; the new century was clearly – even then – the American century, with the pace of change in the rest of the world being set by the USA in every arena. As James Fenimore Cooper acknowledged in one of the first American historical novels, *The Pioneers*, published in 1823, time moves at a different rate in America: 'Five years had wrought greater changes than a century would produce in countries where time and labor have given permanency to the works of man'.[1]

Wharton could thus exploit the drama generated by a clash of cultures as it is enacted within a society, as the exclusivity of the first families of old New York is breached and battered by the rising generations whose money had been made in the new manufacturing or financial industries. Whilst her own roots were in the 'Reservation', as Ralph Marvell calls Washington Square in *The Custom of the Country* (*CC* 74), she could understand the power and the energy of the new – nothing, after all, could be more American than innovation and experimentation. Madame Olenska, in *The Age of Innocence*, comments: 'It seems stupid to have discovered America just to make it into a copy of another country...Do you suppose Christopher Columbus would have taken all that trouble just to go to the Opera with the Selfridge Merrys?' (*AI* 242).

As has been noted in Chapter 1, Wharton's lexis is deeply indebted to the natural and social scientists, and it is with the anthropologist's eye and language that she registers the irresistible forces of change and development and chronicles the lives of both the survivors and the failures in old and new New York; for example, the financial and social ruin of Lily Bart's father in *The House of Mirth* is starkly recorded: 'To his wife he no longer counted: he had become extinct when he ceased to fulfil his purpose' (*HM* 35). Such figurative language and points of reference are extended further in *The Age of Innocence* in particular by the setting of crucial scenes in the novel in key sites of historical or cultural interest. From the opening scene at the old Opera House through the visit to the Patroon House to the clandestine meeting between Newland

Archer and Ellen Olenska in the Metropolitan Museum, Wharton deploys her protagonists in locations that give precision to the time and place but also point back or forward to significant cultural developments and derelictions.

The House of Mirth, upon publication in October 1905, attracted a good deal of critical attention – both positive and negative – and became an instant best-seller. Wharton had been working, somewhat intermittently, on the book during the two previous years and it began its serialization in *Scribner's Magazine* in January 1905 before she had actually completed it. Novels that exposed the underside of life in New York were not new on the American literary scene – Stephen Crane's *Maggie: A Girl of the Streets*, which depicted life in the slums and the descent of the heroine into prostitution and death, had been published in 1893, and in 1900 Theodore Dreiser had his *Sister Carrie* end her career as an actress in New York, having been started on the road to fame and fortune by living as the mistress of various professional men. Novels that exposed the wrong side of 'the social tapestry' (*HM* 301) of the upper echelons of society were, however, a distinct novelty in American literature. Wharton was uniquely placed to describe the current state of a social set peopled by long-established American families, those who could count 'Signers' of the Declaration of Independence as their ancestors and whose ordered world was about to be thrown into disarray by the power of the fantastically rich 'new-comers on the social stage' (*HM* 132) from the new class 'of big money-makers from the West, soon to be followed by the lords of Pittsburgh' (*BG* 6). Just as Crane and Dreiser had chosen to expose the hypocrisies that stifle and pervert the course of women's lives at the bottom of the social pile in their novels, so Wharton puts Lily Bart at the heart of her narrative in order to communicate a similar message about leisure-class American life at the turn of the century.

Lily Bart, unmarried and dangerously close to 30 years old at the beginning of the story, has been on the marriage market in her native New York since the age of 18 and is still procrastinating over her choice of a husband whilst the pool of available men is growing ever smaller. From the opening page Wharton emphasizes the extraordinary glamour of Lily Bart, first glimpsed standing out from the crowd in Grand Central

Station by the constitutionally inadequate male lead in the novel, Lawrence Selden, a dilettantish bachelor who is sometimes a suitor but more often a critic of Lily and her way of life. This glamour, however, throughout the course of the narrative, becomes less and less viable as a currency. The novel looks at the marriage market in transition between an insular complacency, where like marries like and families form alliances through the union of their offspring, and a more cut-throat world where wealth is a surer guarantor of success than beauty and background. In her book *The Social Construction of American Realism*, Amy Kaplan makes the point that the influx of new money and families into New York at the turn of the century meant that 'Social life was thus gradually moving out of the private dining hall and exclusive ball of the Astor Four Hundred Club[2] to the public stage of the hotel and restaurant where anyone with wealth could come to see and be seen';[3] and it is this enormous shift in the location and conduct of the leisure-class life that is so expertly drawn by Wharton in the novel.

Two of the titles with which Wharton toyed before settling on *The House of Mirth* – which itself comes from Ecclesiastes 7: 4: 'The heart of the wise is in the house of mourning; but the heart of fools is in the house of mirth' – were 'The Year of the Rose' and 'A Moment's Ornament', both of which foreground Lily and her ephemerality rather than the society from which she originates. Although Wharton is specifically charting the course of Lily's downfall, the text provides a much wider picture of a society in transition. A rapidly changing New York is Wharton's chief subject and Lily is a representative of that which is lost in the sprint towards the twentieth century and the abandonment of what Wharton terms in *A Backward Glance* 'the formative value of nearly three hundred years of social observance' (*BG* 5). There are women in the novel who are better equipped than Lily to deal with life in the modern world and these are the women who are adapting to the new opportunities offered by a professional life or who realize that marriage can also be conducted like a profession or trade. Wharton gives us Gerty Farish, a representative of the new breed of middle-class women, who, like Wharton's contemporaries, Jane Addams or Charlotte Perkins Gilman, throws herself into various forms of social work; and she also gives us Bertha Dorset, a woman who is willing to abuse the security that her marriage to the rich dull George Dorset gives her, taking lovers and exploiting to the limit the social power she wields, and ultimately causing the exclusion of Lily from the charmed circle of high society.

Forced by her shrinking income to live more and more by her wits, Lily does attempt to adapt and change, specifically in ways that reflect the movement, already mentioned, of the social elite into a more public, less exclusive, and showier mode of operation. The majority of the most crucial incidents in the novel, in terms of the narrative progression of Lily's slide into obscurity and poverty, are occasions where she is exposed – in public – as having misjudged the extent to which she is qualified or permitted to be a participant in the changing social order. A good example of this is the part she plays in the *tableaux vivants* organized by the Wellington Brys, a wealthy couple new to the city who wish to make an entry into high society, whose house was 'so recent, so rapidly evoked . . . that one had to touch the marble columns to learn they were not of cardboard, to set one's self in one of the damask-and-gold arm-chairs to be sure it was not painted against the wall' (*HM* 143). The portrait that Lily imitates is 'Mrs Lloyd' by Joshua Reynolds, which, whilst displaying her beauty to glorious effect, is rather too revealing of her figure and also, crucially, her availability. As Lily's cousin, Jack Stepney, acknowledges in his comment, 'Really, you know, I'm no prude, but when it comes to a girl standing there as if she was up at auction' (*HM* 171), there is no doubt in anyone's mind that Lily is now publicly vendible and her appearance in this picture leads directly to her representation in another frame, the Trenors' doorway, 'silhouetted against the hall-light' (*HM* 175). This time, however, the easy assumption for those who witness this scene has more serious implications for Lily – that she has taken up the role of Gus Trenor's mistress – and it is an assumption that leads Lily towards a series of ever more ignominious and very public humiliations.

The first of these occurs when she is turned off the yacht *Sabrina* by Bertha Dorset, who, having invited Lily aboard to distract her husband, George, whilst she, Bertha, pursues an affair with Ned Silverton, becomes aware that Lily knows too much and so manufactures a charge of impropriety against her. Bertha Dorset is also responsible for Lily's next public failure as she ruins Lily's position with the Gormers by wielding her superior social powers, 'insinuating horrors' (*HM* 275) about her so that the only position she can obtain, the post of secretary to Mrs Norma Hatch, whose home is the 'Emporium Hotel', takes her beyond the pale to a world where 'Mrs Hatch and her friends seemed to float together outside the bounds of time and space. No definite hours were kept; no fixed obligations existed: night and day flowed into one another in a blur of confused and retarded engagements' (*HM* 300). Wharton sets up the scene at the Emporium as a copy of the old social world but curiously inverted: 'Lily had an odd sense of being behind the social tapestry, on the side where the threads were knotted and the loose ends hung' (*HM* 301), and, as Lily discovers after having left Mrs Hatch, it hardly matters whether she is there or not, she had no duties to perform and, long after she had left, those who wish to believe ill of her still think she is working with Mrs Hatch in some sort of conspiracy to debauch young Bertie Van Osburgh.

Honest toil is finally the only recourse left open to Lily, but she even fails to earn a decent living trimming hats; she is, by her own account, 'a very useless person' (*HM* 336), simply unfit for survival in the competitive modern world. The events that lead up to Lily's death are, from beginning to end, fuelled by what Wharton termed the 'force of negation' (*HM* 52), which will, ultimately, destroy all and everything in its path; Lily is in the vanguard of extinction. In anthropological terms the inhabitants of old New York are all representatives of an endangered species, but it is moral inertia rather than physical incapacity that causes them to self-destruct. It is inevitable, therefore, that into the moral vacuum of the New York streets the restless and voracious energy of Undine Spragg, at once villain and victim in Wharton's 1913 novel, *The Custom of the Country*, will pour, as she takes what she wants from the old order on her way towards no higher goal than the gratification of her huge appetite for pleasure. Lily Bart dies with her morals and her principles intact; she refuses to use the Dorset–Selden letters as a means to re-enter society; she will not bear witness against Bertha nor will she stay with Norma Hatch once she realizes the object of her marital ambitions. Whilst Lily cannot bring herself to marry, Undine cannot stop getting married; she has no scruples to speak of and certainly none of Lily's personal fastidiousness. As she tosses the telegram that tells her that her husband is lying close to death in New York into the waste-paper bin, so she clinches her role as Peter Van Degen's mistress, all the while noting – dispassionately – that, in the extremity of desire for her, his face 'looked as small and withered as an old man's, with a lower lip that trembled queerly...' (CC 301).

It is possible to expand on the central differences between *The House of Mirth* and *The Custom of the Country* via Wharton's depiction of the central female protagonists. Just as the events of the earlier text follow on from Lily's refusals, either to marry simply for money or to use what she knows to gain power over others, the drama of *The Custom of the Country* flows exclusively from Undine's willingness to exploit – without shame or scruple – whatever opportunity or person is likely to bring her the most money and power. Undine Spragg is the rightful heiress of the mode of conduct set by Bertha Dorset – one of a newly mobilized army of bored, clever, ill-educated women who have no other occupation than the acquisition of clothes, jewellery, lovers, and husbands. Wharton's most magnificent creation, Undine Spragg-Moffat-Marvell-de Chelles-Moffat, is, as we are told, 'the monstrously perfect result of the system' (CC 208); she is pitiable, admirable, and contemptible in equal measure, but doomed to restlessness, always in search of something more. Where the tragedy of Lily Bart – inevitable from the first page of this most naturalist of Wharton's novels – is played out against a social backdrop that Lily both understands and does not wish to undermine, the tragic wastes that Undine leaves behind are as nothing to her. She destroys civilizations as she destroys people – an exaggeration of course, but an exaggeration that highlights another significant difference between the two novels: *The Custom of the Country* is hyperbolic; it is Wharton's first full-length satire, and it marks a shift into a satiric mode that she was to make distinctively her own, particularly in the novels of the twenties: *The Glimpses of the Moon* (1922), *Twilight Sleep* (1927), and *The Children* (1928).

The 'chronicle-novel' is the proper medium for the relent-lessly paced story of Undine Spragg; its breathless sweep through civilizations old and new allows Wharton to register deficiency after deficiency in both the social world and Undine's understanding of it. The explanation of the derivation of

Undine's name given by Mrs Spragg illustrates beautifully Wharton's method of exposing the hermeneutic void behind modes of behaviour and conduct. Mrs Spragg's account of her being named after her father's patented hair-waver glaringly omits the classical derivation – from the story of the water nymph who could gain a soul only by marrying a mortal and bearing a child. Undine is not averse to getting married, as we rapidly discover, but, as she is incapable of committing herself to any of her husbands, she remains, unequivocally, soul-less. In a discussion of the novel in his essay 'The New Novel', Henry James pinpoints the 'satiric light' as the 'only one in which the elements engaged could at all be focused together'[4] and this illumination is crucial to Wharton's characterization of Undine. Satire is always in dialogue, the revealed always intimating the extent of the unrevealed: the text is structured so that what is missing from the social picture or lacking in Undine herself provide unrelentingly ironic points of reference.

Wharton's work in these novels is very much concerned with the question of appearance, not simply the way a woman looks, although this is obviously crucial in both cases; however, where words are often shown to fail or be inadequate to the purpose in hand, appearance, which is often merely the semblance of reality, takes over. The Wellington Brys' house – 'Mrs Bry thinks her house a copy of the *Trianon*; in America every marble house with gilt furniture is thought to be a copy of the *Trianon*' (*HM* 174) – could be simply a remarkable *trompe-l'œil*; the Spragg family live in hotel rooms that are 'known as one of the Looey suites' (*CC* 4), and so it is the appearance of promiscuity that undoes Lily Bart and the appearance of innocence that allows Undine to marry Ralph Marvell. What is seen is invariably a façade; what things are called bears no relation to their derivation and thus they lose their meaning. It is not insignificant that Edith Wharton calls the ocean liner that carries the New Yorkers back and forth across the Atlantic the '*Semantic*' (*CC* 349), as the Atlantic seems to signal the breadth and depth of the gulf of potential misunderstandings between nations as well as social groups, misunderstandings that are expressed with particular vehemence in this novel by Raymond de Chelles in a biting denunciation of American cultural imperialism (*CC* 545).

Satire flourished in American letters from its earliest days, the focus often being political and cultural clashes between New and Old Worlds. Washington Irving, for instance, whom Wharton remembers in her autobiography as being a writer acceptable in genteel New York circles because 'he was a gentleman, and a friend of the family' (*BG* 67–8), wrote in a satiric vein that exploited to the full the differences between European and American cultural assumptions. Wharton works in an updated version of this cross-cultural exposure of follies; she is writing of a society that is simultaneously contemptuous of and in thrall to its past – both European and American. Charles Bowen, a man who moves knowingly and ironically between old New York and fashionable Paris, casts a sardonic eye on the behaviour of Americans abroad:

> The dining-room of the Nouveau-Luxe represented, on such a spring evening, what unbounded material power had devised for the delusion of its leisure: a phantom 'society', with all the rules, smirks, gestures of its model, but evoked out of promiscuity and incoherence while the other had been the product of continuity and choice. And the instinct which had driven a new class of world-compellers to bind themselves to slavish imitations of the superseded, and their prompt and reverent faith in the reality of the sham they had created, seemed to Bowen the most satisfying proof of human permanence. (*CC* 273)

There is no compassion in this account, nor even dispassion, such as that with which Bowen notes, in his role as 'sociologist', 'that poor Ralph was a survival, and destined, as such, to go down in any conflict with the rising forces' (*CC* 280). The underlying thrust of Wharton's satire on America at play in Paris – as articulated by Bowen – is a bitter reminder of the message of her work in the non-fiction: that it is wasteful of human ingenuity and aesthetic worth if the past is not valued and preserved whilst also being sensitively adapted to new purposes.

The language used to describe the conduct of the inhabitants of Undine Spragg's world focuses on a gap between the real and the imitation – 'delusion', 'promiscuity', 'incoherence', 'slavish imitations', 'sham' – and, as such, could not be more dismissive of this 'phantom "society"'. In this text Wharton seems emphatic that there is a world elsewhere that is authentic, that is not concerned with mere display, but ascertaining the location of this world raises some difficult questions for the reader of her work. No one in the society depicted in *The Custom of the Country* is immune from criticism and her satire is not confined to the 'new class'. As the reviewer for the *New York Times Review of Books* noted:

> The Marvells and Dagonets of Washington Square are mere ghosts of a narrow past, futile, bloodless, out of touch alike with the 'Invaders' who have swarmed into and captured New York society, and with the people who are doing the real, worth-while work of the world. The possessors of certain aesthetic tastes and a fine sense of probity, but expert in the 'vocabulary of evasion', shirkers to the very backbone, every one of them'.[5]

So, if 'real' life is not to be found in the 'Nouveau-Luxe' or the 'Reservation', then where is it? Wharton had got around this difficulty in *The House of Mirth* by locating the authentic in the working-class home of Nettie Struther, a woman who had, by the conventional wisdom, forfeited her chances of a respectable, comfortable life by having fallen victim to an unscrupulous seducer who then abandoned her. In Nettie's case, however, the fact of her very public fall actually enables her and her husband to put the past behind them; as she says, 'I knew he knew about me' (*HM* 343) and his knowledge of her disgrace means that the worst is acknowledged and incorporated into the principles of their shared life. The visit to the tenement is an epiphanic moment for Lily Bart – 'her first glimpse of the continuity of life had come to her that evening in Nettie Struther's kitchen' (*HM* 348) – but it comes too late to save her from a lonely death. There is no equivalent to the home of Nettie and George Struther on offer in *The Custom of the Country*. Whilst the unremitting nature of the satire lets us know that there should be something better elsewhere, that there must be an essential way of being that allows some more dignity to the individual than that afforded by the relentless quest for greater material satisfaction, no one and nothing here escapes criticism. Even Raymond de Chelles, Undine's third husband and representative of 'the Frenchman of his class, embodying in his lean, fatigued and finished person that happy mean of simplicity and intelligence of which no other race has found the secret' (*CC* 275), is inadequate to the task of embodying, even for Wharton the Francophile, a viable alternative.

The Custom of the Country makes uncomfortable reading, not simply because it is difficult to sympathize consistently with any of the protagonists, but because the novel speaks of too many absolutes – there is no value placed on the process of change, the renegotiation of authority that accompanies great social upheaval. Wharton gives credit to Undine for her performativity, her understanding, for instance, that to enter a social set you have to appear to be in tune with it. Time after time Undine's plasticity enables her to get the thing she wants: 'she had not been ten minutes at table before she found that to seem very much in love, and a little confused and subdued by the newness and intensity of the sentiment, was, to the Dagonet mind, the becoming attitude for a young lady in her situation' (CC 91). Undine is a chameleon; when Charles Bowen calls her the 'monstrously perfect result of the system: the completest proof of its triumph' (CC 208), what is acknowledged is her transformative power – her actions are catalytic to the formation of a new world where well-mannered restraint, and the power of traditions invented by the few for the purpose of excluding the many, are the deities that preside no more. Undine's restless energy is the force of the future; her actions – loathsome though some of them undoubtedly are – expand future possibilities for women. When Mr Dagonet asks Undine what she wants, her reply 'Why, *Everything!*' (CC 96) is not taken seriously enough – what Undine wants, Undine gets, but, as she herself acknowledges, 'things she was entitled to always came to her as if they had been stolen' (CC 488).

In an attempt to predicate cultural difference in *The Custom of the Country* – between prior and current New Yorks, between Europe and America – Wharton does not make enough of the fact that the transactions between generations that produce casualties also produce negotiated settlements, as is evidenced in her other great novel of New York, *The Age of Innocence*. Katherine Mansfield, reviewing *The Age of Innocence* in the *Athenaeum* in December 1920, notes the fine line that Wharton treads in the novel: 'To evoke the 'seventies is to evoke irony and romance at once, and to keep these two balanced by all manner of delicate adjustments is so much a matter for her hand that it seems more like play than work.'[6] Wharton's fiction patrols, sometimes uneasily, a borderline between cultures and

31

ages: she began her writing career in earnest at the turn of the century and her enduring subject is the cross-cultural. In her work in the historical novel, however, she could make a virtue of the crossing of boundaries; she restages the past both to accredit and to estrange it – hence it becomes possible to 'evoke irony and romance at once'. As far as Wharton was concerned, the American historical novel became possible only because of the great upheavals of the First World War; she says in *A Backward Glance*: 'It was growing more and more evident that the world I had grown up in and had been formed by had been destroyed in 1914, and I felt myself incapable of transmuting the raw material of the after-war world into a work of art' and the writing of *The Age of Innocence* provided her with 'a momentary escape' (*BG* 369–70).

Although the novel is still centrally concerned with portraying the conditions of the lives of girls and women, the centre of consciousness and of attention here is male: Newland Archer, scion of a family as well established as Ralph Marvell's and equally as fastidious in his tastes and conduct. Archer is very much a safe pair of hands to whom to entrust the story of old New York; he is the paradigmatic 'middle-of-the-road' hero, as described by Georg Lukács in *The Historical Novel*[7] in discussion of the writing of Sir Walter Scott. Like Scott, Wharton understood that the best person to represent the spirit of the age is not the epic hero, the famous politician, or artist, but the person who can demonstrate what it is to be subject to the uncertainties produced by great social change rather than the person driving through reform. Newland Archer's generation is interstitial – dividing nineteenth- from twentieth-century New York – and, although Archer distances himself from some of the more reactionary opinions of society at large, he is still, ultimately, more reflective than active. His expressed beliefs may be those of the socially advanced, but he is, in terms of both family and profession, irreducibly a spokesman for his class and for the status quo.

In *The Age of Innocence* Wharton is concerned to ensure that the bourgeois origins of the inhabitants of the 'tight little citadel' of New York are fully explicated. Economic security here derives from commercial rather than aristocratic sources, and when Mrs Archer talks about her ancestors as 'respectable

English or Dutch merchants, who came to the colonies to make their fortune' (*AI* 46–7), it is plain that the distance between the Archers and those they fear – the incomers who would bring new enterprise capital into the city at the turn of the century – is not significant; generation will give way to generation; the pace and the inevitability of change are built into every structural nuance of the text. In *The Age of Innocence* Wharton makes a virtue of the fact that it is really only in confrontation, or at the very least in comparison, that a culture is validated as authentic. It takes the experience of Ellen Olenska, representative European here, to shock Newland Archer into a sense of his nation, his class, and his personal stake in cultivating what is best about them; it is Ellen Olenska who is able to explain to him the alternative – the disagreeable taste of 'happiness bought by disloyalty and cruelty and indifference' (*AI* 172).

The story of *The Age of Innocence* is a simple one: Newland Archer is engaged to May Welland; he meets Ellen Olenska, the estranged wife of a European nobleman, and falls in love with her, but it is too late to change his plans to marry and he and Ellen separate. After his marriage he meets her once again, as they are thrown together for a variety of family reasons, and they realize they are still in love. They are contemplating how to achieve a future life together when May, acting on the merest suspicion that she might be pregnant, tells Ellen that she is, at which point Ellen determines to return to Europe to live alone. May and Newland hold a dinner party for Ellen on her last night in the country, at the end of which May tells Newland about the baby. The narrative then speeds forward twenty-six years, bringing the action of the book up to the turn into the twentieth century, as Archer accompanies his eldest son, Dallas, on a visit to Paris, where Ellen Olenska lives. The novel closes as Archer, sitting beneath her window, finds himself unable to keep the appointment to see her made for him by his son, and then, as the shutters on her balcony are closed, he returns alone to his hotel room.

Upon the bare bones of this love triangle Wharton is able to hang the complex anatomy of a society that can be confidently asserted only because it predicates a rare moment of solidarity in the class she portrays in the process of self-destruction in *The House of Mirth* and *The Custom of the Country*. In identifying the

1870s as the culmination of a historic period – here in *A Backward Glance*:

> Social life, with us as in the rest of the world, went on with hardly perceptible changes till the war abruptly tore down the old framework, and what had seemed unalterable rules of conduct became of a sudden observances as quaintly arbitrary as the domestic rites of the Pharaohs. Between the point of view of my Huguenot great-great grandfather, who came from the French Palatinate to participate in the founding of New Rochelle, and my own father, who died in 1882, there were fewer differences than between my father and the post-war generation of Americans (*ABG* 6)

– she claims, at once, tradition and obsolescence. Additionally the in-built self-reflexivity of Newland Archer's narratorial presence – with 'his readings in anthropology' that 'caused him to take such a coarse view of what was, after all a simple and natural demonstration of family feeling' (*AI* 66) – points to a perspective startlingly original for his time but fifty years out of date when compared with Wharton's own. This obsolescence in itself is then instrumental in Wharton's strategy: the narratorial imperative points the reader towards an understanding of the unremitting processes of realignment that attend social issues like boundaries between the public and the private, the designation of high and low culture and gender or class-based distinctions, as well as signalling the constant variation and change in the way in which they are expressed.

The Age of Innocence is, in many ways, a text that brings together all the various strands in Wharton's work in perfect harmony. Her writing, whether in the short story, novella, or full-length novel, is always absorbed by the question of how best to use a form that is consonant with her subject but that will also add complexity and depth. She worked in the genre of the historical novel intermittently – at the beginning of her career in *The Valley of Decision*, in the middle in *The Age of Innocence* and the four novellas collectively published as *Old New York* (1924), and in her last, unfinished, novel, *The Buccaneers* (1938). As can be seen in the earlier discussion of Wharton's travel books, her sense of the past, of the aesthetic and moral imperatives that can be carried forward and adapted to new uses, is always active at the very heart of her own artistic practice and creed. In *The Age of Innocence* she exploits the generic opportunities of the historical novel to the full: this is not merely a costume drama, set in a nebulous moment of the past that is irrelevant to the action; instead, this is a narrative in which the contending forces are whole – cultural as well as individual. Wharton's great triumph in this novel is the effective communication of her recognition that people do not conduct their lives in a void; they are contingent beings who bear witness not only to their age but to the daily reinvention of tradition. For example, in the chapter following Lawrence Lefferts's denunciation of those members of society who countenance new people: 'If things go on at this pace... we shall see our children fighting for invitations to swindlers' houses, and marrying Beaufort's bastards' (*AI* 341), we learn that Dallas Archer is, indeed, to marry Fanny Beaufort, child of a liaison with 'the notorious Fanny Ring' and 'nobody wondered or reproved' (*AI* 355).

When Newland Archer makes the decision to leave Paris without seeing Madame Olenska, it is because he 'honoured his own past, and mourned for it'. To try to attain that which he has, over the course of a long life, come to think of as 'the flower of life' (*AI* 350) in old age would invalidate what had gone before, decisions made according to a code of conduct that, in itself, had conferred relatedness and authenticity upon his existence. Archer is, at the end, as he was in the beginning, 'the dwindling figure of a man to whom nothing was ever to happen' (*AI* 228), but, like Edith Wharton, he is in possession of a past that may have 'bent and bound him' (*AI* 355) but that also gave him the intellectual and emotional security to see beyond it.

35

3

The Shorter Fiction

Throughout her career Edith Wharton was a prolific writer of short stories and novellas; her first published fiction was a short-story collection entitled *The Greater Inclination* (1899) and the last book of new fiction she published before her death was also a collection of tales, *The World Over* (1936). Her experimentations with the form of the short story and the novella shadowed her work in the writing of full-length fictions; she was able to tease out problems of genre, style, setting, and theme in the shorter fiction, working with the historical, the gothic and ghostly, with manners and with local colour in ways that were of direct use to her in the structuring and management of material in her longer narratives.

Wharton often reflected, in correspondence and in her critical writing, on the characteristics and the utility of the short-story form; it was a genre in which she felt comfortable and confident. In a letter to Robert Grant, written in response to his comments on her novel *The Fruit of the Tree*, published in 1907, she says:

> As soon as I look at a subject from the novel-angle I see it in its relation to a larger whole, in all its remotest connotations; & I can't help trying to take them in, at the cost of the smaller realism that I arrive at, I think, better in my short stories. This is the reason why I have always obscurely felt that I didn't know how to write a novel. I feel it more clearly after each attempt, because it is in such sharp contrast to the sense of authority with which I take hold of a short story. (*L.* 124)

Wharton not only used the short story as a benchmark against which to judge her success or otherwise with the full-length novel, however. She relished working inventively within the constraints of the short story form whilst also pushing it to its limits in the novella. Including her New England texts: *Ethan Frome* and *Summer*, Wharton published eleven novellas, the first being *The Touchstone* in 1900 and the last the four, issued under the title of *Old New York, False Dawn, The Spark, The Old Maid,* and *New Year's Day*, published in 1924. The novellas, in themselves, engage with a range of different generic possibilities, the earliest three to be published, *The Touchstone, Sanctuary* (1903), and *Madame de Treymes* (1907), are firmly set in the midst of contemporary leisure-class American life, as conducted at both home and abroad; 'Bunner Sisters' is a tale of two working-class sisters in New York which was written in 1892 but not published until 1916; *The Marne* (1918) is an insubstantial tale written for propaganda purposes during the First World War; the New England novellas, self-evidently, are texts that are indebted to the traditions of regional writing; and the novellas of the *Old New York* sequence are historical narratives, each with a subtitle that reflects the decade of their nineteenth century setting.

Many of Wharton's early short-story collections have titles that steer the reader towards a consideration of the work and ideas of the natural and social scientists as significant influences in the fiction. In her own copy of *Evolution and Effort* (1895) by Edmond Kelly she underlines the meaning of the phrase 'the greater inclination', the title of her first published collection of short fiction.[1] Her next volume was entitled *Crucial Instances* (1901), which is a quotation from a discussion of 'The Laws of Inheritance' in Charles Darwin's 1871 *The Descent of Man*,[2] a text to which she pays even more direct tribute in the title of her third collection, *The Descent of Man and Other Stories* (1904). These are not chance or casual allusions to the work of Darwin and others: Wharton, as has already been discussed, was profoundly influenced by social and natural science, and her language and themes reflect the reading she did in the subject. Amongst the extant books from her library are works by Darwin, Huxley, Haeckel, Kelly, Lock, Spencer, Tyndall, Westermarck, and others, and in the short stories the direct results of such reading are plainly discernible in Wharton's use of language, choice of themes, and narrative structure.

The general tenor of the comments made about *The Descent of Man and Other Stories* on publication initiated what would become a regular charge made against Wharton by American reviewers: that her work had nothing to do with portraying the lives of real people. Such reviews were a source of dismay for Wharton, as she makes plain in this letter to William Crary Brownell, the literary consultant for the publisher, Charles Scribner's Sons, in June 1904:

> I return the reviews with many thanks. I have never before been discouraged by criticism, because when the critics have found fault with me I have usually abounded in their sense, and seen, as I thought, a way of doing better the next time; but the continued cry that I am an echo of Mr. James (whose books of the last ten years I can't read, much as I delight in the man), and the assumption that the people I write about are not 'real' because they are not navvies and char-women, makes me feel rather hopeless. I write about what I see, what I happen to be nearest to, which is surely better than doing cowboys de chic... (*L.* 91)

As an example of what so infuriated Wharton, one reviewer, writing for the *Independent*, had commented 'nowhere, either in her ideas of virtue or vice, does she come into contact with normal life'.[3] In consideration of *The Descent of Man and Other Stories*, however, it is possible to interrogate and refute this charge, focusing particularly on two tales,'The Mission of Jane' and 'The Other Two'. Both these stories deal with commonplace domestic situations; both stories are concerned with the dynamics of family or married life and demonstrate the influence of evolutionary theory on Wharton's work. Her intellectual and creative engagement with natural science – which, as already discussed, dramatically changed the way in which she viewed and then wrote about the world[4] – grounds her writing here in common experience, just as it does in many of the early short stories and novellas, no matter who or what she takes for her subject.

In 'The Mission of Jane' Wharton's deployment of the language of evolution brings a sharp edge of detachment to her depiction of human relations. Structured into the story is the superior central consciousness of Julian Lethbury: he operates from 'the standpoint of scientific observation' (*ROS* 57) and there is no question but that, within this domestic hierarchy, men are higher up the evolutionary scale than women. Wharton's use of social-scientific language in this story of middle-aged, middle-class parenting is calculatedly merciless; it enables her to incise the power relations within the household. As Mr Lethbury's intellectual superiority is unchallenged, even his wife's axioms become a testament to her failure to adapt and change: 'Most of his wife's opinions were heirlooms, and he took a quaint pleasure in tracing their descent' (*ROS* 51). The 'primitive' nature of the woman is emphasized throughout the story, the constant refrain of limitation, of arrested development, proscribes Mrs Lethbury, whose intellectual and emotional narrowness is configured by her husband thus: 'there was a pathos in the struggles of her swaddled mind, in its blind reachings towards the primal emotions' (*ROS* 54). Wharton returns time and time again throughout her writing career to a store of metaphor and language from natural science in order to depict the leisure-class woman of the late nineteenth century. The short stories feature the same type of anthropological descriptors she uses to denote the limitations of May Welland in the 1920 *The Age of Innocence*, who is feared by her husband to be comparable to 'the Kentucky cave-fish, which had ceased to develop eyes because they had no use for them. What if, when he had bidden May Welland to open hers, they could only look out blankly at blankness?' (AI 81).

Wharton's setting in the majority of her short fiction may well be the comfortable homes of the leisure classes, but she is not necessarily treating lives that are much more sophisticated than those depicted in the work of the leading naturalist writers of her age. In no different measure, for instance, from the inhabitants of Polk Street in Frank Norris's *McTeague*,[5] published in 1899, Mrs Lethbury is described as 'stupid, limited, inflexible', needing 'very elementary things. She was as difficult to amuse as a savage' (*ROS* 53). Wharton's short stories and novels draw on a fund of metaphoric language more commonly encountered in naturalist fiction – by definition, fiction that is usually concerned with the depiction of varying degrees of low life. When the reviewers accused her of knowing nothing about ordinary life, they levelled that charge against fiction in which she treated working-class life like *Ethan Frome* – 'It is to be hoped that when Mrs Wharton writes again she will bring her great talent to bear on normal people and situations'[6] – as well as against the fiction set amongst the leisure classes, all the while ignoring the common ground between her work and that of writers like Norris and other contemporaries like Theodore Dreiser and David Graham Phillips. All of these writers might be said to be obeying the injunction from reviewers and commentators that the American novelist should write about 'the man with the dinner-pail' (GAM 652), as Wharton herself pejoratively describes it in an article published in the *Yale Review* in July 1927. Here, in the ironically titled essay 'The Great American Novel', she revisits the topic of her 1904 letter to Brownell – that is, the expectations of the American reviewers and, in particular their prescription as to what might constitute the 'canon' of American literature:

> The novelist's – any novelist's – proper field, created by his particular way of apprehending life, is limited only by the bounds of his natural, his instinctive interests. The writer who sees life in terms of South Seas cannibals, as Herman Melville did, will waste his time (as, incidentally, Melville did) if he tries to depict it as found in drawing-rooms and conservatories; although this by no means implies that the cannibal is intrinsically a richer and more available subject than the inhabitant of drawing-rooms. No subject is foreign to the artist in which there is something corresponding to a something within himself. (GAM 649)

Wharton claims, as she always claimed, that content and form, style and setting, are inextricably linked and that they are matters of individual choice and even aptitude for the artist. In 'The Great American Novel' she is simply enumerating another version of the method advocated by Darwin for investigating 'The Laws of Inheritance' – here in the section from which she derives the title of her second volume of short stories: 'As it was impossible even to estimate in how large a number of cases throughout the animal kingdom these two propositions held good, it occurred to me to investigate some striking or crucial instances, and to rely on the result.'[7] In the writing of her short stories, in particular, she sought to depict the 'crucial instances' through which she could shed some light on the human condition. Again, Wharton's ambitions are not discernibly distinct from those of the Naturalist writers, who are described, here in Donna Campbell's words, as being concerned with 'the accurate and detailed representation of ordinary human beings, a fascination with tracing the workings of heredity, and a belief in the shaping power of the environment'.[8] Wharton is, however, primarily absorbed by relations between men and women and, centrally, the impact upon the institution of marriage of social change and – in particular – the expansion of opportunities for women. She sees a future where women are either intolerant of the limitations imposed upon them or become obsolete in a world that has moved on and made them, like Mrs Lethbury, unfit for any purpose other than as 'the epitome, the consummation, of centuries of animal maternity' (*ROS* 57).

The story 'The Other Two' features a woman who has, using the restricted means at her disposal, managed to find a way to adapt and change, in order to improve her social standing and economic position. Mrs Waythorn in 'The Other Two' is '"as easy as an old shoe" – a shoe that too many feet had worn. Her elasticity was the result of tension in too many different directions. Alice Haskett – Alice Varick – Alice Waythorn she had been each in turn, and had left hanging to each name a little of her privacy, a little of her personality, a little of the inmost self where the unknown god resides' (*ROS* 45). Wharton shows Mr Waythorn becoming aware of his own complicity in the professionalization of Alice's role as a bride/wife; what attracted him to her – her ability to be the perfectly and endlessly obliging partner – is also what ultimately arouses his contempt, a contempt that is directed as much towards himself as towards her. Alice, however, is an index of the evolving nature of the social constitution. She is welcomed as an agent of change because no change is overtly signalled; hostesses do not even have to adjust their guest lists to avoid inviting husbands two and three to the same event. Alice Waythorn is an example from a society in the process of 'adaptation', being perfectly 'adapted' (*ROS* 31) herself to move on up the social register, learning, if not 'to shed her past like a man' (*ROS* 45), then to gloss over its continuing difficulties with the successful practice of the 'art . . . of concessions, eliminations and embellishments; of lights judiciously thrown and shadows skilfully softened' (*ROS* 46).

The husbands in the two stories I have discussed, whilst having sufficient leisure to cultivate an ironic distance from their wives and their trivial pursuits, are as dissatisfied, as full of discontent, as any other member of the human race; they have the intellectual capacity to satirize their own situations, but this does not remove them from the compromises and shifts necessary to conduct the business of living. Another story set amongst the moneyed classes, 'The Choice', published in 1908 in the *Century* magazine, is described by Bert Bender in his study *The Descent of Love: Darwin and the Theory of Sexual Selection in American Fiction, 1871–1926* as focusing on 'one of the two key principles of sexual selection, female choice',[9] where the apparently unsatisfactory husband, the boorish, self-centred Cobham Stilling, is actually the one who survives in a dramatic underwater struggle with his wife's lover. Choices, as Wharton constructs them, are rarely a matter of individual will; they are usually compromises, accommodations or even impositions. The word 'choice' is less to do with self-will than with bowing to the inevitable, an inevitable that is often executed in the public eye.

Wharton was not alone in her exploration of the social and syntactical implications of developments in natural and social science; other prominent women in the decades before and after the turn of the century like Charlotte Perkins Gilman also used the evolutionary model, both in fiction and non-fiction, to illuminate the condition of women in the social world. Gilman, however, is distinct from Wharton in her purpose: she is first and foremost an educator not an observer, a reformer not a chronicler. In her essay 'The Economic Basis of the Woman Question', published in 1898, Gilman describes the forces of social evolution that are deemed to apply to the dynamic industrial and commercial world but not to the domestic sphere:

> So in our social world today, men and women who are familiar with liquefied air and Roentgen rays, who have accepted electric transit and look forward with complacence to air ships, people who are as liberal and progressive in mechanical lines as need be hoped, remain sodden and buried in their prehistoric sentiment as to the domestic relations. The world of science and invention may change; industry, commerce and manufacturing may change; but women and the home are supposed to remain as they are, forever...[10]

Wharton's anthropological eye is more detached, more sardonic, than Gilman's. Whilst Gilman's rhetorical skills are ranged against injustices in the treatment of women and inequalities between the sexes, using evidence from social-scientific research to build an argument for massive social change, so Wharton dispassionately depicts relations at a point of crisis between the sexes using the language and insights of the evolutionary scientists. She is thus able to complicate, as has already been discussed in the context of *The Age of Innocence*, her picture of society, particularly when working with the retrospective view. Many of her stories deal with the after-effects of the path not taken, the bold step not attempted and the consequent – and inevitable – regret. When a woman attempts to break out from the confinement of a loveless marriage, as in the story 'The Long Run', first published in the *Atlantic Monthly* in February 1912, the man she loves is not brave enough to risk all for love and regrets his cowardice for the rest of his life; in other stories like 'Souls Belated', from *The Greater Inclination*, Wharton shows a different side to the failure of marriage, where the woman is caught between her need to be free and the conflicting desire to have her social and moral existence sanctioned by the prevailing code of standards and conduct. Wharton paints a picture of obscure European resorts peopled by those dispossessed of their social identity; hoping to find a place safe from the public gaze, they find only that no such space exists. In the absence of the marriage contract there is also an absence of meaning and authenticity, as Lydia Tillotson comes to understand: 'I begin to see what marriage is for. It's to keep people away from each other. Sometimes I think that two people who love each other can be saved from madness only by the things that come between them – children, duties, visits, bores, relations – the things that protect married people from each other' (*ROS* 24).

In substantial numbers of her stories her protagonists have to find ways and means to live with the knowledge of their own emotional, moral, or aesthetic insufficiencies. The earliest novellas are also predicated on a dramatic situation that has arisen because of a previous failure of understanding or nerve: in *Madame de Treymes*, John Durham fails to marry Fanny Frisbee when he has the chance and is subsequently prevented from doing so; in *The Touchstone*, Stephen Glennard's failure of commitment to Margaret Aubyn and subsequent betrayal of her memory contaminates his marriage to Alexa; and in *Sanctuary* Kate Orme's life is constrained by the moral compromise she makes in marrying Denis Peyton.[11] In her ghost stories, a genre to which she returned regularly throughout her career, Wharton often uses the device of the prior event or act as the inspiration for or cause of the supernatural intervention. In 'Afterward', published in 1910, again in *Century Magazine*, the ghost of a wronged business partner comes to claim the life of Ned Boyne; in 'Kerfol', published in 1916 in *Scribner's Magazine*, the tyrannical Lord of Kerfol is savaged to death by a pack of ghost dogs, dogs he had murdered one by one; in the late story 'Pomegranate Seed', published in the *Saturday Evening Post* in 1931, Kenneth Ashby is denied any future prospect of happiness in a second marriage by his dead wife, Elsie, who seeks to reassert her former dominance over him from beyond the grave. In the story 'Bewitched', which featured in the collection *Here and Beyond*, published in 1926, Wharton returns to the themes she exploited so well in *Ethan Frome*, the wasting of the human spirit in a loveless marriage, the failure of hope in a harsh and impoverished landscape and climate. In this story Wharton uses the generic conventions of the supernatural tale to expose the shifts and lies to which people resort when the social organization has no room to accommodate the ambitions and desires of those known as 'the handsomest girls anywhere round', handsome girls who have run 'wild' (*ROS* 155) and will ultimately be subdued in the frozen earth.

Ethan Frome is perhaps the best known of Edith Wharton's works, having achieved an enduring popularity with all kinds of readers. Both this novella and its sister volume, *Summer* – known to Wharton and her friends during the period of its composition as 'Hot Ethan'[12] – are set amongst the Berkshire Hills of Massachusetts, the area of the country in which Wharton and her husband built their American home, the Mount. Both these novellas focus on existence in small, isolated towns, which are, as described in *Summer*, 'abandoned of men, left apart by railway, trolley, telegraph, and all the forces that link life to life in modern communities' (*S*. 125). Obsolete even at the start of the so-called American Century, the most striking features of these locations are their superannuation and decay; they have been bypassed by all the channels of communication that signify modern life. These communities are peopled by those for whom every day is a question of finding the means to ensure survival, unlike the majority of Wharton's novels and stories, which treat the lives of the leisure classes. As already mentioned, Wharton was damned by the reviewers if she did not treat the lives of 'normal people' and damned if she did, and, whilst the reviews of the novella were, in the main, positive, they did lament the desolation and 'remorselessness'[13] of the narrative as if Wharton were breaking some kind of professional code of conduct. As the editors of *Edith Wharton: The Contemporary Reviews* say in their introduction, the charges being made against her were about a failure of moral not artistic integrity; her fiction was said to be 'bleak, disagreeable, and lacking in moral uplift. . . . in the review media, a morally uplifting spirit seemed to be required'.[14]

There is no doubt that *Ethan Frome* is a tragic tale and the intensity of the moral drama is heightened by the starkness of the winter setting and the economic climate of neglect and decay. The lives of all are frozen by inarticulacy, by poverty of opportunity and the bareness of both interior and exterior landscapes. The story cannot be expressed by those who live 'in a depth of moral isolation too remote for casual access,' (*EF* 33), and so it is told, in a structure comparable to Emily Brontë's *Wuthering Heights*, by an outsider who comes to Starkfield to carry out contract work and is given the story 'bit by bit, from various people' (*EF* 27). The story that he tells is a straightforward one; a farmer, Ethan Frome, struggling to make a living from his New England holding, is caught in a loveless marriage with his cousin, Zenobia, whom he had met when she came to nurse his mother through her final illness. Ethan falls in love with a penniless relative of his wife, Mattie Silver, who has come to live with them as their all-purpose 'help' after the death of her feckless father. When Zeena resolves to send Mattie away, Ethan and Mattie decide to commit suicide rather than attempt to make a new life in a different part of the country; they are primarily held back by the legacy of shame and struggle that they would leave to Zeena. Their attempt at joint suicide by smashing their sled into a tree goes horribly wrong and they are both brought back from the brink of death to live on, crippled and miserable, and making, with Zeena, a hideous threesome inextricably bound to each other in poverty at the farmhouse.

The dramatic tension of *Ethan Frome* is fuelled, in common with many of Wharton's other short fictions, by the prior event, and here again it is the most common of prior events – the unsuitable marriage. Ethan Frome's decision to marry his cousin, Zenobia Pierce, because 'he was seized with an unreasoning dread of being left alone on the farm' (*EF* 61) after the death of his mother, is the point from which all the action follows. The narrative structure here, however, complicates our understanding of that prior event, as the tale is told in retrospect; the full horror of the tragedy of all the wasted lives, of the misery and pain of their daily existence, is presented at the outset. The narrator compiles the information he has had from various sources into a story haunted by the lame figure of Ethan Frome and the voices of his women 'droning querulously' (*EF* 38). The scene in the farmhouse at the beginning of the novella shadows the story of Ethan and Mattie Silver's growing romantic love, and emphasizes the inevitability of the failure of their desperate bid to escape from the most basic moral imperatives of their society. In her autobiography Wharton cites two definite influences upon her New England writings – Nathaniel Hawthorne and Emily Brontë – and she takes care to align herself with those particular writers as against others who might – in her view – have produced a different literary version of New England

> For years I had wanted to draw life as it really was in the derelict mountain villages of New England, a life even in my time, and a thousandfold more a generation earlier, utterly unlike that seen through the rose-coloured spectacles of my predecessors, Mary Wilkins Freeman and Sarah Orne Jewett. In those days the snow-bound villages of Western Massachusetts were still grim places, morally and physically: insanity, incest and slow mental and moral starvation were hidden away behind the paintless wooden house-fronts of the long village street, or in the isolated farm-houses on the neighbouring hills; and Emily Brontë would have found as savage tragedies in our remoter valleys as on her Yorkshire moors...New Englanders...had for years sought the reflection of local life in the rose-and-lavender pages of their favourite authoresses and had forgotten to look into Hawthorne's. (*BG* 293–4)

Without examining in detail Wharton's efforts to distance herself from the work of regional writers such as Freeman and Jewett,[15] it was clearly important to her that her work should be placed in both American and European mainstream traditions, and the structure, language, and imagery of *Ethan Frome* owe much to the work of Hawthorne and Brontë. Whilst it is in many ways her most indigenous work of fiction in terms of scene and setting, *Ethan Frome* connects with the widest of themes, that of needless human suffering and waste. Enacted here is a struggle between past and present, between the imperatives of duty and those of passion, between the individual and the community – not at first sight, admittedly, distinctly different concerns from those that drive the narrative in *The Age of Innocence*, a novel firmly set in Wharton's own upper-middle-class New York. What is distinct is the social class and situation of the protagonists, and yet, in this, the most local of her fictions, Wharton achieves a wide range of reference, to other writers, to other landscapes, to other possibilities and codes of conduct.

Ethan Frome and its companion novella, *Summer*, tell of a bare and desolate interior and exterior landscape; the New England portrayed here is a place empty of the signs of material comfort that so abound in the majority of Wharton's fiction. There are none of the barometers of taste in evidence by which readers find their way around the mansions of the established or of the newly rich, as in *The House of Mirth*. The making of meaning for the occupants of the Frome household is reduced to the bare essentials by poverty – of imagination and expression as well as economic opportunity. Wharton herself, in her 1922 introduction to a new edition of the novella, used the language of interior decoration to describe 'the difficulty of presenting [the protagonists] in the fullest relief, yet without an added ornament, or trick of drapery or lighting'. She describes the 'deep-rooted reticence and inarticulateness of the people' (*UCW* 260), a reticence so profound that Zeena can soar only to heights of emotion in a lament for her broken pickle dish, whilst Ethan considers that Mattie's appreciation of the view: 'It looks just as if it was painted!' takes the 'art of definition' (*EF* 43) to the furthest limits of eloquence. The occupants of the Frome farmhouse and the community of Starkfield are alike circumscribed by severe deprivation, and the language and structure of the text reinforce this at every turn.

In *Summer* Wharton takes the isolation of the community one stage further by demonstrating the dehumanization of the landscape that has taken place; the town of North Dormer is in a state of decay both architectural and social; everywhere there are traces of a time when a different kind of community spirit had been in evidence. From the quality of the now mouldy books in the town library to the vestiges of architectural refinement in the crumbling fabric of the once fine houses that Lucius Harney sketches as he and Charity Royall wander around the countryside surrounding North Dormer, the text is replete with examples of neglect and decay, with images of abandonment, of both people and things. Wharton, in this traditional tale of seduction – country girl lured by city gent into a relationship that he has no intention of sustaining – shades the narrative with multiple layers of irony. In fact, T. S. Eliot, reviewing *Summer* in the *Egoist* in January 1919, recognized the vitality of the satiric mode in Wharton's production of the local: 'This novel will certainly be considered "disgusting" in America; it is certain that not one reader in a thousand will apprehend the author's point of view. But it should add to Mrs. Wharton's reputation as a novelist the distinction of being the satirist's satirist.'[16] Lawyer Royall, Charity's guardian and the man to whom Wharton gives all the best lines, makes a speech at the festival of 'Old Home Week' in which the concerns that drive much of the narrative forward are publicly aired. Whilst the event itself, heralded by Wharton as a 'form of sentimental decentralisation' (*S.* 209), is subject to much sardonic comment, the speech that Lawyer Royall delivers is nevertheless founded on the kind of principle of commitment to place that reverberates through much of Wharton's fiction, from *The House of Mirth* to *The Buccaneers*, her last, and incomplete, novel. Although the tribute Lawyer Royall pays to small towns like his own is hedged about with demurrals and acknowledgements of what must be given up in order to live away from the metropolitan centre, he also articulates a broader notion linking the individual and the community: 'Believe me, all of you, the best way to help the places we live in is to be glad we live there.' (*S.* 223). Up against this pious hope, however, is the reality that the kind of small town portrayed here is one that no one seems content to live in – the disjunction between the kind of rhetoric used in and around the event of 'Old Home Week' and the petty, narrow-minded vocabulary of most of the citizenship providing most of the satiric thrust of the narrative. The only things that enliven the community are gossip and envy; Charity is spied on and her movements reported, good fortune attracts as much opprobrium as bad, and the spirit in which Charity and Lawyer Royal return to North Dormer as a married couple is hardly one that presages a life full of family and civic fulfilment. *Summer*, like *Ethan Frome*, is a bleak and pessimistic tale. The daily aspect of war-torn France, from which Wharton composed the novella, was a constant reminder to her of the fragility of the grasp with which mankind holds onto the landscape and the ease with which civilizations can fail, and it is hard to believe that this sense of human transience did not feed directly into the manner and mode of the composition of *Summer*.

In her *Old New York* series of novellas, published in 1924 and including *False Dawn*, *The Old Maid*, *The Spark*, and *New Year's Day*, Wharton returned, as is evident from their title, to the city of her birth, to the mid-nineteenth century and the leisure-classes, who seemed, at that point, to be permanent and central fixtures of the social scene in the city. However, like many of Wharton's historical fictions, these novellas are – amongst other things – commemorative, and part of what is being commemorated is New York as a small town in which everyone knows everyone else and where *New Year's Day* is marked by 'over-eating, dawdling, and looking out of the window: a Dutch habit still extensively practised in the best New York circles' (*NYD* 8). The person being observed from the window of West Twenty-Third Street is Lizzie Hazeldean, the focus of attention in this story of the Seventies: a woman who becomes, in her own words, 'an expensive prostitute' (*NYD* 114), in order to provide her dying husband with material comforts otherwise beyond her financial reach. The narrator of this retrospective account of the precise 'topographies' (*NYD* 4) of old New York society is a sympathetic young man, like Newland Archer, at once a part of and set apart from his own tribe by virtue of a more liberal attitude and imagination.

The failure of old New York to understand or tolerate difference is the abiding theme throughout the four novellas in the sequence. In *The Old Maid* Charlotte Lovell, like Lizzie Hazeldean, has done one unspeakable thing: in this case she has borne a child out of wedlock, and, like Lizzie, she must pay for her transgression throughout the rest of her life. In order to keep her daughter, Tina, with her, Charlotte first conceals the little girl as one amongst many in an orphanage and then pretends to be

Tina's aunt as the girl is absorbed into the family of Delia Ralston, her cousin. The daily misery of watching her daughter call another woman 'mother' is compounded by the fact that Charlotte is well aware that her lover, Clem Spender, the father of her child, was actually in love with Delia Ralston and that he sought only transient comfort not fulfilment in her arms. The legacy of pain and bitterness that is Charlotte's portion as an 'old maid' is set to be re-enacted in the life of Tina, whose mysterious origins are regarded as a sufficient bar to her marrying into a respectable family in a society where respectability is all. It is only Delia's decision to adopt Tina, give her the Ralston name, and endow her with Lovell money that means that, instead of being 'ruined' by Lanning Halsey, a young man 'handsomer and more conversable than the rest, chronically unpunctual, and totally unperturbed by the fact', (*OM* 110), she can be married to him, her burgeoning sexuality constrained within marriage and motherhood. The accommodation of Tina within the boundaries of respectable society is paid for with the agony of silence in which Charlotte, her birth mother, must live; in order to avoid ostracism she denies the natural relation between herself and Tina and becomes the thing she hates, the 'old maid', in her attitudes and actions as well as in her public persona.

All four of the novellas share a concern with the shifts and compromises, the suffering and bitterness in store for the individual who is out of step with the age in which he or she lives. Charlotte's determination to keep and protect her child to the point of risking public disgrace, Lizzie's resolution to sleep with a man for whom she feels nothing but contempt in order to secure ease and comfort for her beloved husband, these actions push at the limits of the woman's life in the mid-nineteenth century. In the other two novellas, which both have male protagonists, Lewis Raycie's championing of the taste and teachings of John Ruskin in *False Dawn* and Hayley Delane's difference – here articulated by the young, admiring narrator of *The Spark*: 'I could never look at him without feeling that he belonged elsewhere, not so much in another society as in another age' (*Sp.* 7) – put them outside the pale of conventional conduct. These two novellas are less successful than *The Old Maid* and *New Year's Day*, as they are perhaps more concerned with prosecuting an agenda – to emphasize the indifference of old New York to both politics and aesthetics – than with constructing a compelling story; the 'twist in the tale' at the close of both stories is productive rather more of bathos than pathos. However, all four of the *Old New York* texts extend the portrait of that city and that society, developing themes that run throughout Wharton's shorter fiction and exploring, as in *Ethan Frome* and *Summer*, the enduring price to be paid for the act of rebellion – the 'great – or abominable thing; rank it as you please' (*NYD* 150), as the narrator of *New Year's Day* says of Lizzie Hazeldean's unconscionable act.

Wharton never ceased to write short fictions, even when in the midst of composing her longest and most complex novels, and, as previously mentioned, the last two books she published before her death were collections of stories. She felt comfortable and confident in the genre and she paid close and detailed attention to the business of composition, working towards the achievement of a form that was also expressive of content. In her short stories Wharton felt the presence of her readers in a transactional sense, as she says in her Preface to the 1937 volume, *Ghosts*: 'But when I first began to read, and then to write ghost stories, I was conscious of a common medium between myself and my readers, of their meeting me halfway among the primeval shadows, and filling in the gaps in my narrative with sensations and divinations akin to my own . . . for reading should be a creative act as well as writing' (*GS* 2). In her short stories and novellas Wharton was rightly concerned with the mechanics of the text, and, for this reason, it is in the shorter fiction that she was able to pose the kind of structural and linguistic questions that would engage her readers in the making of both meaning and significance.

4

The International Scene

There are many ways of organizing critical considerations of Wharton's writing; it is possible, for instance, to shape a discussion around form, as I have done in the previous chapter in talking about the shorter fiction, around generic concerns, like Wharton's use of the historical novel, around place, as in my chapter on 'Writing New York', or simply according to chronology. The choice to bring an author's work into a particular focus can shape a critical argument distinctively and in this chapter I intend to bring together fictions that not only have a European setting but that crucially implicate that setting in the narrative and structure of the text. In addition, these texts can also be explored productively in terms of the various literary influences on Wharton's work that they make manifest. Whilst, to a certain extent, the vast majority of Edith Wharton's fiction can be said to be engaged in some way or another with the international scene, there is a distinct and interesting group of texts that are set substantially, if not entirely, in Europe, and I propose to treat them as having discrete concerns. It is true to say that in all her fiction, from her earliest New York novel, *The House of Mirth*, onwards, there is usually an international dimension in terms of both story and setting and this is, indeed, inevitable, because of the social class she is mainly concerned with: members of the American leisure classes have always travelled extensively in Europe. In some texts, like the 1928 novel, *The Children*, the setting is almost exclusively European, but the concerns that drive the narrative are quintessentially American, and discussion of them belongs, for the purposes of this study at least, with the other novels of the 1920s and 1930s that treat contemporary American society. The novels that I want to consider here begin and end Wharton's career as a writer and also mark her expatriation to France and her involvement in the First World War. Her first published novel, *The Valley of Decision*, has its subject and setting in the Italian eighteenth century; the action of her novel of 1912, *The Reef*, takes place in England and France, although the chief protagonists are American; the war novel, *A Son at the Front* (1923), is set in France but is similarly peopled by Americans; and her last, unfinished novel, *The Buccaneers*, published posthumously in 1938, is concerned, after Book One, with the entry of a group of young American women into aristocratic English society.

What all these texts have in common is their intense engagement with European culture, with the European city, the landscape, but, above all with art, particularly visual art and letters. Part of the point, for instance, of writing *The Valley of Decision*, as far as Wharton was concerned, was to educate her audience about the Italian eighteenth century. As she said in a letter to Sally Norton on 13 February 1902, one of her difficulties lay in the fact that she could not rely on her readers knowing anything about the period or place: 'I imagine the real weakness of the book is that I haven't fused my facts sufficiently within the general atmosphere of the story, so that they stick out here & there, & bump into the reader' (*L.* 57). Wharton's anxiety about the integration of fact, of topographical detail, within the 'story', whilst it has some justification, is largely misplaced. Her Italian novel is very accomplished and much underrated; it is the product of a good deal of historical research but it is also a good piece of storytelling, albeit one with clearly discernible pedagogic intentions. As with the Italian travel books, discussed in an earlier chapter, Wharton had something to tell her audience in this novel. She wanted both to communicate a sense of her enthusiasm for the aesthetic delights of the Italian city and landscape and to paint a picture of a long-established civilization at an important turning point in its history – a turning point that embraces the forces of change as well as acknowledges the value of tradition. This confrontation between past and future, change and stasis, innovation and tradition is, in one way or another, at the heart of all the narratives I discuss in this chapter. In most cases Wharton portrays the effect of such a confrontation on the individual and it is in the relationship between the person and the place, the person and the culture, that the struggle is enacted. This is nowhere more dramatically played out than in Wharton's first novel, *The Valley of Decision*, a text in which she experiments with a number of the themes that would endure in her fiction, no matter which genre, landscape, culture, or time she was working within.

There were a number of important precedents for Wharton in the methodology she needed to grasp before she could write a novel with a setting so remote from her own time, place, and cultural mores. Amongst American writers there were a number who had written novels with Italian locations, for instance: James Fenimore Cooper's *The Bravo* (1831), Nathaniel Hawthorne's *The Marble Faun* (1860), and Henry Blake Fuller's *The Chevalier of Pensieri-Vani* (1890). Other important influences include Charles Eliot Norton, distinguished Harvard professor and father of Wharton's friend, Sally Norton, who had published a number of learned books on Italian art and architecture as well as a translation of Dante's *The Divine Comedy*; and the work of the European writer Vernon Lee, in particular, her 1880 *Studies of the Eighteenth Century in Italy*, to which Wharton pays tribute in *A Backward Glance* (*BG* 133). In terms of the influence of Italian writers on her life and letters, Wharton's library bears eloquent testament to her lifelong passion for Italian literature. She learned Italian at an early age, and her biographer, R. W. B. Lewis, tells us that, with her friend, Emelyn Washburn, she read her way through many of the classics of European literature: 'In the warm weather, the girls climbed through Emelyn's bedroom window onto the library roof and read Dante aloud together.'[1] Among the books in the Italian language in her collection are volumes of Boccaccio, D'Annunzio, Dante, Leopardi, Machiavelli, Manzoni, Petrarca, and Serao, as well as *Tragedie* by Vittorio Alfieri, in a copy inscribed 'Edith Jones May 22nd 1877'.[2] Alfieri actually features as a character in *The Valley of Decision* as an important influence on the central protagonist, Odo Valsecca, and the use of Alfieri in the narrative is one of the devices through which Wharton grounds her tale in historical fact whilst concomitantly acknowledging her debt to one of the authors who inspired and informed the composition of her novel. Writings of the period – both fiction and non-fiction – inevitably provide the chief inspiration for *The Valley of Decision*, and it is therefore highly appropriate that the character that acts as historical referent in the text should be one of the sources for it.

At various points in her career Wharton chose to build a fiction around an encounter between one of her protagonists and a great and influential artist, an artist, in each case, who had a significant effect upon her own writing. As already mentioned in the previous chapter, two of the novellas in the *Old New York* sequence of historical fictions have such a meeting as their foundation: Hayley Delane's friendship, during the civil war, with Walt Whitman in *The Spark* and Lewis Raycie's surrender to the influence of the teachings of John Ruskin in *False Dawn*. The role of Alfieri in *The Valley of Decision* anticipates this later use of the artist as enlightener or catalyst to individual or whole-cultural change, but the portrait of the artist here is one that also exposes the folly of simplistically identifying the person with the writing. Alfieri, as Wharton draws him, is completely ideologically compromised; on the one hand, he is 'the tragic poet who was to prepare the liberation of Italy by raising the political ideals of his generation' (*VD* 102), whilst on the other he is a self-obsessed reactionary: 'It was his fate to formulate creeds in which he had no faith: to recreate the political ideals of Italy while bitterly opposed to any actual effort at reform, and to be regarded as the mouthpiece of the Revolution whilst he execrated the Revolution with the whole force of his traditional instincts' (*VD* 531–2). In this way Wharton is able to complicate her use of both her source material and the role of the artist himself; there is a fundamental scepticism advanced here, as the contradictions between the poet and the poetry highlight the complications and difficulties attendant upon the acceptance of any single version of the past. There are sources of historical and cultural authority, there are precedents, but the task facing the new interpreter of the Italian eighteenth century, as Wharton saw it, was to be a partner in dialogue with her predecessors whilst exploring, in style and subject, beyond their boundaries.

The plot of *The Valley of Decision* carries the reader through a number of generic shifts. Not only is Wharton writing a historical novel; she is composing a *Bildungsroman* and a travel guide in which she is able to meld techniques and themes from non-fiction with fiction. The central protagonist, Odo Valsecca, appears to the reader first as a physically neglected and culturally deprived child, in the line of succession to the Dukedom of Pianura but apparently distant enough from the title to be left in obscurity until the death of his father brings him into more proximate relation to the centre of power. As he is educated as befits his new status, so the reader is led through a cross-section of Italian society: Odo associates, on his travels, with a cast of characters from the highest to the most lowly, through the toils of a post-feudal society that is struggling to reconcile new freedoms with old structures, on a guided tour of Italian painting and sculpture, archaeological digs, and a number of different cities and principalities. Once he becomes Duke, Odo attempts, in spite of his own preference for caution, to bring about radical reforms, and in this he is urged on by his mistress, Fulvia Vivaldi, the intellectual daughter of a Professor of Philosophy at the University of Turin, described by Alfieri as 'one of your prodigies of female learning, such as our topsy-turvy land produces' (*VD* 148). As one of the central features of the reforms is to put limits on the power of the Church, enough public opposition is mustered by the forces of conservatism, both sacred and secular, to cause the new constitution to fail, and, in the process, Fulvia is shot dead by a protester. Odo is eventually forced to abdicate and departs alone from his palace, returning briefly to the farmhouse at Pontesordo where he had spent his early childhood, to attempt some kind of reunion with 'his early hopes and faiths...his old belief in life' (*VD* 656) before riding on toward Piedmont as the new day dawns. This brief outline does not, obviously, do justice to the complexity of the narrative or to Wharton's detailed, vivid, although occasionally creaky, recreation of life in eighteenth-century Italy. There are many points of comparison that could be made between the issues that are rehearsed in the Italian novel and those that feature repeatedly in Wharton's American fictions, especially the conflict between tradition and change. However, central to the conception and the design in *The Valley of Decision* as well as in *The Reef*, *A Son at the Front*, and *The Buccaneers*, are the place and influence of art – visual and textual – in the wider culture. In *The Reef* there are a number of matters that are driven by aesthetic considerations, including a larger structural question rather than a plot-related concern – that is, the extent of the influence of Henry James upon this particular novel. In *A Son at the Front* a painter takes centre stage in a text that is fundamentally absorbed by the aesthetic values of French culture, and in *The Buccaneers*, like *The Valley of Decision*, it is the process of exposure to an indigenous art and architecture that provides much of the momentum of the narrative.

Edith Wharton often drew attention to the points of likeness between herself and Henry James; as she says in *A Backward Glance*, 'The truth is that he belonged irrevocably to the old America out of which I also came, and of which – almost – it might paradoxically be said that to follow up its last traces one had to come to Europe' (*BG* 175). They came from the same country and social class, they both expatriated themselves to Europe, they both treated the subject of the American abroad, they both wrote travel books, they both wrote novels, short stories, and criticism, they were friends, they had many friends in common, Henry James being responsible for introducing Edith Wharton to the man with whom she would have a passionate love affair – Morton Fullerton. All of these likenesses and even intimacies do not, however, mean that she was his creature, except in one instance – that of *The Reef*, in which she loses her voice, finds Henry James's, and then regains her own in time to write *The Custom of the Country*. In terms of structure, the difference between the two novels can be summarized in Wharton's own words from *A Backward Glance* as 'the chronicle-novel' in which she would chart 'the career of a particular young woman ... to whatever hemisphere her fortunes carried her ... record her ravages and pass on to the next phase' versus a novel like *The Reef*, which was concerned with 'the elaborate working out on all sides of a central situation' (*BG* 182–3).

Henry James had written to Wharton in August 1902, before their friendship had really begun, to make a response to *The Valley of Decision*. After spending a good deal of time in syntactical toils in which he demurs from making direct comment on the novel, he then reaches the point of giving her advice about her choice of subject in the future:

> my desire earnestly, tenderly, intelligently to admonish you, while you are young, free, expert, exposed (to illumination) – by which I mean while you're in full command of the situation – admonish you, I say, in favour of the *American Subject*. There it is round you. Don't

pass it by – the immediate, the real, the ours, the yours, the novelist's that it waits for. Take hold of it and & keep hold, & let it pull you where it will ... Profit, be warned, by my awful example of exile & ignorance.[3]

Wharton's response to this advice was to produce *The House of Mirth*, truly a book 'tethered in native pastures',[4] to use another Jamesian phrase. The seven years between *The House* and *The Reef* were very much spent in native pastures, with *The Fruit of the Tree* in 1907 and *Ethan Frome* in 1911, to name but two. *The Reef*, however, was not Wharton's first venture into the French subject, and both her novella of 1907, *Madame de Treymes* and her travel book, *A Motor-Flight through France*, published in 1908, owe a great deal to Henry James's novel, *The American*, published in 1877 and his travel book, *A Little Tour in France* (1883). In neither case, though, is the Wharton text subsumed by the Jamesian precedent. She is working in the same genres, bringing an intelligence of his prior entries into their conventions to her work, but she is not simply replicating his texts. In contrast, *The Reef* does signify a loss of voice for Wharton and is, in my view, one of the chief causes of the charges of imitation that have been made against her. In reading this novel you could be forgiven for believing that Wharton never attained a coherent voice of her own in either fiction or criticism; both its subject and language are a deferral to James, and, in contrast to the dismissive treatment he gave to *The Custom of the Country* only a year later, he lavished praise upon *The Reef* in a letter of 1912: 'the finest thing you have done; both *more* done than even the best of your other doing, and more worth it through intrinsic value, interest and beauty'.[5]

The novel is in many ways a reprise of James's 1881 novel, *The Portrait of a Lady*, a novel that Wharton admired immensely and often referred to in her various writings about James and his work. The character of Fraser Leath, the expatriate collector of snuff boxes – is visited in flashback by his widow, Anna. Leath is clearly a pale and factitious version of Gilbert Osmond, their daughter Effie plays the part of Pansy Osmond, Adelaide Painter the part of Henrietta Stackpole, and, whilst the two stories do not follow exactly the same path, there are enough resemblances to show Wharton, unfortunately, at a disadvantage. The secret that is to be revealed is not, in this case, a prior event, as it is in the case of the liaison between Osmond and Madame Merle in James's novel. The brief affair that George Darrow has with Sophy Viner at the beginning of the novel – which comes back to haunt them both when Darrow resumes his role as suitor and then fiancé to Anna Leath and Sophy becomes first the governess to Effie and then fiancée to Owen, Anna's stepson – is slight in comparison with the depravities and deceptions that characterize the relationship between Osmond and Merle and its aftermath. It is not only a debt in terms of plot, however, that Wharton owes to James here, and, whilst there are some positive things about the effect of the Jamesian precedent in *The Reef* – like the treatment of the international scene and the descriptions of Givré and the account of Anna's relationship with the house – there are also many negative features and most are located within the prose style. Edith Wharton could not avoid the work of her American precursors in the European or transatlantic subject and she uses her literary ancestors wisely and well in the majority of her writings. In *The Reef*, however, her prose becomes mannered and overdetermined, especially in Book One, which deals with the affair between Darrow and Sophy Viner, and where she relies very heavily on a pseudo-Jamesian set of stylistic tricks, like the use of parentheses, of hesitation, and the deployment of a multiplicity of adverbs just like those James uses in his 1902 letter of advice to Wharton, the novelist at the start of her career as a novelist.

There are, nevertheless, good reasons to read *The Reef*, not least for its particular version of the expatriate experience in France, the picture it paints of the difficulties of changing cultures, and the resultant affectations, accommodations, and compromises that have to be made in order to authenticate an existence so far removed from one's origins. The literary forebears who are wrestled with in this text are those whom James cites as sufferers in 'exile & ignorance' – *The Reef* marking a significant moment in Wharton's own life as she made her permanent move to France, the Mount having been sold in 1911. Also evident in the text, as it is in *A Son at the Front*, is a veneration for the seriousness with which the French protect and promote their cultural heritage. As discussed in Chapter 1, Wharton had a proselytizing zeal behind her presentation of French culture, and *A Son at the Front* is, in common with her non-fiction, centrally concerned with the promotion of a full comprehension of the importance of the civilization of France. In ways distinct from *The Reef*, the later novel celebrates French culture in both straightforward and allegorical modes; the behaviour of every French citizen, putting nation before personal safety, the cause before personal satisfaction, is contrasted implicitly and explicitly with the failure of America to become involved in the war. The gradual change in the attitude of the US government, coming to crisis point with the sinking of the Lusitania, is allegorized by Wharton in John Campton's changing view of the war and his part in it. He moves from a total insularity, from a desire to detach himself and his son from any involvement in the European war, to a recognition of a commitment that is international: 'If France went, western civilization went with her; and then all they had believed in and been guided by would perish' (SF 366). This changing awareness of his larger cross-national responsibilities is paralleled by his growing recognition of the legitimacy of other people's involvement in his son's life, in particular that of the boy's stepfather, Anderson Brant.

The overarching allegory in the narrative is the dramatization of the opposition between the claims of the individual as against those of the collective, an opposition that is perfectly enacted, of course, in the business of fighting a war in which solidarity and recognition of a community of interests is crucial. Up until the point of entry into the war by America, made literal by the march past of American troops at the climax of the novel, the allegory divides cultures into those who privilege the individual above all else – the American – and those who prioritize the collective – the European. Crass as these divisions might seem, they carry the whole weight of Wharton's argument here that no nation or civilization can stand alone, and it is France that is, again, made the repository of all that is to be both venerated and imitated: 'An Idea: that was what France, ever since she had existed, had always been in the story of civilization; a luminous point about which striving visions and purposes could rally... to thinkers, artists, to all creators, she had always been a second country' (*SF* 366). In order to emphasize the enormity of the sacrifices necessary to ensure the continuation of such a model, the text is littered with the dead bodies of a generation who must suffer and die in order to reaffirm the faith. George Campton, as Wharton writes in the notebook in which she made her plans for the novel, 'Dies on July 4th as first American troops march through Paris' (SN); he is the Isaac who must be sacrificed for Abraham's blindness. George, who resisted all his parents' attempts to keep him away from the fighting and in a safe job behind the lines, can be allowed to die once the 'brown battalions' of American soldiers arrive to replace him and his unflinching commitment.

Wharton's view of the war and of French civilization, as has already been discussed in an earlier chapter, was straightforwardly conservative, and the allegory in *A Son at the Front* is easily dismissed as belated and simplistic in its morality. It would be misleading, however, to generalize beyond this text, which did have the war and its cataclysmic effects on the everyday business of life, the physical rents and tears in the fabric of civilization, at the heart of its narrative drive. Wharton was, in many ways, at her most American when trying to educate her fellow countrymen and women about the texture, rather than the appearance, of life in another culture. As R. W. B. Lewis says, when describing her attitudes during the war, 'She remained quintessentially American in her way of conducting herself – and never more so than when she was virulently criticizing certain aspects of America as against its superior manifestations'.[6] The war, in this novel, provides the pretext for the same homage to place, to the preservation of the felt relationship between individual and location and through that location to all kinds of other lives, that is embedded in *The Valley of Decision* and *The Reef*. It is in *The Reef*, in fact, that such a sense of rootedness, of belonging, is perhaps expressed most roundly, here in the description of Anna Leath's mature relationship with her French house, Givre:

> Then, with the passing of years, it had gradually acquired a less inimical character, had become, not again a castle of dreams, evoker of fair images and romantic legend, but the shell of a life slowly adjusted to its dwelling: the place one came back to, the place where one had one's duties, one's habits and one's books, the place one would naturally live in till one died: a dull house, an inconvenient house, of which one knew all the defects, the shabbinesses, the discomforts, but to which one was so used that one could hardly,

after so long a time, think oneself away from it without suffering a certain loss of identity'. (*R* 82–3)

This long, single sentence, describing, modifying, qualifying, justifying, and eulogizing certainty of location, is as poignant a tribute to the sustaining power of place as can be found in the whole of Wharton's work; this is the 'centre of early pieties' missing from such as Lily Bart's life as she whirls 'rootless and ephemeral' through *The House of Mirth*. What Wharton described in that novel as the most destructive force in Lily's life is the absence of a sense of self in relation to people and place; she goes on:

> In whatever form a slowly-accumulated past lives in the blood – whether in the concrete image of the old house storied with visual memories, or in the conception of the house not built with hands, but made up of inherited passions and loyalties – it has the same power of broadening and deepening the individual existence, of attaching it by mysterious links of kinship to all the mighty sum of human striving'. (*HM* 348)

All the key words articulated as absences from the life about to expire in *The House of Mirth* are crucial in all the novels discussed in this chapter and nowhere is this more evident than in Wharton's last, unfinished novel, *The Buccaneers*.

This text revisits the territory mapped out in *The Valley of Decision*, confronting not only the clashes between past and present, adaptation and tradition, but also between cultures, clashes that are actually exploited to much comic effect, especially in poking fun at the ignorance of the English aristocracy. The trope of the house – from the farmhouse at Pontesordo that enshrines for Odo Valsecca all 'his early hopes and faiths', to Givre, repository of Anna Leath's most clearly articulated belief in the value of commitment to people as well as place – is most fully realized in Annabel (Nan) St George's sensuous awareness of the atmosphere at Honourslove: 'In his answers to her questions she had detected a latent passion for every tree and stone of the beautiful old place – a sentiment new to her experience, as a dweller in houses without histories, but exquisitely familiar to her imagination' (*B*. 136). This is a book written in the open spirit that characterizes Wharton's first full-length fiction; like Odo Valsecca, Nan St George is our guide through a particular alien territory – in this case, the stately homes of England. As she becomes sensitized to the beauties of the English countryside and to the value of tradition, so she also, however, becomes aware of the stultifying effects that an unblinking adherence to the past can have. Indeed, in the ending planned for the novel, but which she did not live to write, Wharton has her heroine abandon duty and obligation, incurring public disapprobation and personal shame, to pursue love with 'the right man at last'[7] beyond the shores of the land she has learned to love.

So, in *The Buccaneers* the themes and issues that have been traced throughout the texts already discussed in this chapter are writ large; the blend of genres that characterized the progress of Odo Valsecca through the Italian landscape, at once historical novel, *Bildungsroman* and travel guide, are re-enacted as Nan St George makes her way through the labyrinth of the English class system, stopping off in places with names that resonate with historical meaning like Runnymede and Tintagel. As she lies awake listening to 'the long murmur of the past breaking on the shores of a sleeping world' (*B* 134), so she is absorbing both the lesson of history and the imbrication of individual lives with specific topographies in the process of making that history. Wharton had completed twenty-nine chapters of the novel and had also made a full plan of the story before her death; both novel and plan were published in 1938 by her literary executor, Gaillard Lapsley, together with a brief introduction and lengthier afterword. The story follows the progress of a group of American girls, daughters of 'new money' and thus excluded from the houses and social events of the established families of New York, who are painted here as willing to do business with those businessmen whom Wharton called 'the Invaders' in *The Custom of the Country* but not willing to socialize with their women. Repeatedly rebuffed by New York society, the girls move on and mount an 'invasion' (*B* 159) of London society, ending by marrying into the premier aristocratic families of England.

The centre of consciousness in the novel is the woman appointed as governess to Nan St George, one Laura Testvalley, born and bred in England but of Italian descent and closely related to the real artist who features – albeit obliquely – in this novel, Dante Gabriel Rossetti – here described by Laura as 'a widower, and very stout [who] has caused all the family a good deal of trouble' (*B* 90). Despite this report of his unprepossessing appearance, the poetry of Rossetti is used throughout the narrative as a touchstone; it is one of the 'magic casements' (*B* 166) through which Nan's aesthetic sensibility is shaped and provides an aesthetic link between Nan and Laura and between them both and the men of the Thwarte family. It is Laura's status as an outsider herself that gives her particular insights into the situation of the girls in both their native and their adoptive countries. The picture painted of the old New Yorkers in this novel is of a group of nervous, narrow, and hidebound conformists who are seen entirely from the perspective of the outsiders, primarily Laura, and who are not, therefore, shown to advantage. This view of the negative side of old New York forms an interesting contrast to the picture of her own social background painted by Wharton in her autobiography, *A Backward Glance*, published just four years before *The Buccaneers*. Where the autobiography asserts repeatedly 'the value of duration ... against the welter of change' (*BG* 5), the novel takes the side of those who would breach the defences of 'the old manners and customs' (*BG* 6), with Laura leading the charge: 'Miss Testvalley, after that visit, felt that she had cast in her lot once for all with the usurpers and the adventurers. Perhaps because she herself had been born in exile, her sympathies were with the social as well as the political outcasts – with the weepers by the waters of Babylon rather than those who barred the doors of the Assembly against them' (*B* 68).

It seems clear from the way in which the characters and plot were developing in the novel when compared to the plan, that the 'little brown governess' (*B* 235) was occupying more of the narrative space than Wharton seemed to have intended originally. There are few working women in Wharton's fiction; where they occur they are hangers-on, like Carry Fisher in *The House of Mirth*, or have suffered a reversal of fortunes, like Justine Brent in *The Fruit of the Tree*, and, whilst governesses are frequent and well-established figures in English letters of the nineteenth century, the focus on such as Laura is unique in Wharton's fiction. As a writer she was generally concerned not with the employees but rather with the occupants of the grand houses of New York's elite. The portrayal of such a working woman is just one of the many distinct twists on her familiar themes and concerns in *The Buccaneers*; there are a number of interesting differences between this novel and her previous work. The particular set of attributes, personal and professional, that Laura brings to the tale – an understanding of the conditions of exile, of responsibility for dependent relatives as well as her own living, an active aesthetic sensibility, emotional independence and maturity – are significantly in advance of any other woman in her fiction; even Ellen Olenska in *The Age of Innocence*, one of Wharton's most complex and compelling women, is a dependent on the goodwill of her grandmother and responsible for no one but herself.

In her autobiography Wharton talks about the governess as having walked fully formed into her imagination:

> Laura Testvalley. How I should like to change that name! But it has been attached for some time now to a strongly outlined material form, the form of a character figuring largely in an adventure I know all about, and have long wanted to relate. Several times I have tried to give Miss Testvalley another name, since the one she bears, should it appear ever in print, will be more troublesome to my readers than to me. But she is strong-willed, and even obstinate, and turns sulky and unmanageable whenever I hint at the advantages of a change. (*BG* 202)

In his afterword to *The Buccaneers*, Gaillard Lapsley makes much of the 'tenacity and ambition of the middle-aged governess who had taken possession of the novel' (*B* 369) and not only suggests that Nan St George would have been consigned to a minor role but implies that Wharton might have found it difficult to deny this distinctive and unlikely heroine the kind of fulfilment that seems to be promised in a relationship with Sir Helmsley Thwarte. In the plan Laura loses, as Lapsley puts it, 'the great prize, the chance in October of what had been denied to her in May, ease, rank and the companionship of a cultivated man who was also her lover' (*B* 370), but she is the final facilitator of the consummation of the love between Nan St George and Guy Thwarte. This climax, again unique in Wharton's fiction, unites lovers who are forbidden by law and custom to be together; unlike Newland Archer and Ellen Olenska, the guilty couple run away together to a place outside the specific geography of Wharton's fictional territory. In *The Age of Innocence*, when Ellen

Olenska admonishes Newland Archer for having proposed that they run away together to a place where they can be unrecognized and alone, she says: 'Oh, my dear – where is that country? Have you ever been there?...I know so many who've tried to find it; and, believe me, they all got out by mistake at wayside stations: at places like Boulogne, or Pisa, or Monte Carlo – and it wasn't at all different from the old world they'd left, but only rather smaller and dingier and more promiscuous' (*AI* 293). No such scruples afflict Nan and Guy as they make their escape, but Laura, 'the great old adventuress, seeing love, deep and abiding love, triumph for the first time in her career...goes back alone to old age and poverty' (*B* 359).

In *The Buccaneers*, despite its anti-establishment ending, there is a conciliatory and mediating spirit abroad. In this, the last of Wharton's fictions, the tensions between ancient and modern, youth and age, individual and society, as well as between cultures and their distinct imperatives, are ameliorated in the even-handed appreciation of the old alongside an embrace of the new. The book was generally well received on its publication in both the United States and Great Britain and the eminent critic Edmund Wilson, writing in the *New Republic*, combined praise for the character of the governess with an appreciation of the author herself:

> Miss Testvalley is much the best thing in the book; and there is a particular appropriateness and felicity in the fact that Edith Wharton should have left as the last human symbol of her fiction this figure who embodies the revolutionary principle implicit in all her work. As the light of her art grows dim and goes out before she has finished this last novel, the image still lingers on our retina of the large dark eyes of the clever spinster, who, like her creator, in trading in worldly values, has given a rebuff to the values of the world; in following a destiny solitary and disciplined, has fought a campaign for what, in that generation, would have been called the rights of the heart[8]

– an epitaph of which both Laura Testvalley and Edith Wharton might have approved.

5

Living in America

In this chapter I will be discussing texts that are concerned with life in early twentieth century America – the first published in 1907 and the rest in the 1920s – and that are controversial in some way or other, in their engagement either with taboo or with contemporary public discussions about subjects as various as euthanasia, factory reform, and religion. From *The Fruit of the Tree*, published in 1907, through *The Glimpses of the Moon* (1922), *The Mother's Recompense* (1925), *Twilight Sleep* (1927), to *The Children* (1928), Wharton is concerned with morality in the modern world and, in particular, how variation and change in the moral climate affect the role of women in society. As novels they are part-reactionary, part-revolutionary, venturing into territory that is controversial and shocking but also demonstrating allegiance to a clearly visible set of traditional moral standards.

For many years critical opinion has placed all of these novels firmly in the second rank of Wharton's achievement, a judgement that is, in many ways predicated on the assumption that the texts are written by someone alienated or estranged from the subject of her fiction – that is, the society of her native land. I would like to argue that the central difference between these novels and those judged to be of greater artistic worth is chiefly the transparency of their morality: they all clearly and unflinchingly promote a well-defined aesthetic and ideological position. In articulation of their particular concerns a fairly histrionic mode of delivery is common to all these texts and they offer, in many ways, very straightforward accounts of conflict between clearly delineated contesting forces. The dramas are played out in a variety of different settings – from the seedy Riviera lodging house to the avant-garde New York salon, from the *Nouveau Luxe* hotel in Paris to the industrial town of Hanaford – and are all structured around social discordance and personal confusion. The novel, *Twilight Sleep*, for instance, is essentially predicated on the gross disjunction between the surface – the world in which Pauline Manford is preoccupied by the organization of a prestigious dinner party or the best way to reduce the size of her hips – and the underside, where her family are plunging ever more fearfully into a chaos of infidelity, incest, and murderous intent. The fact that two such worlds coexist, each real, one directly acknowledged, one unacknowledged, and each deeply antipathetic to the other, is Wharton's subject in this, and, indeed, all of these novels.

A novel that Edith Wharton published in 1907, *The Fruit of the Tree*, has been subject to much critical re-examination, particularly in relation to issues of social class and gender, both being of crucial importance to the narrative here. *The Fruit of the Tree* is the least consistently satiric of all the texts under discussion in this chapter, but, in spite of this, a variety of human frailties are mercilessly exposed, not least, and as ever, the destructiveness of 'separate spheres' of activity for men and women. The monstrous appetite of such as Undine Spragg for self-gratification is not on display in this novel, but one of the major narrative lines is fuelled by the consequences of the ignorance of women about the economic structures that support or restrict their spending. As Wharton makes plain, every dispute between John Amherst and his wife is provoked by their contrasting views about the uses to which money should be dedicated. She cannot answer his questions about the management of the mills:

> As the easiest means of escaping them, she had once more dismissed the whole problem to the vague and tiresome sphere of 'business,' ... Her first husband – poor unappreciated Westmore! – had always spared her the boredom of 'business', and Halford Gaines and Mr Tredegar were ready to show her the same consideration; it was part of the modern code of chivalry that lovely woman should not be bothered about ways and means' (*FT* 182–3).

The effects of this 'modern code of chivalry' are visible everywhere in Wharton's work, in both fiction and non-fiction: for instance, she considers the economic and intellectual infantilization of the American woman in her 1919 study *French Ways and their Meaning*.[1] In *The Fruit of the Tree* Wharton sets up a simple contrast between the two female leads, the rich, spoiled Bessy Westmore and the middle-class but impoverished Justine Brent, who trains as a nurse in order both to earn a living and to play an active role in the alleviation of suffering. This novel is unique in Wharton's work in its attempt to portray the lives of the working class alongside the leisure class and to make explicit the ways and means by which the two are interconnected, with the latter being sustained in largely useless luxury by the toil of the former. This is not to make any great claim for Wharton as a social reformer or as a radical political thinker, but it is to make a claim for her as a writer with ambitions both to produce a social problem novel in the tradition of English writers such as Gaskell or Dickens and to acknowledge the complexity of the American scene by demonstrating her imaginative engagement with all its aspects. Where in *The House of Mirth* Selden expresses the 'confused sense that [Lily Bart] must have cost a great deal to make, that a great many dull and ugly people must, in some mysterious way, have been sacrificed to produce her' (*HM* 5), in *The Fruit of the Tree*, the price of everything is clearly visible, from the cost of Bessy's ignorance, expressed here by Mrs Ansell: 'Isn't [Bessy] one of the most harrowing victims of the plan of bringing up our girls in the double bondage of expediency and unreality, corrupting their bodies with luxury and their brains with sentiment, and leaving them to reconcile the two as best they can, or lose their souls in the attempt' (*FT* 281), to the price of Justine's moral and practical decisiveness in ending the course of treatment that has been prolonging Bessy's life despite all humane considerations.

There is some confusion of plot in *The Fruit of the Tree*, which is produced by the number of issues that are in contention, but the skeleton of the narrative is straightforward. Most of the action takes place in Hanaford, a mill town in western Massachusetts. The deputy manager of the mill, John Amherst, is an idealist who wishes to promote better working and living conditions for the operatives, an ideological position that puts him in conflict with the manager and those who speak for the owner, who is a young widow, Bessy Westmore. Once Bessy and John meet, however, they are instantly attracted to each other, and, after a whirlwind courtship, they marry; but the marriage almost immediately comes under the strain of cross-purposes.

John's devotion to the mill and its employees and Bessy's devotion to pleasure are soon shown to be anti-pathetic, added to which, the child they have dies and the fragile ties of sentiment and passion are quickly broken. The third lead actor in the drama of the novel is Justine Brent, an old schoolfriend of Bessy's who comes to Amherst's attention when she nurses a Hanaford worker who loses an arm after it was caught in dangerously positioned mill machinery. Justine weaves in and out of the narrative; at one minute she is working as a hospital nurse, then she returns to occupy an uncertain position between guest and employee at Bessy's Long Island home, taking care of Bessy's daughter from her first marriage, and, in some respects, acting as a conciliator between John and Bessy, trying to heal the rifts between them. Justine is on hand when Bessy has a terrible riding accident and is one of those who is responsible for caring for her. As John Amherst is in the deep South, managing a mill, there is no one to prevent the doctor in charge of Bessy's care from inflicting terrible suffering on the injured woman in order to keep her alive and Justine takes the treatment and the law into her own hands by administering a dose of morphine large enough to put Bessy out of her misery.

As Justine stays on with the family as companion to Cicely, Bessy's daughter, she is thrown in the way of John Amherst again and they realize their powerful affinities and marry. Unlike the marriage between Bessy and John, this union is based on perfect harmony of intellectual and spiritual concerns, but, when the doctor who cared for Bessy in her final days reappears and blackmails Justine, she is forced into a position where she must reveal the truth of what she did, both to Bessy's father and to John, and the relationship is ruined. After a period apart, however, they are reunited, although the understanding between them is never to be restored: 'Nothing was left of that secret inner union which had so enriched and beautified their outward lives. Since Justine's return to Hanaford they had entered, tacitly, almost unconsciously, into a new relation to each other: a relation in which their personalities were more and more merged in their common work, so that, as it were, they met only by avoiding each other' (*FT* 623).

In her essay 'Architectonic or Episodic? Gender and *The Fruit of the Tree*', Katherine Joslin points to the overarching simplicity of Wharton's allegory in this novel: 'The *hand* of labor is mangled and therefore helpless to effect social change; the *back* of the mill owner is crushed and therefore incapable of supporting the responsibilities of management in its relationship to labor; the *head* of the mill, the manager, then weds the *heart* of the novel, the nurse.'[2] This very simplicity, however, is in tension with the actual complexity of many of the issues that are opened up for discussion in the novel, as there is insufficient space for any of the matters of substance, for example, euthanasia, to be anything other than plot devices. There is a similar problem in the 1922 novel *The Glimpses of the Moon*, where the matter in contention is the marriage contract, a contract apparently freed from all its social, legal, and religious moorings in order to be reconstructed as a career move, or, more simply, a contract of employment, from which one can obtain release as soon as a better job offer comes along. Between *The Fruit of the Tree* and *The Glimpses of the Moon* there may be only fifteen years but they are years full of the most tremendous domestic and international upheaval, including, of course, the First World War. The latter novel, however, shows few signs of anything other than the most superficial engagement with the turbulence of modernity and, as such, is an anomaly in Wharton's work.

The novel itself is quite entertaining and, in many ways, satirizes leisure-class society in a manner that was to become familiar in the work of writers like F. Scott Fitzgerald and Evelyn Waugh. The leading characters, Susy Branch and Nick Lansing, are a romantic comedy version of Lily Bart and Laurence Selden who are allowed a happy ending. They meet, they fall in love, they marry – even though neither of them has inheritance or income – they live off their friends in a variety of resort settings, and eventually fall out over the moral shifts and compromises that must be made, chiefly by Susy, in order to pay back their variously dissolute friends for their financial support. Nick is then taken up by a nouveau riche, mid-Western culture-hungry family as a companion/guide to their European travels and looks set to marry the heiress if he so desires; whilst Susy becomes engaged to an English aristocrat, being urged by her friends to announce her nuptials before actually divorcing Nick so as to be sure of securing her prize. In the final resolution, however, neither can go ahead with their 'chance to do better' (*GM* 21), as their moral scruples prevent them from marrying for money when they are already married for love. In stark contrast to the tone of the majority of the writing in the novel, which is clearly satiric, they are reunited in a declaration of confidence in marriage, the family, love, and loyalty quite at odds with the Zeitgeist. The controversial in this novel – the darkness of betrayal and heartlessness of the creed of individual fulfilment at all costs, here expressed through the expedient making and breaking of marriages – is glossed over and ameliorated in a sentimental conclusion. In *The Glimpses of the Moon* Wharton does not penetrate beyond the most cursory glimpse at the pain and confusion of the individual left behind in the scramble for personal gratification or social success. In contrast, her novel of 1925, *The Mother's Recompense*, is almost entirely concerned with the superannuated individual, with the consciousness of social and emotional failure as well as with the dynamics of personal responsibility in the face of both personal and shared shame.

This novel begins and ends in exile. The narrative charts the progress of the outsider, the social outcast who having made a bid for freedom from the constraints of traditional society is cast adrift without any means of material or spiritual support. Kate Clephane, having escaped from a claustrophobic marriage by absconding with a lover, soon decides in favour of a solitary life albeit a life spent acknowledging 'the long long toll [she] had to pay to the outraged goddess of Respectability' (*MR* 29). Drifting between European resorts, living as economically as she can, she has one lapse from the business of expiation over the course of her twenty years in exile, in the form of an affair with a younger man, who is, however, the man with whom her daughter will fall in love. There are other women in Wharton's fiction who have relationships with younger men; in the short story 'The Muse's Tragedy', published in *Scribner's Magazine* in 1891, a young, aspiring writer becomes infatuated with Mrs Anerton, a woman chiefly known as an inspirational figure for the great poet Vincent Rendle; in *The Touchstone*, a novella published in 1900, Stephen Glennard, the younger man beloved by Margaret Aubyn, a writer of genius, betrays her memory by publishing her letters to him, letters that reveal the fact that he never loved her; in 'The Pretext', a short story of 1908 also published in *Scribner's Magazine*, a middle-aged, respectable New England wife is attracted to a visiting Englishman, Guy Dawnish, who, despite breaking off his engagement to a girl at home with the excuse of having formed a new attachment in America, never declares his love nor reappears. Disappointment is the refrain in all these stories and Wharton does not change the tune in *The Mother's Recompense*; all the women in these stories are in some way defrauded by their attachment to the younger man, either directly or indirectly, but only in the novel is the disparity and dissonance in age highlighted in so dramatic a way – that is, through the fact that Chris Fenno has a sexual relationship with the mother and subsequently with the daughter.

The plot of *The Mother's Recompense* holds no particular surprises except the central core of the sexual relationship of the mother and daughter with the same man. Wharton worked and reworked variations on the theme of the prodigal mother and her return to the New York society that had previously ostracized her in both short stories and novel plans throughout her career, though none has illicit sex as an issue in quite the same way as in *The Mother's Recompense*. In 'Autre Temps', a story of 1911, the woman in question, Mrs Lidcote, returns to New York when she hears the news that her daughter is to divorce and remarry. Ostracized as she has been for twenty years after her own divorce from her husband, she fears that the same fate is about to befall her child. However, it soon becomes plain that, whilst Leila, her daughter, is allowed a second chance, nothing has changed with regard to the attitude of New York society to her own situation. She is shunned by old and young alike and is forced to return to Italy before she becomes a serious embarrassment to her daughter. In some ways the story is proleptic of the novel, but the moral drama here is one that points to a fairly simple hypocrisy in the social world, whilst the core of the moral dilemma in the novel is obviously much more vexed, raising as it does questions of incest as well as illicit sexual attraction. These are questions that are also under scrutiny in *The Children* and in *Twilight Sleep*. In the latter novel, Lita Wyant, like Chris Fenno, who sleeps with both mother and daughter, sleeps with (step)father and son. A significant and shocking number of the confusions of the age are expressed through intergenerational cross-currents of desire and Wharton makes various assaults on the subject with varying degrees of

73

frankness. In the manuscripts that Edith Wharton left to Yale University in her will there is a plan for a story entitled 'Beatrice Palmato', and there is also a fragment, headed 'unpublishable' in Wharton's handwriting, which describes, in full and explicit detail, oral and penetrative sex between a father and daughter. The critic Cynthia Griffin Wolff conjectures that, since such an account could have no place in a published story, the detail of the sexual encounter is 'the suppressed horror that lay *behind* the action of the tale and made it understandable'.[3] Incest as a motif, as a sign of the kind of secret that might lie at the heart of a series of otherwise inexplicable events, is employed by Wharton in a variety of ways in the later fiction. She does not need to give us the details of the sexual relationship between Kate and Chris Fenno for the simple reason that the basic fact of the affair is sufficient to silence Kate with shame. She could not trade the information of her affair with Chris Fenno for a place in mainstream society even if she wanted to, as there are too many taboos surrounding the revelation of her own history; it becomes clear to her very quickly, as it did to Mrs Lidcote, that only the young seem to be entitled to change sexual partners or, indeed, to feel desire. One of the most uncomfortable sensations for Kate Clephane, as Wharton depicts her caught on the horns of the most terrible dilemma, is her uncertainty about her own feelings towards her daughter: does she want to separate her from her lover because she wants to protect her or because she is jealous of her? In all sorts of ways Ann's love affair and marriage to Chris Fenno provide final and irrefutable proof to Kate of her own obsolescence; as Ann walks down the aisle, so she must return to the nether-world of the Riviera, renouncing her claim on any kind of romantic or sexual fulfilment.

It is just such personal and social obsolescence that Pauline and Dexter Manford are struggling with in *Twilight Sleep*. Dexter Manford solves his middle-aged crisis of sexual confidence by indulging in an affair with his daughter-in-law, whilst Pauline is forced to rely on a troop of firemen for her kicks:

> Pauline stood smiling, watch in hand, as the hook-and-ladder motor clattered up the drive and ranged itself behind the engine. The big lantern over the front door illuminated fresh scarlet paint and super-polished brasses, the firemen's agitated helmets and perspiring faces, the flashing hoods of the lamps.... She dominated them all,

grave and glittering as the goddess of Velocity. 'She enjoys it as much as other women do love-making,' Manford muttered to himself'. (*TS* 297)

Kristin Lauer, in her essay 'Can France Survive this Defender? Contemporary American Reaction to Edith Wharton's Expatriation', formulates the 'four entrenched prejudices that we might call the four fallacies of contemporary Wharton criticism'.[4] The 'four fallacies', as Lauer describes them, are: critical assignment of her work as slavish imitation of Henry James, discussion of her work in the separate and unequal category of 'lady novelist', the audience resistance bred by her class background and expatriation to Europe, and finally her intellectual aloofness, her apparent concern with high culture at the expense of that which was deemed to be her proper, American subject. The majority of these complaints have been examined already in this study – the extent of James's influence, for instance, being fully considered in the discussion of *The Reef*. However, it is possible to cite the example of *Twilight Sleep* to refute the rest. Nothing could be less like the work of Henry James than the satirical focus of *Twilight Sleep* and indeed, of the majority of the novels discussed in this chapter, concerned as they are with the weaknesses in a society or its members. The novel treats the American not the international scene, and the horrors that would remain unexpressed in James's fiction are not only brought to the surface in this text but they are exposed in all their sordidness. This exposure of the sordid also provides the grounds for dismissing the critical tendency to discuss Wharton as if she were a genteel 'lady novelist'; there is no delicacy here, no decorum, only corruption and cynicism. As for Wharton's expatriation, as Millicent Bell has pointed out, what could be more American than living abroad as an American, defining oneself as always in opposition to an alien society?[5] Finally, the charge that Wharton was concerned only with matters of high culture is refuted on every page of *Twilight Sleep*, with the novel's unremitting preoccupation with matters of basic human weakness and corruption, as a plot summary will demonstrate.

Twilight Sleep concerns one family, but a family enlarged and ultimately distorted by the two marriages of Pauline Manford, who forms the centre of interest in the narrative. Pauline comes originally from the mid-west, her money deriving from her family, who made a fortune from mining in Pennsylvania and subsequently in bicycle and car manufacture. She marries first into old New York in the person of Arthur Wyant, and, on discovery of his infidelity, marries her divorce lawyer, the up-and-coming Dexter Manford. Pauline has a child from each marriage – a son, Jim, from the first, and a daughter, Nona, from the second – and when the novel opens they are both adult enough for Jim to be having problems with his own marriage to Lita Cliffe, and for Nona to be unhappily attached to a married man whose wife refuses to divorce him. Jim and Lita have just had a baby and it is from the place in which Lita gives birth that the novel takes its name: treatment at the 'most perfect "Twilight Sleep" establishment in the country' having enabled her to feel no pain but simply to have 'drifted into motherhood as lightly and unperceivingly as if the wax doll which suddenly appeared in the cradle had been brought there in one of the big bunches of hot-house roses she found every morning on her pillow' (*TS* 14). Jim's stepfather, Dexter Manford, in an attempt to curb Lita's ambitions to divorce Jim and establish herself as a movie actress, takes upon himself the role of her protector, a role that, when combined with a personal crisis of confidence in his own sexual attractiveness, soon develops from the fatherly to the romantic and they embark upon an affair. Whilst Nona is vaguely aware of most of what is going on, Pauline is not; she is much too busy pursuing a variety of good causes, organizing social events that are designed to enhance her prestige in New York society, as well as subscribing to a motley collection of physical and spiritual cures for her feelings of inner emptiness. Despite Pauline's blindness to the affair that is being conducted under her nose, her ex-husband, Arthur Wyant, knows what is going on and he decides to take the direct action which he sees his son, Jim, as too weak and unmanly to take for himself. Whilst all the family except Jim are at their country home, Cedarledge, he breaks in and, in his attempt to shoot Manford, he wounds Nona, who has tried to intervene. The account of the night's events that is then invented for the benefit of the public has Nona saving Lita from an armed burglar and the arrival in the room of Manford only after the shot was fired and the assailant frightened off. The novel ends with the illusion of order reimposed on the extended family group as Arthur Wyant is sent away for a rest cure, Lita and Jim on a tour of Europe, and Pauline and Dexter Manford on a trip around the world. Nona is left to recuperate as best she can, alone as she is with the most painful of memories and feelings of total disillusion.

Twilight Sleep is the published text in which Wharton is most explicit about intergenerational sexual relations and, again, about incest or near-incest. One of the participants, Lita Wyant, is – in the Undine Spragg tradition of Wharton heroine/villains – both the clearest of villains and the clearest of victims. Like Bessy Westmore in *The Fruit of the Tree*, she has been brought up to regard the pursuit of pleasure as her right and due; she has no empathy, no love, no loyalty, and no scruples. Lita is frank and open because she has no sense of right and wrong, no sense that there might be things that are unsayable and relationships that might be taboo. She is a bundle of appetites, underscored and driven by vanity and perverseness in her targeting of Dexter Manford as her next lover, believing him to be, as she informs a scandalized Pauline, her husband's real father. The only voice speaking against such reckless pursuit of individual pleasure is that of Nona; a contemporary of Lita's but a girl made wise beyond her years by the weight of responsibility that falls upon her in the absence of adequate parents. The subject of the abnegation of parental duty was to absorb all of Wharton's attention in her next novel, *The Children*, where the assorted parents of the extended Wheater family are so remiss that the children declare themselves independent of them, seeking to set up an alternative family structure that cannot be destabilized by divorce or remarriage.

As in the earlier *The Glimpses of the Moon*, the setting for *The Children* is resort Europe, a country populated by people with too much money, too much self-absorption, and no sense of responsibility or morality. Into this 'wilderness', as Wharton calls the world in which the children of the title move – 'The real wilderness is the world *we* live in; packing up our tents every few weeks for another move . . . And the marriages just like tents – folded up and thrown away when you've done with them' (*C* 23) – comes Martin Boyne, an engineer returning after a long absence from fashionable society, who is selected by the assorted children to be their guardian. The children in question are all connected to Cliffe and Joyce Wheater, friends of Martin Boyne's youth. The eldest is Judith, 15 years old at the start of the novel, followed by twins, Terry and Blanca – these three deriving from the first marriage of Cliffe and Joyce; following on are two step-siblings – Bun and Beechy – who are the children of an Italian nobleman to whom Joyce was briefly married, and Zinnie, the child of Cliffe's marriage to a film star; the last child, Chipstone, is the offspring of Cliffe and Joyce's second marriage to each other. The competing appetites that have both produced the tribe of children and have kept them on tenterhooks – as custody battles and disputes over money rage around them – are portrayed in a kind of burlesque style, which belies, again in the mode of *The Glimpses of the Moon,* the seriousness of the destruction of human life and hope which is the inevitable end result of the way in which the adults conduct themselves. Even the eminently sensible and staid Martin Boyne, the piece of security to whom the children cling, is infected by the promise of endlessly renewable youth as he entertains hopes of being not Judith's parent but her lover. Despite his long-standing commitment to a woman of his own age, Rose Sellars, Martin prefers to retreat from the mature relationship and the shared community of taste, of culture, and of generation, to the role of a guardian with unlimited access to Judith, who, however, interprets his offer of marriage as an offer to adopt her. This is the final incest or near-incest plot to feature in the novels of Wharton's later career and its role here is to indicate not so much Martin's innate corruption but his inability to remain unaffected by the constant valorization of youth that surrounds him and, concomitantly, his failure to take on a responsibility that might in some way restrict the range of interpretations to which his largely unexciting life is subject. He proposes to Judith probably knowing that he will be rejected, and what he finally fails to understand, as do most of the other adults in the novel, is the nature of the freedom that might be gained through commitment. The novel ends: 'Two days after-ward, the ship which had brought him to Europe started on her voyage to Brazil. On her deck stood Boyne, a lonely man' (C. 347). Stark as it is, his end is in his beginning, he leaves as empty-handed and hearted as he began, a fate he shares with the majority of those who people Wharton's fictions of the 1920s.

6

Edith Wharton and her Books: A Writer in her Library

Apart from her last historical novel, *The Buccaneers*, Wharton would be absorbed, from the publication of *The Children* onwards, with the telling of the writer's life, both in fiction – in the linked narratives, *Hudson River Bracketed* (1929) and *The Gods Arrive* (1932) – and in her own autobiography, *A Backward Glance*. Crucial and central in that telling is the place and influence of the printed word, the literary influences that not only awakened and sustained Wharton herself as an artist but that she places at the heart of the life story of her fictional writer, Vance Weston. Whilst the moral and social concerns that animated the novels of American life discussed in the previous chapter do not disappear, they are more incidental to the structure of both the novels and the autobiography. All three books can be seen as continuing with the anti-modernist and reactionary drift of Wharton's work in the 1920s: the strongest impetus for the writing of the fiction, for instance, is the promotion of the argument she put forward to her publishers, Appleton, in an outline of *Hudson River Bracketed*: that the cultural conditions of American life are not conducive to the production of great art. As she said: 'I want to try to draw the experiences of an unusually intelligent modern American youth, of average education and situation, on whom the great revelation of the Past, which everything in modern American training tends to exclude, or at least to minimize, rushes in through the million channels of art, of history, and of human beings of another civilisation' (*SHRB*).

Wharton's ambition in *A Backward Glance*, as discussed in Chapter 1, is to commemorate not interrogate the social structures of old New York. Whilst she celebrates the access to culture that relative freedom to explore her father's library gave her as a child, she also pokes fun at the fear and loathing in which her family and social circle held the practitioners of any creative art. The autobiography is an embattled text, but the obstacles that she describes as having been thrown in the way of her own youthful artistic ambitions are as nothing compared to the difficulties with which she freights the intellectual and creative development of Vance Weston. From humble beginnings in Euphoria, Illinois, through a crash course in the art and architecture of Western civilization – mediated through 'a fairly good specimen of what used to be called a "gentleman's library" ... with additions, naturally, from each generation' (*HRB* 68) – through artistic success and failure, romantic fulfilment, disillusion, infidelity, and reconciliation, Vance Weston ends sadder and wiser, persuaded of the virtues of tradition and continuity, both in personal and aesthetic terms. *Hudson River Bracketed* and *The Gods Arrive* are interlaced with many of Wharton's own most fiercely held beliefs about life and art, and her distrust of 'modern American training' is palpable in the text. What is celebrated unequivocally in these novels, however, particularly in the first, is the role of the printed word in the account of Vance's maturation. As in her own case, the expression of the individual artist's indebtedness to the work of others, and in particular to a wide range of poetic works, is here portrayed as more than an acknowledgement of pleasure or even of influence; it is an enabling principle that endows personal and artistic enlightenment as well as a means of expression. In both her personal writing and in her fictional accounts of the artist, she uses literary language and citations from the work of other writers in order to fill the gaps, to cross the divide where her own invention cannot equal the sublimity of the moment of realization or change. She figures the debt to the work of other artists in terms of illumination: Vance Weston sitting in the library at the old house, the Willows, comes across Coleridge's 'Kubla Khan' for the first time and hears 'a new music, a music utterly unknown to him, but to which the hidden chords of his soul at once vibrated' (*HRB* 63). In her earlier, aborted attempt at drawing the portrait of an artist, 'Literature', she has Richard Thaxter, as a small child, being transfixed by the 'rain of celestial syllables' (Lit. 2), which is David's lament for Absalom, and in her own autobiographical fragment, 'Life and I', she describes the life-changing effects of her first experience of 'The Lays of Ancient Rome' – 'The movement of the metre was intoxicating: I can still feel the thump thump of my little heart as I listened to it! . . . But this increase of knowledge was as nought compared to the sensuous rapture produced by the sound and sight of the words' (L&I 9). In each case the encounter with the poetry provides the crucial moment of recognition of the intrinsic worth of the words for and in themselves and, beyond that, of the writing life as enmeshed in and expressed through literary encounters or recognitions.

From her account of the small girl who returned to New York from her years in Europe, 'to enter into the kingdom of [her] father's library' (BG 43), through to the mature, successful artist reflecting on *The Writing of Fiction*, much of Wharton's sense of her own work and worth can be understood in relation to her books and to the acts of writing and reading. Wharton found both a community and a voice in literature; she entered into a shared world of artistic tradition when she read and wrote and the volumes in her library communicate a sense of intimacy with Wharton herself, with the essence of her personal and professional being, driven as she was from first to last by 'Letters' (*BG* 119).

One of the books that is of special interest in Wharton's library and that I want to mention in conclusion of this study of her work, is her copy of *Leaves of Grass*, inscribed to her by Walter Berry: ' "Who can stray from me?/I follow you whoever you are from the present hour." Washington April 1898'.[1] The markings in the book follow almost exactly the list of lines and poems given in the outline of a study of Whitman's poetry Wharton had planned to write and, indeed, had mapped out in some detail (Notes). In her *Leaves of Grass* she marked poems in the list of contents and also side- or under-scored individual lines or stanzas and stylistic and linguistic features. The themes she tracks through the poetry in her markings declare her affinities both as reader and writer with Whitman, and this declaration of affinity is not limited to her interactions with this poet: everywhere in the pages of the books she owned are testimonials to the way in which her literary life 'interpene-trated', to use one of her favoured words, both her quotidian and her professional existence. For instance, she writes 'back' to the editor of *Sages et poètes d'Asie* (1916), Paul-Louis Couchoud, adding six haikus of her own to the endpapers, which make touching and tender reading, for example:

> My little old dog:-
> A heart beat
> At my feet.

There are other interpolations in a variety of different volumes but the most characteristic intervention is the line or lines drawn in the margin, described here in a 1901 letter from Wharton to Sally Norton and cited in George Ramsden's Introduction: 'I send you back the little book with a faint scratch here and there to show you the detached things that struck me...this is the nearest approach to talking over a book together.'[2] Wharton's edition of Shakespeare's Sonnets, for example, which Ramsden believes was acquired in Paris in the winter/spring of 1906–7, when her affair with Morton Fullerton began, is heavily marked, and among the lines underscored are these from Sonnet 110:

> Most true it is that I have look'd on truth
> Askance and strangely: but, by all above,
> These blenches gave my heart another youth,
> And worst essays proved thee my best of love.

The expression of passion, love that combines intellectual and physical attraction, and, above all, the renewal of youth that love seemed to promise, these are the themes traced through her markings in Shakespeare's Sonnets. Her feelings, as expressed through those markings, leap off the page, as Shakespeare's words become her words, as they take on the significance of events in her life and her art. In other volumes there are on-the-spot translations of work written in French and German; indeed, as mentioned in the Introduction, some of her marginalia are in French or German.

However, returning to Whitman, in her notes for the article she was planning she writes:

> He has the direct vision: his characterization of natural objects is extraordinarily suggestive; he sees through the layers of the

conventional point of view and of the conventional adjective, straight to the thing itself, and not only to the thing itself, but to the endless thread connecting it to the universe. He hears 'the poor grass plot and plan/What it will do when it is man.' This sense of the absolute behind the relative gives to his adjectives their startling, penetrating, quality, their ultimateness. (Notes)

The features of Whitman's work that she wishes to explore are therefore his 'sense of continuity', his transmission of the generic behind the specific, and his 'unexpectedness' – particularly his syntactic 'unexpectedness'. Put simply, his ability to arrest, confront, change, and yet build on the experience of the reader is for her the essence of his genius, and, as so often in Wharton's expressed relationship with art and artists, what she admires about Whitman is also revelatory of her own creed, a creed that finds repeated exposition in her personal writings – letters, journals – as well as in her critical work.

One of the patterns that emerges from her markings in the text of *Leaves of Grass* is her emphasis on Whitman's confidence that he can render any experience poetic and of benefit to humanity, for example, from 'Starting from Paumanok': 'And I will show that whatever happens to anybody it may be turned to beautiful results'.[3] Wharton also repeatedly highlights the poet's self-reflexivity, the manifold allusions to the making of the poem, and, most significantly, the use of figurative language deriving from the lexical, from speech and writing as well as from the publishing, reading, and possessing of books. She marks the line in 'I Saw in Louisiana a Live Oak Growing': 'Without any companion it grew there uttering joyous leaves of dark green',[4] in 'Song of Myself' she encloses the line: 'Do you know O speech how the buds beneath you are folded?'[5] and, from 'So Long!', she picks out:

> Camerado, this is no book,
> Who touches this touches a man,
> (Is it night? Are we here together alone?)
> It is I you hold and who holds you,
> I spring from the pages into your arms.[6]

Wharton clearly has a sensual awareness of the language, of the presence of the 'man' in his language; love and desire, both suggested and protested – the lyrical capaciousness of Whitman's patriotic and erotic verse charges her critical and creative juices.

The Edith Wharton who planned to write an essay on Walt Whitman is a confident manipulator as well as interpreter of language. The cadences of his verse often echo in her own writing, especially when she is describing the effects of the war in Europe. The only phrase picked out in the Whitman poem 'Assurances' – 'the inherences of things'[7] – is the line at the top of her essay plan; what is valued most especially in Whitman by Wharton is the direct assault he makes upon 'the intrinsic quality of the thing described', the expression, with all the self-consciousness of the maker of the book, of the essential through which the universal can also be discerned. In a letter to Henry James of March 1915 Wharton talks of 'those big summing-up impressions one meets at every turn. I shall never forget the 15 mile run from Verdun to that particular ambulance, across a snow-covered rolling country sweeping up to the white sky, with no-one in sight but now & then a cavalry patrol with a blown cloak struggling along against the wind' (*L.* 351). The lone soldier, exposed at once as both prosaic and sublime, stark against the windswept landscape, encapsulates the experience and the effect of war, on the individual, the landscape, and the observer. In such a description Wharton forces her reader back to the essentials of both the humanized and the natural landscape, to 'the inherences of things'.

In some ways it could be considered perverse to concentrate on Wharton's relationship with Whitman in discussing her library, which must be seen, in its entirety, as a testament to Wharton's long and loving relationship with the classics – old and new – of European literature. However, one of the things that reading Wharton reading Whitman does is to direct attention back to the American Wharton, towards a celebration of 'the large unconscious scenery of my land with its lakes and forests', which she highlights in 'When Lilacs last in the Dooryard Bloom'd'.[8] The word 'unconscious' here is a good example of what she calls, in her notes for the essay, 'the allusive adjective, which while not describing the concrete object as it presents itself to the eye, suggests it as it presents itself to the imagination'. This 'indirect association' – which she compares twice with Keats's description of Ruth standing 'amid the alien corn' in 'Ode to a Nightingale' – is a pared-down version of the informing principle – yet again – of her idea of what great art should achieve. The line describing her native land contains, for Wharton, the essence of the American landscape; the very simplicity of its scenery contains and suggests the un-humanized and therefore boundless possibilities of that landscape for the human imagination. Wharton's response to Whitman is positive; it reaches for the sublime in the American scene brought before her by the poetry and is a salutary reminder that the letter to Sally Norton that complains of 'the wild dishevelled backwoods look of everything when one first comes home!' (L. 84) cited in Chapter 1 is not the only view of her native land to be expressed or felt by Wharton.

The sense of isolation that is communicated throughout Wharton's autobiographical writings is illustrated in the interactions visible between the author and her books, but it is concomitantly ameliorated by the sense of connectedness she clearly felt with other readers and also with the writers. To borrow a phrase she uses in the essay fragment 'Italy Again', the books made literal for her her own descent from 'the great genealogical tree of the arts' (IA). The reading of Whitman placed alongside the work she did in preparation for her essay on the poet expresses something of Wharton in her books which is often missed – it communicates an adult enthusiasm. Whitman, 'the great patient rugged joys'[9] of Whitman that she marked in the 'Song of the Redwood Tree', brings out the best in the American Wharton. The relationship between the two, as communicated through her markings of the verse, actually effects one of those 'summing-up impressions' she wrote about to Henry James. An exploration of the 'scratches' in Wharton's volume of Whitman's Leaves of Grass can be said to encapsulate the experience of the library as a whole; in the lone book, so closely and sensitively marked, can be found, in true Whitmanian style, 'the intrinsic quality of the thing described'. For Wharton, words – especially the language of poetry – were, 'visible, almost tangible presences' in her life; (L&I 10); recognition of what she could achieve came to her through the written word, to which she, in turn, dedicated her life.

Notes

INTRODUCTION

1. R. W. B. Lewis, *Edith Wharton* (London: Constable, 1975), 151.
2. George Ramsden, *Edith Wharton's Library: A Catalogue* (York: Stone Trough Books, 1999), 38.
3. Ibid. 63.
4. Details of all the books cited here are given in the Bibliography.

CHAPTER 1. TRAVEL BROADENS THE MIND

1. The majority of the marks – underlinings and lines in the margins – that Wharton made in her copy of Henry James's 1907 volume *The American Scene* are all made in sympathy with negative remarks on the impression given by features of the American landscape and customs. For instance, in the chapter 'New York Revisited', she marks: 'It is indubitably a "great" bay, a great harbour, but no one item of the romantic, or even of the picturesque, as commonly understood, contributes to its effect. The shores are low and for the most part depressingly furnished and prosaically peopled' (*The American Scene* (1907; repr. Bloomington and London: Indiana University Press, 1968), 73–4).
2. R. W. B. Lewis, *Edith Wharton* (London: Constable, 1975), 272.
3. See Alan Price, *The End of the Age of Innocence: Edith Wharton and the First World War* (London: Robert Hale, 1996), for a comprehensive account of Wharton's war work.
4. Kristin Olson Lauer, 'Can France Survive This Defender? Contemporary American Reaction to Edith Wharton's Expatriation', in Katherine Joslin and Alan Price (eds.), *Wretched Exotic: Essays on Edith Wharton in Europe* (New York: Peter Lang Publishing, Inc., 1993), 88.
5. James Tuttleton, Kristin Lauer, and Margaret Murray (eds.), *Edith*

Wharton: The Contemporary Reviews (New York: Cambridge University Press, 1992), 301.

6. For a full discussion of the development of Wharton's writing of the self, see Chapter 6, ' "Literature" or the Various Forms of Autobiography', in Janet Beer Goodwyn, *Edith Wharton: Traveller in the Land of Letters* (Basingstoke: Macmillan, 1990).

CHAPTER 2. WRITING NEW YORK – OLD AND NEW

1. James Fenimore Cooper, *The Pioneers* (1823; repr. New York: New American Library, 1964), 43.
2. In his biography of Edith Wharton, R. W. B. Lewis gives an account of the origins of the social group called the 'Four Hundred' as 'the number of people who could be fitted comfortably into Mrs Astor's ballroom at Fifth Avenue and Thirty-fourth Street... Ward McAllister, Mrs Astor's social entrepreneur, declared that number to represent the maximum size of the whole of genuine New York society' (*Edith Wharton* (London: Constable, 1975), 36).
3. Amy Kaplan, *The Social Construction of American Realism* (Chicago: University of Chicago Press, 1988; repr. 1992), 93.
4. Henry James, 'The New Novel' (1914); repr. in *Selected Literary Criticism*, ed. Morris Shapira (London: Peregrine Books, 1968), 387.
5. James Tuttleton, Kristin Lauer, and Margaret Murray (eds.), *Edith Wharton: The Contemporary Reviews* (New York: Cambridge University Press, 1992), 205.
6. Ibid. 291–2.
7. Georg Lukács, *The Historical Novel*, trans. Hannah and Stanley Mitchell (London: Peregrine Books, 1969), 38.

CHAPTER 3. THE SHORTER FICTION

1. George Ramsden, *Edith Wharton's Library: A Catalogue* (York: Stone Trough Books, 1999), 169.
2. Charles Darwin, *The Descent of Man* (1871; repr. New York: Appleton, 1895), 233.
3. James Tuttleton, Kristin Lauer, and Margaret Murray (eds.), *Edith Wharton: The Contemporary Reviews* (New York: Cambridge University Press, 1992), 79.
4. In *A Backward Glance* Wharton pays tribute to the influence of Egerton Winthrop, who had introduced her 'to the wonder-world of nineteenth century science. He it was who gave me Wallace's "Darwin and Darwinism", and "The Origin of Species", and made

known to me Huxley, Herbert Spencer, Romanes, Haeckel, Westermarck, and the various popular exponents of the great evolutionary movement' (*BG* 94).

5. The opening of Norris's *McTeague* describes McTeague, the car-boy turned dentist, as 'immensely strong, stupid, docile, obedient' (*McTeague* (1899; repr. Oxford: Oxford University Press, 1995), 7). Edith Wharton definitely owned Frank Norris's novel, *The Pit*, published in 1903; see Ramsden, *Edith Wharton's Library*, 91.
6. Tuttleton *et al* (eds.), *Edith Wharton: The Contemporary Reviews*, 183.
7. Darwin, *The Descent of Man*, 233.
8. Donna Campbell, *Resisting Regionalism: Gender and Naturalism in American Fiction, 1885–1915* (Ohio: Ohio University Press, 1997), 9.
9. Bert Bender, *The Descent of Love: Darwin and the Theory of Sexual Selection in American Fiction, 1871–1926* (Philadelphia: University of Pennsylvania Press, 1996), 323.
10. Charlotte Perkins Gilman, 'Economic Basis of the Woman Question' (1898), collected in Aileen S. Kraditor (ed.), *Up From the Pedestal: Selected Writings in the History of American Feminism*, ed. (Chicago: Quadrangle Books, 1968), 175–6.
11. See the discussion of the novellas in the chapter 'Edith Wharton and the Coherence of the Novella: From Initiation to Disillusion', in Janet Beer, *Kate Chopin, Edith Wharton and Charlotte Perkins Gilman: Studies in Short Fiction* (Basingstoke: Macmillan, 1997).
12. R. W. B. Lewis, *Edith Wharton* (London: Constable, 1975), 396.
13. Tuttleton *et al* (eds.), *Edith Wharton: The Contemporary Reviews*, 186.
14. Ibid., pp. xiv–xv.
15. See the discussion of Wharton's relationship with writers of local colour in the chapter 'Edith Wharton, Literary Ghosts and the Writing of New England', in Beer, *Kate Chopin, Edith Wharton and Charlotte Perkins Gilman.*
16. Tuttleton *et al* (eds.), *Edith Wharton: The Contemporary Reviews*, 263.

CHAPTER 4. THE INTERNATIONAL SCENE

1. R. W. B. Lewis, *Edith Wharton* (London: Constable, 1975), 28.
2. George Ramsden, *Edith Wharton's Library: A Catalogue* (York: Stone Trough Books, 1999), 2.
3. Lyall H. Powers (ed), *Henry James and Edith Wharton: Letters 1900–1915* (London: Weidenfeld & Nicolson, 1990), 34.
4. Lewis, *Edith Wharton*, 126.
5. Powers (ed.), *Henry James and Edith Wharton: Letters 1900–1915*, 238.
6. Lewis, *Edith Wharton*, 406.
7. From a letter to Royall Tyler quoted by Lewis (*Edith Wharton*, 421), in

which she describes her feelings on the purchase of her house in the South of France, Ste Claire du Vieux Château.

8. James Tuttleton, Kristin Lauer, and Margaret Murray (eds.), *Edith Wharton: The Contemporary Reviews* (New York: Cambridge University Press, 1992), 553.

CHAPTER 5. LIVING IN AMERICA

1. In a discussion of the differences between American and French women Wharton declares that the social world occupied by most American women 'bears not much more likeness to real living than the exercises of the Montessori infant' (*FWM* 102).
2. Katherine Joslin, 'Architectonic or Episodic? Gender and *The Fruit of the Tree* in Clare Colquitt, Susan Goodman, and Candace Waid (eds.), *A Forward Glance: New Essays on Edith Wharton* (London: Associated University Presses, 1999), 70.
3. Cynthia Griffin Wolff, *A Feast of Words: The Triumph of Edith Wharton* (New York: Oxford University Press, 1977), 307.
4. Kristin Lauer, 'Can France Survive this Defender? Contemporary American Reaction to Edith Wharton's Expatriation', in Katherine Joslin and Alan Price (eds.), *Wretched Exotic: Essays on Edith Wharton in Europe* (New York: Peter Lang Publishing, Inc., 1993), 80.
5. Millicent Bell, 'Edith Wharton in France', in ibid. 64.

CHAPTER 6. EDITH WHARTON AND HER BOOKS: A WRITER IN HER LIBRARY

1. George Ramsden, *Edith Wharton's Library: A Catalogue* (York: Stone Trough Books, 1999), 141.
2. Ibid., p. xix.
3. *Walt Whitman: The Complete Poems*, ed. Francis Murphy (London: Penguin Books, 1975), 57.
4. Ibid. 159.
5. Ibid. 89.
6. Ibid. 513.
7. Ibid. 462.
8. Ibid. 355.
9. Ibid. 236.

Select Bibliography

WORKS BY EDITH WHARTON

The Decoration of Houses (With Ogden Codman Jr.) (New York: Charles Scribner's Sons, 1897).

The Greater Inclination (New York: Charles Scribner's Sons, 1899).

The Touchstone (New York: Charles Scribner's Sons, 1900).

Crucial Instances (New York: Charles Scribner's Sons, 1901).

The Valley of Decision (New York: Charles Scribner's Sons, 1902).

Sanctuary (New York: Charles Scribner's Sons, 1903).

The Descent of Man and Other Stories (New York: Charles Scribner's Sons, 1904).

Italian Villas and their Gardens (New York: The Century Co., 1904; repr. New York: da Capo Press Inc., 1988).

Italian Backgrounds (New York: Charles Scribner's Sons, 1905).

The House of Mirth (New York: Charles Scribner's Sons, 1905; London: Oxford University Press, 1936).

Madame de Treymes (New York: Charles Scribner's Sons, 1907).

The Fruit of the Tree (New York: Charles Scribner's Sons, 1907).

The Hermit and the Wild Woman and Other Stories (New York: Charles Scribner's Sons, 1908).

A Motor-Flight through France (New York: Charles Scribner's Sons, 1908).

Artemis to Actaeon and Other Verse (New York: Charles Scribner's Sons, 1909).

Tales of Men and Ghosts (New York: Charles Scribner's Sons, 1910).

Ethan Frome (New York: Charles Scribner's Sons, 1911; repr. London: Constable, 1976).

The Reef (New York: D. Appleton & Co., 1912).

The Custom of the Country (New York: Charles Scribner's Sons, 1913).

Fighting France: From Dunkerque to Belfort (New York: Charles Scribner's Sons, 1915).

Xingu and Other Stories (New York: Charles Scribner's Sons, 1916).

The Book of the Homeless (ed.) (London: Macmillan & Co., Limited, 1916).

Summer (New York: D. Appleton & Co., 1917; repr. London: Constable,

1976).

The Marne (New York: D. Appleton & Co., 1918).

French Ways and their Meaning (New York and London: D. Appleton & Co., 1919).

In Morocco (New York: Charles Scribner's Sons, 1920).

The Age of Innocence (New York and London: D. Appleton & Co., 1920).

The Glimpses of the Moon (New York and London: D. Appleton & Co., 1922).

A Son at the Front (New York: Charles Scribner's Sons, 1923).

False Dawn (New York and London: D. Appleton & Co., 1924).

New Year's Day (New York and London: D. Appleton & Co., 1924).

The Old Maid (New York and London: D. Appleton & Co., 1924).

The Spark (New York and London: D. Appleton & Co., 1924).

The Writing of Fiction (New York and London: Charles Scribner's Sons, 1925).

The Mother's Recompense (New York and London: D. Appleton & Co., 1925).

Here and Beyond (New York and London: D. Appleton & Co., 1926).

Twilight Sleep (New York and London: D. Appleton and Co., 1927).

The Children (New York and London: D. Appleton and Co., 1928).

Hudson River Bracketed (New York and London: D. Appleton and Co., 1929).

Certain People (New York and London: D. Appleton and Co., 1930).

The Gods Arrive (New York and London: D. Appleton and Co., 1932).

Human Nature (New York and London: D. Appleton and Co., 1933).

A Backward Glance (New York and London: D. Appleton-Century Co. Inc., 1934; repr. London: Constable & Co., 1972).

The World Over (New York and London: D. Appleton-Century Co. Inc., 1936).

Ghosts (New York and London: D. Appleton-Century Co, 1937; repr. as *The Ghost Stories of Edith Wharton* New York: Charles Scribner's Sons, 1973).

The Buccaneers (New York and London: D. Appleton-Century Co., 1938).

The Letters of Edith Wharton, ed. R. W. B. Lewis and Nancy Lewis (London: Simon & Schuster Ltd, 1988).

Edith Wharton: The Uncollected Critical Writings, ed. Frederick Wegener (Princeton: Princeton University Press, 1996).

The Reckoning and Other Stories, ed. Janet Beer (London: Pheonix Paperbacks, 1999).

BIOGRAPHY

Lewis, R. W. B., *Edith Wharton* (London: Constable, 1975).

Benstock, Shari, *No Gifts from Chance: A Biography of Edith Wharton* (London: Penguin Books, 1994).

Griffin Wolff, Cynthia, *A Feast of Words: The Triumph of Edith Wharton* (New York: Oxford University Press, 1977).

CRITICISM AND OTHER WORKS

Ammons, Elizabeth, *Edith Wharton's Argument with America* (Athens, Ga.: University of Georgia Press, 1980). A study that focuses on Wharton's portrayal of women within the particular conditions of American society.

Beer Goodwyn, Janet, *Edith Wharton: Traveller in the Land of Letters* (Basingstoke: Macmillan, 1990). This book considers Wharton's fiction and non-fiction with particular regard to the landscapes that inform and illuminate her subjects.

Beer, Janet, *Kate Chopin, Edith Wharton and Charlotte Perkins Gilman: Studies in Short Fiction* (Basingstoke: Macmillan, 1997). As well as a brief introductory chapter that considers all three writers, there are two chapters dedicated to a discussion of Wharton: one considers her novellas and the other the short fiction that she set in New England.

Bender, Bert, *The Descent of Love: Darwin and the Theory of Sexual Selection in American Fiction, 1871–1926* (Philadelphia: University of Pennsylvania Press, 1996). A study of a number of authors, including Wharton, in terms of the influence of Darwin's theories of sexual selection on their writing.

Campbell, Donna, *Resisting Regionalism: Gender and Naturalism in American Fiction, 1885–1915* (Ohio: Ohio University Press, 1997). A detailed examination of the relationship between naturalism and local colour in turn-of-the-century American writing.

Colquitt, Clare, Goodman, Susan, and Waid, Candace (eds.), *A Forward Glance: New Essays on Edith Wharton* (London: Associated University Presses, 1999). A collection of essays on a variety of aspects of Wharton's work, including discussions of biography, autobiography, and aesthetics; issues of race, class, and gender are also given particular attention throughout the volume.

Darwin, Charles, *The Descent of Man* (1871; repr. New York: Appleton, 1895). Darwin's exegesis of his theories of sexual selection.

Erlich, Gloria, *The Sexual Education of Edith Wharton* (Berkeley and Los Angeles: University of California Press, 1992). A study of selected texts by Wharton via the perspective of familial and sexual influences upon the writer herself.

Fedorko, Kathy, *Gender and Gothic in the Fiction of Edith Wharton*

(Tuscaloosa, Ala.: University of Alabama Press, 1995). Close analysis of a range of Wharton's short stories and six of her novels through gothic convention in order to explore 'gender tension' in the fiction.

Goodman, Susan, *Edith Wharton's Women: Friends and Rivals* (Hanover and London: University Press of New England, 1990). A re-evaluation of certain of Wharton's writings alongside close scrutiny of her relationships with women – both friends and family.

James, Henry, *The American Scene* (Bloomington and London: Indiana University Press, 1968). James's impressions of a trip he took to the United States in 1904.

—— 'The New Novel' (1914), repr. in *Selected Literary Criticism*, ed. Morris Shapira (London: Peregrine Books, 1968). A collection of critical essays by Henry James.

Joslin, Katherine, *Edith Wharton* (London: Macmillan, 1991). An introduction to the major novels that provides a detailed feminist reading of Wharton's work.

—— and Price, Alan (eds), *Wretched Exotic: Essays on Edith Wharton in Europe* (New York: Peter Lang Publishing, Inc., 1993). A collection of nineteen essays, the majority of which place Wharton's work in a European context.

Kaplan, Amy, *The Social Construction of American Realism* (Chicago: University of Chicago Press, 1988; repr. 1992). A study of Wharton alongside Theodore Dreiser and W. D. Howells, which looks at the engagement of all three writers with the processes of social change and redefinition in American society.

Kraditor, Aileen S. (ed.), *Up from the Pedestal: Selected Writings in the History of American Feminism* (Chicago: Quadrangle Books, 1968). An edited collection of important documents in the history of the women's movement.

Lukács, Georg, *The Historical Novel*, trans. Hannah and Stanley Mitchell (London: Peregrine Books, 1969). A Marxist study of the form and influence of the historical novel.

Norris, Frank, *McTeague* (1899; repr. Oxford: Oxford University Press, 1995). A novel by one of the leading American naturalist writers.

Powers, Lyall H. (ed.), *Henry James and Edith Wharton: Letters 1900–1915* (London: Weidenfeld & Nicolson, 1990). Correspondence between the two writers charting the course of their friendship.

Price, Alan, *The End of the Age of Innocence: Edith Wharton and the First World War* (London: Robert Hale, 1996). A detailed account of Wharton's active commitment to the war effort in France and the effects of her charity work in both personal and professional terms.

Ramsden, George, *Edith Wharton's Library: A Catalogue* (York: Stone Trough Books, 1999). A detailed guide to the surviving books from Edith Wharton's library, with a Preface by Hermione Lee and

Introduction by George Ramsden.

Raphael, Lev, *Edith Wharton's Prisoners of Shame* (New York: St Martin's Press, 1991). An analysis of Wharton's fiction using insights from the psychology of emotion and, in particular, shame.

Singley, Carol, *Edith Wharton: Matters of Mind and Spirit* (Cambridge: Cambridge University Press, 1995). A contextualization of Wharton's work in the larger traditions of American philosophical and religious thought.

Tuttleton, James, Lauer, Kristin, and Murray, Margaret (eds.), *Edith Wharton: The Contemporary Reviews* (New York: Cambridge University Press, 1992). This volume contains critical responses to the whole range of Wharton's fiction and non-fiction.

Vita-Finzi, Penelope, *Edith Wharton and the Art of Fiction* (London: Pinter, 1990). A study of Wharton's work in the light of her ideas about art and the artist.

Waid, Candace, *Edith Wharton's Letters from the Underworld: Fictions of Women and Writing* (Chapel Hill, NC: University of North Carolina Press, 1991). A critical analysis of six texts with particular reference to Wharton's ideas about the role of the woman writer in America.

Wershoven, Carol, *The Female Intruder in the Novels of Edith Wharton* (Rutherford, NJ: Farleigh Dickinson Press, 1982). A study of the catalytic role played by the intervention of women in Wharton's narratives.

Whitman, Walt, *Walt Whitman: The Complete Poems*, ed. Francis Murphy (London: Penguin Books, 1975).

Wright, Sarah Bird (ed.), *Edith Wharton Abroad: Selected Travel Writings, 1888–1920* (London: Robert Hale, 1995). Extracts from a range of Wharton's travel writing with a Preface by Shari Benstock and Introduction by Sarah Bird Wright.

—— *Edith Wharton's Travel Writing* (Basingstoke: Macmillan, 1997). Subtitled 'The Making of a Connoisseur', this study looks at the formation and application of Wharton's aesthetic principles as they inform her travel writing.

—— *Edith Wharton A to Z* (New York: Checkmark Books, 1998). A useful guide to all aspects of Wharton's life and works.

Index

British Orchids

– a site guide

British Orchids

– a site guide

ROGER BOWMER

THE CROWOOD PRESS

First published in 2008 by
The Crowood Press Ltd
Ramsbury, Marlborough
Wiltshire SN8 2HR

www.crowood.com

British Library Cataloguing-in-Publication Data
A catalogue record for this book is available from the British Library.

ISBN 978 1 84797 002 2

Photograph credits
© Royal Botanic Gardens Kew pages 14 (top); 15-19, 24-27, 32, 33, 37, 38,
42-55, 58-61, 65, 66, 67 (inset), 68, 69, 70, 71, 74, 75 (bottom), 76, 77, 88,
89, 106-111; © Roger Bowmer pages 12-13, 14 (bottom), 20-23, 29, 31,
34-36, 39, 40, 57, 62, 63, 67, 73, 75 (top), 78, 79, 80, 81, 83, 85; 86, 87, 90,
91, 92, 93, 94, 95, 96, 97, 102, 103, 104, 105, 112, 113, 114, 115
© Paul Sterry/Nature Photographers page 64; © Andrew N. Gagg's Photo
Flora 98, 99; Robert Thompson 99, 100; © Sydney Clarke 101.

Typeset by Simon Loxley
Printed and bound in India by Replika Press PVT Ltd

Contents

Introduction

About this book

This book was started as a collection of notes on the flowering sites of British orchids to help the author in his still incomplete task of photographing all the orchids of the UK. The more information that was amassed regarding sites, the more obvious it became that sites, habitat and distribution, together with the particular natural history of any one species, were all linked, as indeed were the larger issues of habitat management and conservation. As more and more books on orchids were read, and more data collected, it seemed useful to try to put all the relevant facts together and to have a single file where most of that information was quickly available. This book is that file.

Each orchid species has its own section, all of which are laid out in the same format, almost in note form. This is because most orchid books are largely concerned with taxonomy (classification), so that information on flowering times is scattered about the text and occasionally absent. So it is with habitat and distribution information in many volumes, and much time can be spent reading through taxonomic niceties to find out where the plants are and when they are in flower. Furthermore these books never give lists of sites as this book does. These are the reasons for offering this information to the wild flower enthusiasts of the UK.

The rarest species of orchid are recorded in the Red Data Books, a series of reference books for all endangered species. For the UK, these are compiled by the Joint Nature Conservation Committee covering Britain and Ireland. Endangered orchids are listed in the volume on vascular plants. In this book, the current situation of endangered orchids is shown in the text where appropriate under the heading 'RDB Status'.

As with all areas of botany, the study of orchids has its own specialized vocabulary; a glossary of terms is provided on page 116 to explain these.

Some basic guidelines

This book represents an opportunity but also a danger. The listing of sites will enable more people to visit them and appreciate the plants. However, it may also cause harm as more feet across the ground damage or destroy a particular species' very special requirements. I take this opportunity to ask all who use this book to behave responsibly. People with bad intentions towards the plants probably know the sites of their intended vandalism far better than I, but I would ask all who are genuinely interested in our wild flowers, and those in this book in particular, to observe the following basic rules.

Cut nothing and dig nothing. The unlicensed removal of any material from orchids listed on Schedule 8 of the Wildlife and Countryside Act (1981) is an offence, as indeed is the unlicensed uprooting of any wild plant without the express permission of the owner or occupier of the land. If you really feel you must have British wild orchids in your garden, there are now specialist nurseries that can supply nursery-raised stock of certain species, hardy in the UK but not all raised from UK native-grown stock.

Watch where you walk and try to avoid any young plants that could be orchids.

When taking photographs be very careful if lying prone; you could be lying on young orchids close to their parents.

Do not cut back foliage that lies across your field of view; rather bend or twist it away and let it spring back when your shot is completed.

Try to minimize time spent around an individual plant to avoid compaction of the ground in a very localized area.

Contact details

Pages 122–137 list sites with their approximate locations and National Grid References and also the name of the body whose protection and maintenance the site enjoys. The Appendices list the various bodies, including local Wildlife Trusts, Nature Conservation bodies, English Nature, The Royal Society for the Protection of Birds and The National Trust.

It is strongly advised that the relevant body be contacted before visiting sites as they may be closed for various reasons, including

A Conservation Scandal!

Our reasonable expectation today is that those people charged with conserving our rare and endangered wildlife would be scrupulous in avoiding any actions that could reduce the plant or animal's chances of survival. It was not always so. Writing in a letter to the June 1994 Quarterly Bulletin of The Alpine Garden Society, Mr Eric Hardy of Liverpool tells of the 'outrageous collection' of the sole flower stem of the Yorkshire Lady's Slipper by a botany lecturer from Leeds University. Mr Hardy writes that from the discovery of the sole surviving Yorkshire plant by his colleague, Mr Jarman, in 1930 up until 1950, the two men kept the site totally secret. They made a series of 150-mile plus round trips from Liverpool every year to check its flowering, to study its fertilization by the *Andrena* species bees and to compare flower colours with those of cultivated plants.

In 1953 Mr Hardy gave a paper to the British Association for the Advancement of Science on the plant, and the three flowers it had produced since 1930. In 1958, after seeing the plant in bud they were dismayed to find that the flower stem, only the fourth to be produced in twenty-eight years, had

been removed. Only eight people knew of the site. The late Dr W.A. Sledge of Leeds University Botany Department admitted taking it for his herbarium, without the courtesy of consulting either Mr Jarman or Mr Hardy. Eric Hardy was threatened with legal action for having the temerity to criticize and condemn what he called 'this autocratic act', which Dr Sledge somehow considered his academic right, and for daring to mention it in unfavourable terms on a television programme. As a result Jarman and Hardy's access to the plant was denied, and their research left in tatters. Dr Sledge's shameful behaviour was covered up by conservation officials and a constant stream of privileged visitors beat a wide path to the site, while life-long conservationists without influence were denied access to the plant. Dr Sledge's herbarium now belongs to Bradford City Museum, where, by appointment, it can be viewed in all its dullness. There are few things in nature as depressing as a herbarium specimen of a beautiful orchid, all colour gone.

Mr Hardy concludes that 'one only has to look through museum herbaria to see how professional herbarium botanists have collected rare plants to the brink of extinction; the ____dale colony of *Cyprepedium calceolus*, for example.'

shooting, the breeding of rare birds and other non-orchid-related events.

Acknowledgements

I would like to thank all those individuals and bodies who helped in the writing of this book. Among the individuals to be thanked are Julie Bowmer, Judith and Jim Millward for putting the handwritten script on to disk, and Pete Jepson and Bryan Cole for reading and correcting my many mistakes and inconsistencies. Dr Margaret Hartley, Curator of Cliffe Castle Museum, Keighley, showed me Dr Sledge's herbarium and Sandra Bell of the Royal Botanical Gardens, Kew, revealed possible further avenues of study. Rob Petley-Jones and Ian Taylor of English Nature in Cumbria gave help and advice, as did Dr Jill Sutcliffe from their Peterborough head office. Of the Wildlife Trusts, I would particularly like to thank the following individuals: John Martin of Avon Wildlife Trust, Nic White of Cornwall Wildlife Trust, Emma Townsend of Devon Wildlife Trust, Kent Wildlife Trust, Norfolk Wildlife Trust, Chris Wynne of North Wales Wildlife Trust, Nottinghamshire Wildlife Trust, Neil Wilcox of Scottish Wildlife Trust. The Wiltshire Wildlife Trust gave me valuable information and advice. I would also like to thank David Noble Rollin of Northumberland Natural History Society, Dr A.J. Richards of Newcastle University, Paul Drummond, Site Warden at Gosforth, Pete Burton, Warden at Sandscale Haws, John Hawley of Sizergh Castle, and John Butterworth and Mark Garland for translations and explanations of difficult Classical words. Many others have given help and advice, and I apologize to anyone whose name I have inadvertently omitted.

British orchids – flowering times

1.	Lady's Slipper Orchid	End May / early June
2.	White Helleborine	End May / end June
3.	Narrow-leaved Helleborine	Mid-May / mid-June
4.	Red Helleborine	Late June / end July
5.	Marsh Helleborine	Early July / early September
6.	Broad-leaved Helleborine	Mid-July / early September
7.	Violet Helleborine	July / August
8.	Slender-lipped Helleborine	Mid-July / mid-August
9.	Dune Helleborine	End June / end July
10.	Young's Helleborine	July
11.	Pendulous-flowered Helleborine	Late June (dune plants); late July / August (coppices)
12.	Dark Red Helleborine	June / July
13.	Ghost Orchid	June / October
14.	Autumn Lady's Tresses	Mid-August / end September
15.	Summer Lady's Tresses	Mid-July / mid-August, but now extinct in UK
16.	Irish Lady's Tresses	Mid-July / end August
17.	Common Twayblade	Early April / late July
18.	Lesser Twayblade	Mid-May / end June
19.	Bird's Nest Orchid	Early May / early July
20.	Creeping Lady's Tresses	Mid-July / late August
21.	Bog Orchid	July / September
22.	Fen Orchid	Mid-June / early July
23.	Coralroot Orchid	Early June / end July
24.	Musk Orchid	Mid-June / early August
25.	Frog Orchid	Early June / mid-September
26.	Chalk Fragrant Orchid	June / July
27.	Small White Orchid	End May / mid-July
28.	Greater Butterfly Orchid	End May / early July
29.	Lesser Butterfly Orchid	Late May / June (woodlands); June / July (moorlands)
30.	Dense-flowered Orchid	Dates around 20 May
31.	Bee Orchid	Early June / late July
32.	Late Spider Orchid	End June / mid-July
33.	Early Spider Orchid	Late April / mid-May
34.	Fly Orchid	May / June
35.	Lizard Orchid	Mid-June / early July
36.	Lady Orchid	Mid-May / early June
37.	Military Orchid	Mid-May / mid-June
38.	Monkey Orchid	Mid-May / mid-June
39.	Burnt Orchid	Early May / mid-June (southern); mid-May / end June (northern)
40.	Green-winged Orchid	Late April / early June
41.	Early Purple Orchid	April / mid-June
42.	Common Spotted Orchid	Mid-May / July
43.	Heath Spotted Orchid	Late May / late July
44.	Early Marsh Orchid	Late May / June
45.	Southern Marsh Orchid	Mid-June / end July
46.	Northern Marsh Orchid	Mid-June / end July
47.	Hebridean Marsh Orchid	May / June
48.	Narrow-leaved Marsh Orchid	Late May / mid-June
49.	Lapland Marsh Orchid	Late May / July
50.	Man Orchid	Early May / July
51.	Pyramidal Orchid	Mid-June / mid-August

1. Lady's Slipper Orchid

Cypripedium calceolus

Botanical Name

Kypris, Venus; *podion*, slipper; *calceolus*, slipper.

Flowering

End May/early June.

Habitat

Steep slopes of rocky valleys, screes and scars of limestone in oak/hazel, oak/ash or oak/ash/hazel scrub, thicket and woods. Extremely rare in UK, but now orchids raised from the sole surviving Yorkshire plant are flowering in and around their original sites in Northern England.

Distribution

Only one location in Northern England – apart from the plants propagated from it, the only surviving truly wild plant grows in Yorkshire. Plants raised from this parent at Kew have also been planted across its former range.

RDB status

The British Red Data Book on vascular plants notes that only one station still exists for this species, which was formerly widespread over northern limestone. The decline is due to picking and uprooting rather than habitat loss.

Natural History

The Lady's Slipper Orchid grows from a rhizome. The 30–50cm (12–20in) stems have several (usually up to five) broad, bright green sheathing leaves and bear one, occasionally two, flowers with brownish purple sepals and petals. These contrast with the large yellow lip in the shape of a pouch, which is 2–3cm (1–1.5in) long, and has orange dots inside. The two lateral sepals are 3–5cm (1.5–2in) long, and twisted. The flowers are visited by small bees of the genus Andrena, which may only be capable of recognizing the flowers as a nectar source when a 'critical mass' appears together. In England the sole remaining plant needs artificial assistance to set seed, but when this is done seed production is very high. Flowering may take fifteen or so years from germination so we have had a long wait for the naturalized Kew-propagated plants to appear in flower. The plant is extremely long-lived; the Yorkshire survivor has been known for at least seventy years, and plants on the continent are known to have lived well over 100 years.

Sites

The surviving Yorkshire site is under the protection of English Nature and is not to be disclosed. Various sites where the Lady's Slipper Orchid was formerly known have been planted with the seedlings raised at Kew and will be disclosed in due course. The Kew programme raised thousands of plants, which are in the care of selected, skilled alpine

gardeners. A plant from the Kew programme flowered in 2001 in the rock garden at The National Trust-owned Sizergh Castle near Kendal, Cumbria. *The Times* reported on 5 December 2001 that over 300 plants from the Kew programme were reported to be flourishing at fifteen sites in Yorkshire, Derbyshire, Cumbria and Co. Durham. Silverdale Golf Club has a plant, which at present is flowering very well; genetic study of this plant indicates that it is of Austrian origin. In 2003 it was dug up by vandals, but luckily sufficient root was left behind for the plant to regenerate and flower the following year.

2. White Helleborine
Cephalanthera damasonium

Botanical Name

Kephalos, head; *anthera*, anther, referring to the anther shape; *damasonium*, name given by Pliny to an unidentified flower.

Flowering

End May/end June.

Habitat

Chalky soils, often in shade under beeches. Mossy, stony ground sometimes favoured.

Distribution

Abundant in its preferred habitats in south and south-east England, it is largely a Home Counties species, decreasing in number the further one travels north. It has been reported in North Lincolnshire, its most northerly station in the UK.

Natural History

White Helleborine has a fibrous rhizome from which thick roots penetrate as much as 60cm (23in) into the soil, sustaining the plant on dry soils and well-drained slopes. There are two rows of oval leaves growing up the stem, which is 15–60cm (6–23in) high. The flower spike is loose, with usually from three to nine flowers, but exceptionally there may be as many as fifteen. The flowers are white or creamy-white and do not appear to open fully as the petals and sepals do not diverge to any

extent. There are yellow marks and ridges on the hypochile and epichile, which are attractive to insects. Charles Darwin noted this in 1862 in his book *On the Various Contrivances by which British and Foreign Orchids are Fertilised by Insects, and on the Good Effects of Intercrossing.* Any orchid enthusiast will derive great pleasure from Darwin's ability to make strong arguments from random observations, and from the strength and clarity of his prose. In spite of all this, most flowers are self-pollinated, and from seed-setting to flowering may take up to ten or twelve years in a new plant.

3. Narrow-leaved Helleborine
Cephalanthera longifolia

Botanical Name

Longifolia, having long leaves.

Flowering

Mid-May/mid-June.

Habitat

Usually in woods on calcareous soils. On boulder clay or blown sand overlying peat in Ireland. In southern England, beech woods; in northern England, ash/oak woodland.

Distribution

Kent, Hampshire, Chilterns, south and west Wales, Cumbria; sporadic in western Scotland.

Natural History

The Narrow-leaved Helleborine, formerly known as the Sword-leaved Helleborine, has a root system similar to that of the White Helleborine – a few thick, fleshy deep-penetrating roots and a mass of thin, wiry ones, which spread into the humus layer at the surface. The majority of plants have one stem of 15–60cm (6–23in). As the name suggests, the leaves are narrow, light green and stand erect. They are 1–3cm (.5–1.5in) wide, and get shorter higher up the stem, until they resemble the bracts of the flowers, while the flower bracts resemble leaves. The white flowers number up to twenty and are carried horizontally, in contrast to the erect flowers of the White Helleborine, and they also are much more open. The epichile has three dark orange grooves and the flowers are insect-pollinated, usually by small species of bees, but seed production is poor in the UK; even the long flower spikes produce few seed capsules. No reliable information is currently available on the period from germination to flowering.

4. Red Helleborine
Cephalanthera rubra

Botanical Name

Rubra, red.

Flowering

Late June/end July.

Habitat

Beech woods on chalk or lime, often close to mature tree trunks. Flowering is dependent on available light, and the plant can survive in a vegetative state when heavily shaded, flowering when light levels improve.

Distribution

The Chilterns, Gloucestershire, Hampshire.

RDB Status

Since 1960 the Red Helleborine has been confined to the Buckinghamshire Chilterns, the Gloucestershire Cotswolds and Hampshire. It has never been a common plant in this country, and because only a small percentage of plants flower it may often be overlooked.

Natural History

Unlike its two white-flowered relatives, the Red Helleborine has a slender root system, which spreads horizontally in the leaf litter rather than vertically. From the root-stock grows a single aerial stem, from 30–90cm (12–35in), but 45cm (18in) is more usual. The leaves are dark green, short and rather limp, and in the UK the flowers are few in number; on the continent there may be as many as fifteen, but five is a reasonable average on UK plants. As a woodland species it is able to survive in a dense, almost lightless environment by reducing or losing its leaves and relying on the mycorrhizal fungus in the root system to supply food. It then becomes a saprophytic, rather than photosynthesizing, organism, producing buds on the roots that develop into normal plants when light levels increase, whether by thinning, by gale damage or similar activity. The petals, sepals and labellum range in colour from bright pink to a

deep purplish pink, and are slightly open. All flower parts are covered in fine hairs. The labellum has a pale centre and the epichile has orange ridges. The flowers are pollinated by small bees, hoverflies and small skipper butterflies. The plant is so rare in the UK that seed set, germination, and the time of growth from germination to maturity are not well understood.

Sites

Red Helleborine is a very rare flowering plant and as such English Nature do not wish to encourage visits to sites, where trampling is likely to cause damage. Individual approaches to the local Wildlife Trust may gain access to the site but we must respect the will of the local body responsible for a species under severe habitat pressure.

5. Marsh Helleborine
Epipactis palustris

Botanical Name

Epignuo, to coagulate (various species have been used in cheese-making); *palustris*, relating to marshes.

Flowering

Early July/early September.

Habitat

Damp areas where there is lime dissolved in the water. The most common habitat is dune slacks, where crushed seashells provide the lime. Almost always in open aspects, avoiding shade, which many other Epipactis species prefer.

Distribution

Throughout England, Wales and Ireland, with the exception of Leicestershire, Nottinghamshire and south-west Yorkshire. Found in eastern counties of Scotland.

Natural History

The Marsh Helleborine has a shallow, thin, creeping rhizomatous root system, which is extremely effective at colonizing wet ground, lying as it does just below the surface, but

above the wet marshy ground, which carries little oxygen. The roots are thus able to obtain a good supply of nutrients, so there is little fungal activity within them. The roots give rise to an aerial stem up to 60cm (23in) high with about six closely spaced leaves, long, narrow and funnel-shaped, clasping the base of the stem. The inflorescence contains about fifteen flowers in a one-sided spike, which are very attractive. The sepals are brown- or purple-tinged, while the petals have a pink or purple mottling over a dull white ground. The hypochile is white with red striped lobes, while the broader epichile has a notched, frilly edge and a yellow spot at its base from which nectar seeps into the cup of the hypochile, and attracts ants, bees, wasps and hoverflies. They then contact the viscidium with their heads, which releases a glue to stick the pollen masses on to them. Although this is an effective mechanism to ensure pollination, by far the most common method of multiplication is vegetative, as the spreading rhizome, lying only 2–3cm (1in) below the surface easily produces new lateral growth buds, from the tips of which aerial shoots appear each year.

6. Broad-leaved Helleborine
Epipactis helleborine

Botanical Name

Helleborine, old name for *Epipactis*.

Flowering

Mid-July/early September.

Habitat

Beech woods, verges of roads through beech woods and on limestone. Limestone pavements and rocky screes, in a similar habitat to Dark Red Helleborine.

Distribution

Very widely distributed throughout England, Wales and Ireland. Distribution is more restricted in Scotland.

Natural History

The Broad-leaved Helleborine has a short thick stock, from which the roots penetrate deeply to obtain moisture on the dry banks and slopes that are its favoured habitat. Plants growing in a humus-rich environment have a high level of mycorrhizal fungus, while plants on mineral-rich soils have little or no fungal activity in their roots. From the root stock up to six stems may arise, up to 80cm (31in) high and carrying from four to ten broad, oval leaves, ribbed and furrowed and spirally arranged up the stem, with two or three basal leaves sheathing the stem beneath them.

The flower spike is rather one-sided and may contain as many as 100 flowers, although between ten and fifty is more usual. The flowers are extremely variable in colour. The sepals and petals can vary from pale green, yellow/green through to a deep wine red, while the outer lip, usually redder than the rest of the flower, can vary from deep pink to purple and occasionally greenish white. The hypochile is dull reddish brown. There are two protuberances at the base of the epichile, which can help in the identifica-

tion of such a variable plant, especially when the flowers are newly opened.

Pollination is by wasps, which seem to find the nectar attractive, but not by bees, which do not seem to be attracted by it. The flowers do not self-pollinate, and the ovaries soon wither away without insect pollination, but still a high percentage of flowers set seed. The time from germination to flowering is at least eight years.

7. Violet Helleborine
Epipactis purpurata

Botanical Name

Purpurata, purple.

Flowering

July/August.

Habitat

Beech woods on chalk and lime, occasionally found in oak woods on sandy soils. Tolerates much lower light levels than *E. helleborine*.

Distribution

Generally southerly and easterly in England, from the Wash, across to Shropshire, down to Dorset, along the south coast to Kent and then back up to East Anglia. Absent from most of Wales, all of northern England, Scotland and Ireland.

Natural History

The Violet Helleborine has a slow growing vertical rhizome from which long roots range as much as one metre (3ft) below the plant to obtain mineral nutrients and water. They are obviously efficient in this task, as they never contain a mycorrhizal fungus. From the rhizome arise clumps of grey/purple stems usually 30–60cm (11–23in) high, but capable of reaching a metre in height in the most robust plants.

The stems usually have between five and ten narrow leaves of a peculiar grey/green colour, spirally arranged and narrower than the broad leaves of the previous species, *E. helleborine*, with which it can be confused if growing in close proximity. The stems bear many flowers in a tight, one-sided spike and the bracts are as long as, or longer than, the flowers, giving the top of the plant a very leafy appearance when combined with its greenish flowers.

The flowers have white petals tinged with green, and the sepals are greenish. The inner lip of the labellum is pink/brown while the outer lip is pale pink inside, shading whiter towards the recurved tip. There are two

smooth pink protuberances at the base of the epichile.

Pollination is effected by wasps, and by autumn most plants have set seed. There does not seem to be a vegetative method of increase, because the rhizomes are vertical rather than horizontal. A debate exists as to whether plants in deep shade are saprophytes.

8. Slender-lipped Helleborine
Epipactis leptochila

Botanical name

Lepto, thin; *cheilos*, lip.

Flowering

Mid-July/mid-August.

Habitat

Beech woods on chalk in southern England.
Populations exist in Lincolnshire, Yorkshire
and Northumberland on zinc-rich and lead-
polluted woodland sites of ancient metal
working activities. Needs shade to flourish.

Distribution

Kent and Surrey, Hampshire, the Chilterns,
Gloucestershire and Devon. North to Shrop-
shire, then on polluted sites in Lincolnshire,
Yorkshire and Northumberland.

Natural History

E. leptochila was only recognized as a separate species in 1919, having been confused
with the many variant forms of *E. helleborine*.
It grows from a deep-set stock which carries
thick roots similar to those of the Violet
Helleborine, but which spread wider and less
deep. The stems are from 15–65cm (6–25in)
usually single, but as many as six may be
seen on established plants in favourable
habitats. The leaves are yellowish green,
rather limp and in two rows. They never
have the red/violet tinge sometimes seen in
the Violet or Broad-leaved Helleborines; this
feature gave the former common name of
Green-leaved Helleborine. The spike may
contain up to twenty-five flowers, of a
generally greenish appearance, the sepals
being pale green and the petals whitish. The
inner lip forms a cup and is greenish pink
outside and glistening reddish brown inside
where the nectar is contained. The epichile is
long and pointed with two greenish bosses at
the base.

The plant is usually self-pollinating and

has the synonym *E. cleistogama*, a cleisto-gamous plant being one which self-pollinates, without the flowers needing to open prop-erly. Wasps have been seen to remove the pollinia of this species. The pollination, seed-setting and development of the plant are not well understood.

Sites

The taxonomy of *E. leptochila*, *E. dunensis*, and *E. youngiana* is in flux at the moment, so any site information is likely to be incorrect as any of the *Epipactis* plants may be trans-ferred to a different taxon.

9. Dune Helleborine
Epipactis dunensis (synonym: *E. leptochila var. dunensis*)

Botanical Name

Dunensis, from a dune-land habitat.

Flowering

End June/end July.

Habitat

Coastal sand dunes, usually in the drier parts. Often on low ridges of sand, which build up around dwarf willow. In Lancashire it grows in the lee of planted Scots pines. Also found inland on old mine spoil heaps heavily contaminated by lead and zinc.

Distribution

The sand dunes of Anglesey, Lancashire and Northumberland, also found inland on polluted sites in north Durham, north Yorkshire, Lincolnshire and Lanarkshire.

RDB status

Dune Helleborine is reported from eleven sand dune sites. The populations are small, and in south Lancashire under severe public pressure. It is, however, locally common there on one NNR (National Nature Reserve).

Natural History

The Dune Helleborine has a woody nut-like rootstock penetrating deep into the sandy soils of its natural dune habitat and the loose open soils of spoil heaps. From the rootstock a few thin wiry roots penetrate the surrounding soils. The stem, up to 50cm (20in), arising from this rootstock has a funnel-like sheath around the base, which distinguishes it from the Broad-leaved Helleborine. Like the Slender-lipped Helleborine, the leaves are yellowish green, but in this species they are stiff and the bracts are shorter than the flowers. The spike is open, bearing up to twenty or so small yellowish green flowers, held horizontally at first and then drooping

---

A note on Lindisfarne Helleborine
Epipactis sancta

Sancta means holy or saintly, and Lindisfarne is also called Holy Island for its connection with St Cuthbert.

Genetic testing at a level way beyond the abilities of amateur botanists has revealed that the plants formerly classified as *E. dunensis* were sufficiently differentiated from that species to warrant being allocated to a separate species. In practical terms this means that an orchid that closely resembles *E. dunensis* growing on Lindisfarne is in fact *E. sancta*. The only visible distinguishing features are rather tenuous for the amateur. The flowers are slightly larger and the base of the stem has a greenish tinge, rather than the violet of *E. dunensis*. It is found on Lindisfarne on the dunes of The Snook at the end, and north of the causeway.

as the seeds develop. The flowers are dull in appearance, greenish yellow with a pinkish labellum. The hypochile is a darker pink and the epichile is broad, with two bosses at its base. The flowers are usually self-fertilized as the sterile stigma withers almost as soon as the flowers open and the pollen masses crumble, which usually leads to self-pollination.

Sites

See the Slender-lipped Helleborine on page 26 for notes on taxonomy.

10. Young's Helleborine
Epipactis helleborine var. *youngiana*

Botanical Name

Youngiana, named for Dr D.P. Young, English botanist, who died in 1972.

Flowering

July.

Habitat

Three sites in Northumberland, also found in Lanarkshire. Yorkshire and Glamorgan records may be of other species.

Natural History

This is a newly discovered (1982) species, at first thought to be a hybrid between *E. leptochila* and *E. helleborine*, but the type description was from a site in Northumberland where *E. leptochila* was not recorded. There is a theory that the Northumbrian *E. youngiana* is a hybrid between *E. helleborine* and *E. phyllanthes* var. *pendula*, while the Scottish plants have a different origin. It is distinctly possible that Young's Helleborine will not be regarded as a separate species for much longer as information from a taxonomist at the Royal Botanic Gardens at Kew suggests that Young's Helleborine's DNA is identical to that of *E. helleborine*, and it can no longer be considered a separate species. It remains, however, an interesting oddity.

As well as being new, the plant is rare, and details of the root system are scarce. The leaves are yellowish green, narrow, with wavy edges and one or two basal sheaths. The flower spike is one-sided, on a slender stem which is softly hairy above the top leaf and smooth below that. It is 30–60cm (12–24in) high, and the flowers, up to twelve in number, have greenish white sepals that are sometimes rose-tinted at their edges. The petals are similarly coloured. Where it grows alongside *E. helleborine*, the lack of pigment in *E. youngiana* is very distinctive.

The inner lip is semi-circular, again whitish green with purple spots, and the epichile is rose pink, and green in the centre; the tip is recurved, and there are two bosses at the base of the epichile, which may hold nectar on their depressed upper surface. The viscidium (the sticky cap which attaches the pollinia to the rostellum) withers before, or just as, the flower opens, so the pollinia fall on to the stigma resulting in self-pollination. This is a similar mechanism to that in *E. dunensis*.

The positive identification of the Broad-leaved Helleborine is difficult for the professionals, so we find it a minefield. *E. helleborine* hybridizes with other *Epipactis* species including *E. atrorubens* and *E. purpurata*. Because of its unusual presence on spoil heaps and other sites heavily contaminated with heavy metals, and a distinctive appearance with very pale, almost colourless flowers, it is now treated as a variety of *E. helleborine*.

11. Green-flowered Helleborine

(Pendulous-flowered Helleborine)

Epipactis phyllanthes

Botanical name

Phyll, leaf-like; *anthes*, flowers.

Flowering

Late June onwards for dune plants; late July/August for coppice plants and spoil heap plants.

Habitat

Three widely different habitats in the UK. In Kent it grows on the chalk in mixed copse, in moderate shade. Welsh plants grow in the open on calcareous dunes, in dry conditions, while in Northumberland it shares the habitat of *E. helleborine* and *E. youngiana*, growing in deep shade on old spoil heaps contaminated with lead and zinc ores.

Distribution

South-east England, North and South Wales, Yorkshire, Lancashire and Northumberland. Also reported from Londonderry. A rare plant in the UK.

Natural History

Sometimes regarded as a new species, the Green-flowered Helleborine has sub-species *E. pendula*, *E. vectis* and *E. degenera*. Other varieties are the Isle of Wight Helleborine (*E. vectensis*), and the Welsh Helleborine (*E. cambrensis*). Not surprisingly, the taxonomy of this plant is difficult!

It has long, fleshy roots, although this varies with habitat. A single stem, (usually) up to 45cm (18in) high, bears sheathing leaves at its base, with between six and sixteen leaves opposed to each other. The stiffly-ribbed leaves have wavy edges.

The flower spike bears up to thirty drooping, greenish, dull flowers. The sepals are green and longer than the petals, which are slightly tinged with white over the green ground colour. The inner lip is hollow and greenish, while the outer lip is white, with pink staining and a tip tending towards green. The flowers do not open fully and are self-fertile or cleistogamous, where the flower is self-fertilized before it opens.

12. Dark Red Helleborine
Epipactis atrorubens

Botanical Name

Atrorubens, deep red.

Flowering

June/July.

Habitat

In the UK almost invariably on bare lime-stone rock, clints, screes, pavement and rocky cliffs.

Distribution

Restricted to the areas where karst features and bare limestone rocks are found, namely West Yorkshire, Derbyshire, South Cumbria and North-west Lancashire in England. Also in North Wales, Wester Ross, Sutherland, Skye and Banffshire.

Natural History

This beautiful orchid grows in what seem to be extreme conditions, appearing out of cracks in seemingly bare rock. It has long, thin roots which can penetrate the vertical cracks and horizontal bedding planes of the limestone, where it finds water and nutrients in the small pockets of humus created by washed down organic material. The thin but mineral-rich soil on which it exists means that fungal activity is low, and the sunny open aspect the leaves enjoy makes photosyn-thesis an efficient provider of energy for the

plant. There is usually one flowering stem, 15–30cm (6–12in) high, which bears up to ten oval leaves, strongly folded and carried in two rows up the stem, making them a very dis-tinctive feature of this species.

The flowers range in colour from a brick red to a beautiful deep wine red shade, and are up to twenty in number. They are attrac-tive to rabbits, deer and sheep, which may be drawn to the vanilla fragrance the flowers

are reported to exude, so there may be no flowers to see when you get there!

The sepals have a green tinge to their wine red base colour, but the petals are a beautiful deep red/purple. The labellum has a greenish inner lip spotted with red, while the outer lip is the deep red of the petals and has a recurving tip and three bright red bosses. The flowers are visited by bees, wasps and hoverflies.

13. Ghost Orchid

Epipogium aphyllum

Botanical Name

Api, over; *pogon*, labellum, referring to the labellum being at the top of the flower; *a*, lacking; *phyllon*, leaf.

Flowering

Extremely variable from June through to October. The plant is reported to flower only after an extremely wet spring.

Habitat

Old oak and beech woods on chalk, growing in the deep leaf litter in the darkest areas of the woods.

Distribution

Oxfordshire, and the Chilterns of Buckinghamshire. Original sites in the UK were in Herefordshire, Worcestershire and Shropshire. The plant may still exist in these old localities and indeed others where it has remained undetected because of its shy flowering, and the difficulty of seeing the small insignificant flowers against the background of the leaf litter.

although one of the current sites bears flowers almost every year. The plants are susceptible to slugs and the depredations of rare plant collecting vandals.

RDB Status

Currently recorded from Oxfordshire and Buckinghamshire only. Formerly known from Hereford and Shropshire, but last recorded there in 1910. It has always been very rare, with long intervals between flowerings,

Natural History

The Ghost Orchid is a very rare plant, although possibly slightly less rare than sightings indicate. It is a saprophyte, obtaining its nutrients not by photosynthesis, but by absorbing them from the decaying

at these positions buds develop, capable of producing a new plant, just as in creeping buttercup or garden strawberries. The runner withers as the new plant develops and is capable of independent growth, or at least growth aided only by its mycorrhizal partner, eventually developing into the flat rhizome of its parent plant.

After about twelve years the rhizome sends up a flowering shoot, provided that the spring has been wet enough to sustain it and its fungal partner to store sufficient energy. When this happens a swelling occurs at the base of the stem, which acts as a reservoir for the flowering shoot. The stem is short, 5–20cm (2–8in) high, usually of a pinkish colour. There are between two and eight flowers with narrow, drooping petals and sepals, yellow with tiny pink/red dots. The labellum is pinkish with deeper pink spots and ridges and is at the top of the flower, as the ovary upon which the flower sits is not resupinate, i.e. it has not twisted through 180 degrees as in most orchid species where the lip is at the bottom of the flower. The spur contains nectar which attracts small bees, but seed production is very low. The vegetative propagation by stolons is very efficient and can produce large stands of the plants.

Sites

Locations are not to be revealed. Because of the largely invisible nature of its growth and spread, just below the leaf litter, the plants are very susceptible to unwitting damage by trampling. Combined with the threat from slugs and unscrupulous collectors, it is only sensible to leave the plants to recover to a greater extent under the protection of the local Wildlife Trusts. A polite enquiry to the local Trust may, or more likely will not, gain more site information; the plants' continued existence must be the priority.

remains of plants and other organic matter, in the same manner as fungi. The plant has no chlorophyll, and so cannot photosynthesize sugars from sunlight, carbon dioxide and water. There is a flattened many-lobed rhizome, which increases in size as the plant matures. From the rhizome, runners spread out through the leaf litter of the forest floor. The rhizome bears no roots, but has long hairs that are infected by a mycorrhizal fungus, a symbiosis from which, presumably, both partners gain an advantage. As the runners spread out beneath the leaf litter, scale-like sheathing leaves develop at intervals and

14. Autumn Lady's Tresses
Spiranthese spiralis

Botanical Name

Spira, spiral; *anthos*, flower; *spiralis*, spiralled.

Flowering

Mid-August/end September.

Habitat

Old chalk grasslands; seaside cliff tops; short turf on calcareous soils.

Distribution

Southern England, especially Wiltshire, becoming less frequent further north. Recorded from West and North Lancashire and North East Yorkshire. In Wales found mainly in coastal counties.

Natural History

Autumn Lady's Tresses grows from one or two rootless tubers. The tuber that bears the current season's flowering remains fat and plump until the flowers have gone, when it withers, and at the same time the second tuber, which will bear next year's flowers begins to swell and fatten.

In autumn a rosette of leaves, usually four or five, is produced and this persists over winter, dying in late spring or the early summer. The flowering stem grows up through the middle of this rosette, but by this time the old leaves have died and the new rosette is forming. The sweetly scented flowers are

arranged in a loose spiral around the stem, and when the buds are tight resemble braided hair. The stem is 7–15cm (3–6in) high and carries from six to twenty flowers, which are white and tubular in appearance as the upper sepal, petals and lip are joined together. The lateral u-shaped sepals sweep back on each side. The lip is frilled, and has a greenish tinge and shines with the nectar which insects collect on their visits.

Seeds are produced abundantly and while the plant does multiply vegetatively the majority of new plants are seedlings.

15. Summer Lady's Tresses

(now extinct in the UK)

Spiranthes aestivalis

Botanical Name

Aestivalis; relating to summer.

Flowering

Mid-July/mid-August.

Habitat

Permanently wet bogs and marshes, usually by running water. Neutral to acid pH, but never on moorlands in the UK.

Distribution

Extinct in UK, but is included in this book for completeness, and in the hope that it might one day be reintroduced. Last recorded sites were in the New Forest.

RDB Status

Summer Lady's Tresses was last seen in Hampshire in 1959; it formerly had four sites there, but by 1930 had diminished due to drainage and vandalism. The last recorded site in Guernsey was in 1914, again lost to drainage and collection, and the last four surviving Jersey plants were dug up in 1926. It is now extinct in the UK.

The situation in continental Europe now follows that in the UK, with the species in rapid decline due to drainage, nitrate fertilizer run-off and habitat destruction.

Natural History

Summer Lady's Tresses has similar tubers to the previous species, although longer at about 10cm (4in) as against *S. spiralis*' 1–3cm (.5–2in). The leaves are erect, unlike Autumn Lady's Tresses' flat rosette, and are yellowish, indicating low chlorophyll levels and a reliance on a mycorrhizal fungus as the main energy source.

The flower stem is 7–10cm (3–4in) high with a loose spiral of up to twenty flowers. They have a similar campanulate appearance to Autumn Lady's Tresses, and the scent is said to be extremely sweet in the evening, whereas *S. spiralis* is day-scented. Pollination is thought to be by aphids attracted by the honey-like scent.

Sites

Although extinct in UK, it is still known in Austria, Czechoslovakia, France, Germany, Switzerland, Holland, Spain, Hungary, Italy and Yugoslavia in mainland Europe, but is declining in all the central regions.

16. Irish Lady's Tresses
Spiranthes romanzoffiana

Botanical Name

Named after Count Romanzoff, Russian minister for Alaska, where the species was first identified. (Alaska was still Russian territory at the time.) He also sponsored a circumnavigating naturalists' expedition.

Flowering

Mid-July/end August.

Habitat

Wet, open ground in full sun by streams, rivers and lakes. In Scotland it is found on rocky, heathery outcrops that are intersected by the drainage gullies in which it grows. Found on soils with a pH below seven. In the UK it is not found on acid bogs although this is a common continental habitat.

Distribution

Mainly found in Western Scotland and the Hebridean Islands, one site in Devon and also in Fermanagh, Tyrone, County Down, Antrim and County Londonderry in Northern Ireland.

RDB Status

Still relatively abundant in some Irish sites, but some sites have been lost to drainage schemes and land reclamation. The Argyll population fluctuates and the species has gone from several of its sites of the 1960s, but has appeared in others. Still to be found in the Hebrides.

Natural History

Irish Lady's Tresses is rather a freak in the UK flora, being a North American species that is found in Europe only in the UK and Ireland.

It has a fleshy, tuberous rootstock, which grows vertically in dry situations, and horizontally in its more usual wet, marshy habitat. The leaves are erect, up to eight in

number, narrow with the edges sometimes rolled. The flowers are in three-spiralled rows, tubular, and usually number about twenty. The petals and sepals forming the tube are creamy white, shading to green, and the lateral sepals are whitish. The labellum is frilled and striped with green, and the tip bends back through 180°. The flowers smell strongly of vanilla, and it is thought that the plants are insect-pollinated. Flowering in established sites is extremely sporadic.

17. Common Twayblade

Neottia ovata (synonym: *Listera ovata*)

Botanical name

Listera, after Lister, English naturalist (1638–1711); *ovata*, oval (leaves).

Flowering

Early April (south)/late July (north).

Habitat

A very adaptable plant with a wide range of habitats; hill pastures and meadows, dune slacks, moist open woodland with base rich soils and on moorland acid soils. Discovered recently on old coalmine spoil heaps and disused railway lines in Scotland.

Distribution

Common and recorded throughout the UK, with the exception of the Shetland Islands.

Natural History

The Common Twayblade has a short, thick rhizome with a mat of fibrous roots from which the stem, hairy and sturdy, grows. The two large, oval, dark green leaves, from which the species derives both its common and botanical name, are a little way up the stem, above the basal sheath. The stem can grow to 75cm (30in) but is usually 20–60cm (8–24in), and as small as 10cm (4in) in the machair of the Hebrides. The flowers usually number fifteen to thirty, and have dull green/brown petals and sepals forming a loose hood. The lip is longer, and a brighter green/yellow. It has a deeply forked strap shape and a groove centrally from which nectar oozes and flows. This attracts a great variety of insects, beetles, flies, wasps and bees, which ensure pollination in the great majority of the flowers.

Lateral buds on the rhizome can develop into new plants; an effective strategy when light levels close down on woodland plants and seedlings cannot develop. When light levels increase, the plant is well adapted to take advantage of the new energy source.

18. Lesser Twayblade
Neottia cordata (synonym: *Listera cordata*)

Botanical name

Cordata, heart-shaped (leaves).

Flowering

Mid-May/end June.

Habitat

There are two distinct and different habitats in the UK. The first is among wet moss on bogs of open moorland, but also in acid soils among pine trees. Also recorded from limestone pavement in Ribblesdale and on the sand of a Wester Ross lochan's beach.

Distribution

A northern species in the UK, most frequent in Scotland and Northern Ireland, but not Isle of Man. Found across northern England and North-West Wales and sporadic sites on the South-West Peninsula in Devon and Somerset.

Natural History

Like many other orchids which grow in damp, mossy conditions, the Lesser Twayblade has fibrous roots and slender rhizomes, which penetrate the frugal material in which it grows to search for food. It is infected with a mycorrhizal fungus, which supplements the little energy derived from photosynthesis.

The stem is short, only 3–25cm (1–10in) high, with the two glossy, light-green, heart-shaped opposed leaves about a third of the way up the stem; above them the stem has short, glandular hairs.

There are three to fifteen short-stalked reddish-brown flowers tinged with green. The labellum is deeply forked, with pointed tips like a snake's tongue. Many small insects visit the flowers and seed is set in the majority of capsules. Root buds may separate from the parent to produce new plants, which can

flower within four years. This vegetative propagation leads to large colonies, which, hidden as they are among the moss and heather cushions, are by no means easy to find, and the species is probably under-recorded. Flowering also is shy, with usually no more than about twenty per cent of a colony in flower in a particular year.

19. Bird's Nest Orchid
Neottia nidus-avis

Botanical name

Neottia, bird's nest; *nidus*, nest; *avis*, bird.

Flowering

Early May/early July.

Habitat

The light-starved inner realms of beech and yew woods where the leaf litter is deep.

Distribution

Found throughout the UK, though more frequent in the southern half. However, it is not common anywhere.

Natural History

The Bird's Nest Orchid is not to be confused with the Yellow Bird's Nest (*Monotropa hypopitys*), a plant of the Wintergreen (*Pyrolaceae*) family, and a similarly saprophytic plant.

There is a rhizome, surrounded by a mass of short, tangled stubby roots which resemble an untidy magpie's nest; at one end of the rhizome grows the sturdy, leafless flowering stem, the only aerial part of the plant. The stem is 17–40cm (6–15in) tall, usually towards the lower end of that range, and bears a few scaly bracts. The whole visible plant is a light yellow-brown. The flowers number from twenty to as many as one hundred, being a similar colour to the stem. The

spike is lax at the bottom, becoming tighter higher up. The sepals and petals form a loose hood, and the lip is large, with two lobes diverging and curving away from each other, with a nectar-secreting depression at its base. The plant has a sickly, honey-like odour and is visited by small flies, which, it is thought, are the agents of pollination.

The plant has no chlorophyll, adapted to an environment where light is in very short supply and has a saprophytic existence,

gaining its energy from the decaying leaves and humus which surround the root-stock, with the aid of a mycorrhizal fungus partner. It seems that propagation is largely vegetative, and the plant can survive in a solely underground fashion for many years, producing new shoots from buds at the tips of the roots.

20. Creeping Lady's Tresses
Goodyera repens

Botanical Name

Goodyera, after Goodyer, English botanist (1592–1664); *repens*, creeping.

Flowering

Mid-July/late August.

Habitat

Ancient, open pinewoods; mixed woods of birch and pine, especially the remnants of the ancient Caledonian forest. Occasionally found among heather by the seashore.

Distribution

Almost exclusively a Scottish plant, it is found nowhere south of Durham and Cumbria, with the exception of Norfolk where it is found growing among the roots of introduced Scots pines. Not common on the Western Isles.

Natural History

Creeping Lady's Tresses grows from stolons that creep through the moss and needle litter of old pine forests. There are a few, short vertical roots heavily infected with the mycorrhizal fungus specific to this plant, *Rhizoctonia goodyera-repentis*.

After seven or eight years of horizontal, subterranean growth, the stolon turns towards the light and a flower stem, 8–35cm (3–13in) high appears. It bears a loose spiral of five to twenty-five creamy-white flowers, which all face in the same direction in spite of the spiral.

The leaves have stalks and are a pointed oval shape. They form a rosette of three to five leaves, which, unusually for a monocotyledon, have net veining.

The sepals are white, hairy outside and form a hood with the petals. The lip is shorter

than the sepals and is pointed. The flowers are sweetly-scented and attract bees, which are thought to pollinate the plant. The usual method of multiplication is by the runners, but seed is the agent by which new colonies are formed. The Norfolk colony has almost certainly been established by human agency, wittingly or not.

21. Bog Orchid
Hammarbya paludosa

Botanical Name

Hammarbya, after Hammarby, Linnaeus' summer residence near Uppsala; *paludosa*, of marshes.

Flowering

July/September.

Habitat

Bogs, wet acid sites with abundant growth of Sphagnum mosses, or reed beds on thick mossy growths.

Distribution

A plant of the Celtic fringes, Ireland, Scotland and Wales being its main strongholds. In the last twenty or so years it has also been recorded from western Norfolk, Northumberland and the Borders, Durham, Cumbria and Devon.

RDB Status

Still known from numerous sites in UK and Ireland, but declining in southern England because of drainage pressure. Under more threat on the continent than in the British Isles.

Natural History

A minute, entirely yellowish-green plant, the Bog Orchid blends in so well with its sphag-

num moss background that it is probably under-recorded.

There are two small pseudobulbs in the sphagnum moss. The lower one dies every year and a new one forms on top of the current year's bulb, in the top layer of the moss. The current growing bulb has basal stem leaves covering it, and on the stem itself are two or three small, elliptical leaves. On the margins of these leaves tiny bulbils form, and these can detach and grow into new plants.

The stem is 2–9cm (.5–3.5in) high and bears up to twenty insignificant green flowers. The most notable feature is the lip that is

at the top of the flower rather than its usual position underneath. Most orchid flowers have the lip at the base because the ovary has twisted 180°. The Bog Orchid, however, has an ovary twisted through 360° to bring the lip back to the top. The petals and sepals are longer than the lip and curve backwards. Insects visit the flowers, which set copious amounts of dust-like seed. The success rate of propagation by seed is unclear, but the plant is well adapted to vegetative multiplication in its wet habitat, where detached bulbils can quickly establish themselves and form new plants.

22. Fen Orchid
Liparis loeselii

Botanical Name

Liparis, glistening; *loeselii*, named for Loesel,
German professor of medicine (1607–1657).

Flowering

Mid-June/early July.

Habitat

Pool edges in fens where soil is always wet,
with alkaline to neutral pH. Never found in
acid bogs.

Distribution

Now only found in two areas of the UK – the
East Anglian Fens, a diminishing habitat,
and in South Wales dune slacks, which
remain moist all through the year.

RDB Status

The species is in rapid decline down from
more than thirty localities to about eight;
some of these are sparse. The main cause is
loss of habitat due to drainage, and even
attempts in Nature Reserves to preserve
water levels cannot insulate them from
the effects of general excessive drainage in
the area.

Natural History

Unlike the previous species found only on
acid bogs with sphagnum moss, the Fen

Orchid grows only on alkaline to neutral
soils. In fens this is where the peat is covered
by water that has leached the lime from solu-
ble chalk. In dune slacks the lime is derived
from crushed seashells.

There is a swollen bulb at the base of
the stem, alongside last year's withering
pseudobulb. The stem, 5–20cm (2–8in) in
height, has two erect, broad glossy leaves,
5–10cm (2–4in) long, and the flowering stem
is round at the base, becoming triangular in
section and multi-angled at the tip, with
the angles extending to form narrow wing-
like projections.

There are usually four to eight flowers, but as many as fifteen in exceptionally well grown specimens; they are dull yellow-green with the lip usually lowest, although like the Bog Orchid it can be uppermost and can also be found in any intermediate position. It is pointed and folded, while the petals and sepals are long and narrow. There is no discernible scent and no nectar so pollination is uncertain, although the plants do set abundant seed. Vegetative multiplication often occurs, when more than one pseudobulb is formed and splits off to form a new plant.

23. Coralroot Orchid
Corallorhiza trifida

Botanical Name

Corallion, coral; *rhiza*, root; *trifida*, three-pointed (shape of labellum).

Flowering

Early June/end July.

Habitat

In its coastal habitats, Coralroot Orchid is found in the slacks of old established dune systems. Inland it is a plant of the mossy undergrowth of birch and pine woodland. It is always found on damp ground.

Distribution

A northern species in the UK, found no further south than Yorkshire. More common in eastern than western Scotland; not found in the Western Isles.

Natural History

Like the Ghost Orchid and the Bird's Nest Orchid, this is a saprophytic plant. It has little or no chlorophyll, so photosynthesis is a dubious energy source. It obtains its food from dead organic matter in the soil around its roots (unlike parasitic plants which actively tap the phloem, the tissue in normal photosynthesizing plants which translocates the sugars formed in the leaves to other parts of the plant).

The plant leads an underground existence, showing above ground only to flower. The rhizome is knobbly, like a lump of coral, and has no roots. It is heavily infected with a mycorrhizal fungus upon which it depends to obtain nutrients.

In most relationships of this nature, which are quite common, the plant benefits from the fungus' ability to decompose the dead organic material, while the fungus benefits from the green plant's products of photosynthesis. Quite who is the winner when the vascular plant does not photosynthesize is problematic.

The stem, 8–15cm (3–6in) high, is usually yellowish-green. Dune plants usually have a reddish tinge to their stems. There is a little chlorophyll present, but no true leaves. Two to five sheathing scale leaves are present, but with little or no green pigment. The flower spike is loose with between five and fifteen flowers, generally yellow with green or red tinges. The petals form a hood with the upper sepal, while the lateral sepals are incurved and slightly downward pointing. The lip is three-lobed, white or pale yellow with red spots at the base.

Various small insects visit the plants, and seed setting is high. As there are no roots or runners, the only method of vegetative propagation is by small pieces of the rhizome separating as parts of the plant die away.

24. Musk Orchid
Herminium monorchis

Botanical Name

Herminium, name given by Linnaeus, who listed it under 'Gods' in his *Philosophia Botanica*, so possibly derived from Hermes; *monorchis*, one root (literally, testicle).

Flowering

Mid-June/early August.

Habitat

Grows among short grass on calcareous soils, such as the short turf on old downland pastures. Often found near old quarry workings. Found on the oolitic limestones of Gloucestershire and Somerset.

Distribution

The UK is at the northern limit of the plant's range, and it is not found north of a line from the Wash to the Gower Peninsula.

Natural History

This plant is so tiny that it can only survive among very short grasses; coarser growth would overwhelm the plant. In spite of the botanical name the plant has up to five small tubers attached by stalk to the main tuber, but if the plant is uprooted the stalks break and there appears to be a single one.

There are two to four strap-shaped leaves and a stem 1.5–10cm (.5–4in) high, carrying as many as one hundred, though usually fewer, yellow-green scented flowers. The petals and sepals do not diverge, but rather form a tube. The lip is the same length as the other flower parts and has three lobes, the central one being longer and also pointed.

Many small insects are attracted to the sweet smell and nectar secretions, and seed is freely set. The plant is well equipped for vegetative multiplication by the separation of the satellite tubers and their stolons from the parent plant, and dense colonies can form in this way.

25. Frog Orchid

Dactylorhiza viridis (synonym: *Coeloglossum viride*)

Botanical Name

Dactyl, finger; *rhiza*, root; *viride*, green.

Flowering

June/August, but in an exceptional year can span May/September.

Habitat

Pastures overlying calcareous soils, old quarry workings, dune slacks in old established dune systems. Becoming more common on the machair of the Hebrides as grazing increases. Found on some golf links in Scotland.

Distribution

Widespread, but local in England and Wales. Patchy distribution from West Midlands and mid-Wales. All of Northern Ireland, but not found in the Isle of Man.

Natural History

A tiny green plant, the Frog Orchid is easily overlooked. There are two divided tubers and a new one develops every year. The stem is 4–30cm (1.5–12in) high, at a slight angle, and the higher parts have a reddish tinge. The leaves are three to six in number; the lower ones sheathing the stem, while the upper, narrower leaves are non-sheathing.

The flowers are green, often with a purplish red tinge, and a spherical spur, which is distinctive. The upper petal and sepals form a loose hood while the lower petals are narrow and hidden by the sepals. The lip is strap-shaped, three-lobed, with the mid lobe shorter. There are yellow pollinia, which are carried away stuck to the heads of small insects attracted by the honey scent. These swivel forward after removal to be in a position to contact the stigma of the next flower visited. Seed is set freely, and the plant relies on it for propagation, as there is no mechanism for vegetative increase.

26. Chalk Fragrant Orchid
(formerly Fragrant Orchid)
Gymnadenia conopsea

Botanical Name

Gymnos, naked; *aden*, gland; *conopsis*, resembling a fly.

Flowering

June/July.

Habitats

Downs and pastures on calcareous soils. There is a subspecies densiflora, which is found on marshes and fens. On the coast it grows on lime-rich established sand dunes, and in the industrial north it can be found on old waste tips that have a high alkalinity from the disposal of lime used in chemical processing.

Distribution

Very widely distributed throughout the UK and recorded everywhere except Middlesex and South-West Yorkshire.

Natural History

The Chalk Fragrant Orchid has a divided, lobed tuber with a small, fungally-infected root system. The stem is 15–45cm (10–18in) high. There are three to five sheathing

leaves, tapering to a point (lanceolate) and two or three narrow pointed leaves higher on the stem. The flower spike is long and tightly packed with scented pink flowers, which have a loose hood of two petals and a sepal; the lip is three-lobed. There is a long, slender, curved spur. Ssp. *densiflora* is generally more substantial, with a longer, more open flower spike. The pollinia are removed by visiting moths and butterflies, which run the gauntlet of crab spiders that hide among the flowers and prey upon visiting insects. Seed-setting is high. The flowers smell sweet, being described as like carnations, or spicy and clove-scented, and range in colour from rose pink through lilac to an occasional magenta bloom. Any large colony will contain a few pure white albino forms.

27. Small White Orchid
Pseudorchis albida

Botanical Name

Pseudo, spurious; *orchis*, orchid; *albida*, whitish.

Flowering

End May/mid-July.

Habitat

Well-drained soils in hilly country, up to 700m above sea level. Found on calcareous and acid moorland among the stubble of burned-off heather. Usually in an open, sunny situation. The Small White Orchid is largely an upland plant, growing on thin soils whether acidic or base-rich. Rough grassland on well-drained but nutritionally poor soils are favoured habitats and it can be found even on road verges. It is generally found above about 150m (450ft) and in Cumbria on Alston Moor it flourishes above 500m (1650ft). In areas of western Scotland it can be found growing at sea level.

Distribution

A northerly plant in the UK, found in North Wales, Derbyshire, Yorkshire, Durham, Cumbria, then southern, central and northern Scotland, including the Inner Hebrides and Western Highlands.

Natural History

The Small White Orchid is a close relative of the previous species and was formerly known as *Gymnadenia albida*. It has two parsnip-like tubers, with vertical roots at the tips and horizontal roots running just below the surface of humus rich soil. Both types of root have a mycorrhizal infection. The stem, which appears about four years after germination, is from 10–20cm (4–8in) high, exceptionally 30cm (12in). There are usually four oblong leaves sheathing the base of the stem, and two rather more pointed non-sheathing leaves higher up. The flower spike is a dense

cylinder of thirty to forty creamy-white or green-tinged white flowers, which all face the same way and are slightly drooping. The lip is three-lobed, with the central lobe longer than the outer lobes. There is a faint vanilla scent that attracts bees, butterflies and wasps. Seed is set in most flowers, and the short period from germination to flowering produces spectacular displays of dense flowering clumps.

28. Greater Butterfly Orchid
Platanthera chlorantha

Botanical Name

Platys, broad; *anthera*, anthers; *chloros*, green; *anthos*, flowers.

Flowering

End May/early July.

Habitat

Woods on calcareous soil. In shade of scrubby woodland growing among the mossy understorey. It is sometimes found in marshy areas or on moorland heaths, but generally the Lesser Butterfly Orchid is the more likely species on acid moors.

Distribution

Common throughout southern England and western Scotland, although it has been recorded from almost every UK county in England, Wales, Scotland and Ireland. Not found in Shetland.

Natural History

This orchid has two small tubers that resemble parsnips, with a long, deeply-penetrating root from the tip and horizontal roots spreading out through the humus layer. The roots and tips of the tubers have a mycorrhiza, *Tulasnella calospora*, which provides energy when the woodland canopy becomes too dense for photosynthesis to take place.

The stem is 20–60cm (8–24in) high with a pair of broad opposed leaves, usually slug-damaged at the base, and about three narrow, more pointed leaves higher up the stem.

The flower spike contains between eight and thirty flowers in a striking arrangement, as their stalks are long, giving the whole inflorescence a substantial appearance. The flowers are white, tinged with green and are quite beautiful when seen in dappled woodland in evening light. The flowers are

night-scented and attract long-tongued species of moths which can reach down to the bottom of the spur, which is up to 3cm (1in) long with the nectar only in the last 5mm (.25in) or so. Seed is set in seventy to ninety per cent of the flowers. The plant can persist in an underground form for many years, putting up an aerial shoot and leaves only when felling, whether natural or by man, allows light once more to reach the plant.

29. Lesser Butterfly Orchid
Platanthera bifolia

Botanical Name

Bi, two; *folia*, leaves.

Flowering

Late May/June – woodland form; June/July – moorland form.

Habitat

Two distinct sorts of habitat, with the plant varying according to the site. In the northern half of the UK it is usually a plant of moorlands, where it grows on both acid and alkaline soils up to 350m (1148ft) above sea level. The plant more usually found in southern Britain grows in damp woods, usually of beech, on chalk. The plants can survive long periods of heavy shading in woodland, reappearing when the canopy is reduced by felling.

Distribution

Found throughout the UK, but not in the Midlands. Not found in the Shetland Isles.

Natural History

Although named Lesser, this orchid cannot be distinguished from the preceding Platanthera by size alone. Its tubers, roots and leaves are similar to *P. chlorantha*. The stem is 15–35cm (6–14in) high, with a spike of between twelve and twenty-five green-tinged, white, night-scented flowers. These are on shorter stalks than *P. chlorantha*, and give a much more compact appearance. The moorland form has a short, compact cylindrical flower spike, while plants in woodland have a looser spike, more nearly resembling that of the Greater Butterfly Orchid. The plants

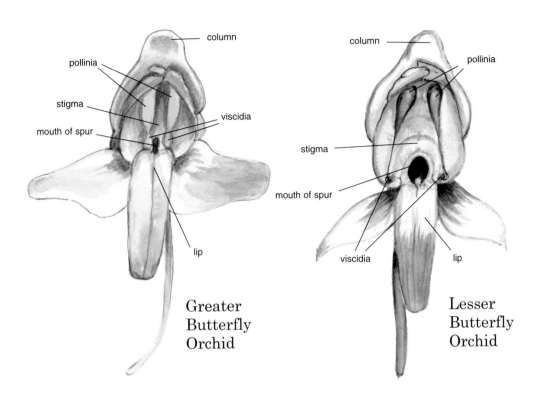

Greater
Butterfly
Orchid

Lesser
Butterfly
Orchid

Illustrations: V. Swinden

have a long, recurved strap-shaped lip and a spur about twice as long as the lip. It is pollinated by long-tongued night-flying moths, which collect the pollinia on their probosces. As the insect flies away, the pollinia twist to a position where they will contact the stigma of the next flower visited. Seed-set is very high.

The easy way to distinguish the two species of Butterfly Orchid is to observe the position of the pollinia (if the insects have left you any to observe). In the Greater Butterfly Orchid they diverge to reveal the opening to the spur, while in the Lesser Butterfly Orchid the pollinia are vertical and parallel, and obscure the entrance to the spur.

30. Dense-flowered Orchid

Neotinea maculata

Botanical Name

Neo, new (species); *tineo*, after Vincenzo Tineo, Sicilian botanist (1791–1856); *maculata*, spotted.

Flowering

Very short flowering period around 20 May.

Habitat

Limestone pavement in Ireland and shell-rich stable sand dunes in the Isle of Man are the only two British Isles habitats.

Distribution

Three counties in Eire; especially on the Burren. The Isle of Man site, discovered in 1967 has the only UK colony.

RDB Status

The plant has maintained a precarious foothold on the Isle of Man since its discovery. There have been new sites found in Eire, so the species may be increasing its range.

Natural History

This orchid develops a small, ovoid tuber each year, then the previous year's tuber flowers and dies. The flowering stem grows up in autumn, from 8–40cm (3–16in) high, and the buds develop early in the New Year. There are two or three oval spreading basal leaves and longer, sheathing leaves up the stem. The Dense-flowered Orchid is a Mediterranean species, and in that habitat the flowers vary greatly in colour, from greenish-yellow through pink to a purplish shade. British Isles plants, however, are creamy white, with an odd exceptional pink example. The spike is 2–6cm (1–2in) high, and one-sided. The flowers scarcely open, and there are fifteen to twenty-five in a spike. The flowers have a vanilla scent, and tiny beetles

of *Malachiidae* species have been observed entering the buds. The flowers are usually self-pollinating, sometimes cleistogamous, although it may be that the beetles are actually doing the pollinating before the flowers open, which they never do properly. Whatever the method, seed-set is efficient and productive.

Sites

Contact Manx Wildlife Trust, as this location is not secure.

31. Bee Orchid
Ophrys apifera

Botanical Name

Ophrys, eyebrows; *apis*, bee; *fera*, carrying.

Flowering

Early June to late July, later in more northerly areas.

Habitat

Only found on lime on open scrubs, short turf on downland, poor stony soil on old lime workings, abandoned quarries, chalk pits and railway cuttings. Found on calcareous sandy soils such as shell-rich dune slacks. Usually in open aspects, but survives deep in beech and ash woods in Kent and Sussex.

Distribution

Locally common throughout England, Wales and Ireland. Not found in Scotland.

Natural History

One of the most striking of our native wild flowers, the Bee Orchid has two globular tubers and a rosette of broad dull green leaves, which persist over winter. From these a stem of 15–50cm (6–20in) in height arises, usually with one or two leaves clasping the stem. The flowers are few in number, but striking in appearance, generally from two to seven, but as many as eleven have been recorded. The sepals are pink and the two upper petals are brown and incurved and resemble insect antennae. The lip is reddish brown, of a furry texture and cushion-like as the side lobes and pointed tip curve backwards. The lip is irregularly marked with bands of brown and gold. (In ssp. *trollii* the tip of the lip does not recurve and its pointed appearance leads to this form being known as the Wasp Orchid.) The whole flower resembles a big furry insect resting on a pink flower. Colour variations in the flower are common and lip markings also vary.

Self-pollination would appear to be the usual fertilization mechanism, despite the insect-like appearance of the flowers. It is efficient, most flowers setting capsules containing as many as 10,000 seeds.

The flowering of the Bee Orchid is something of a mystery. Young plants take on average six to seven years to come to flowering, and are usually monocarpic, i.e. dying after flowering once. However, some recent studies have shown that certain individuals may go on flowering for seven or eight years. Another feature of the flowering of Bee Orchids is the unpredictability of the numbers of flowering specimens on any one site. On Salthill Quarry near Clitheroe there were around ten flowering plants in 1996, but the following year the flowers were too numerous to count. In 1998 the flowering plants were down to very low numbers again, but it is always worthwhile to look for these flowers on known sites.

32. Late Spider Orchid

Ophrys fuciflora (synonym: *Ophrys holoserica*)

Botanical Name

Fuci, bumblebee; *flora*, flowers.

Flowering

End June/mid-July.

Habitat

Short grass over chalk, on open downs, banks and ledges. Cannot tolerate long grass. Its favoured habitat in the UK is usually south-facing, well-grazed turf on relatively poor soils and disturbed ground seems to be an advantage, possibly helping young plants to find a foothold. Long grass will ensure the loss of a colony, so it is important for the site management to keep to a strict grazing regime.

Distribution

In the last one hundred years, there has been only one unconfirmed sighting on the Sussex Downs (1974). In UK the species is restricted to about six colonies in Kent around Wye Downs and towards Folkestone. In Europe it is a plant of central and southern countries, extending eastwards towards Turkey and the Middle East. It is essentially a species of central/southern Europe where it can be found at altitudes up to1300m (4300ft).

RDB Status

Reduced to around ten localities in Kent. Some are still well-stocked, but other sites are down to a couple of specimens. The conversion of downland to methods of farming other than grazing is the main cause of the reduction.

Natural History

This rare plant, in common with the other three Ophrys species, grows from spherical tubers with a 10–30cm (4–12in) high stem rising above a rosette of four or five strap-shaped leaves. Above them on the stem are two or three narrow pointed sheathing leaves and two to six flowers.

The sepals are bright pink with rounded tips and a green vein running through the centre. The two upper petals are short, triangular and covered in velvety hair, with a

reddish-yellow to orange hue. The velvety brown lip is an angular trapezoidal shape, broader at the epichile than hypochile, and it resembles a large bee or spider. At the base of the lip is a yellow pattern, which resembles a piece of a jigsaw puzzle; it outlines a number of brown circles and half circles. The whole pattern is, however, very variable.

The rostellum protrudes prominently above the base of the lip and is tipped with green. On the Continent, where the Late Spider Orchid is much more abundant, the flowers attract male bees of species *Eucera tubercolata*, which attempt to mate with the flowers and so remove the pollinia. This behaviour ceases when the females of the species appear, resulting in hybrids between *Ophrys fuciflora* and *Ophrys apifera*. However, this bee does not occur in the UK. A viable alternative is pollen beetles; for sure, there must be cross-pollination for the UK hybrids to be produced.

33. Early Spider Orchid
Ophrys sphegodes

Botanical Name

Spheg, wasp; *oides*, resembling.

Flowering

Late April/early May. Mid- to late May in a
very good year.

Habitat

Old chalk pastures and downs. Almost always
close to the coast.

Distribution

Kent, Sussex and Dorset are its known
stations. Hampshire, Isle of Wight, Gloucestershire, Berkshire and Suffolk are possibly
areas where it may still be found.

RDB Status

Known from thirteen localities south of the
River Thames. Ploughing and public access
are having a deleterious effect, especially
in Dorset.

Natural History

The Early Spider Orchid grows from two egg-
shaped tubers, as with other British Ophrys
species. It is not likely to be confused with the
Late Spider Orchid as it is much more compact and is a very early flowerer, two months
before its larger and rarer relation. The stem
is usually about 10–20cm (4–8in) high,

although on exposed coastal sites it may be as
little as 5cm (2in). There are three or four
basal leaves and a few leaves clasping higher
up the stem, and all the leaves have prominent veins.

There can be from five to nine flowers on
a spike, but usually there are only two or
three, and these fade rapidly after pollination. The sepals are yellow and broad, with
the upper one often bending forward, while
the petals are slimmer and slightly shorter,
with a reddish-brown tinge to their wavy
edges. The lip is large brown, furry and semi-
circular, unlike any other UK Ophrys. It is

marked in a metallic grey with a variable pattern that often resembles a capital letter H or the Greek letter pi. The column resembles a bird's head and at each side are the thecae, nectar glands that shine like a pair of insect eyes when full of nectar. Despite the obvious attraction to insects for pseudo-copulation and nectar collection, the percentage of flowers setting seed is low, twenty per cent being a very high rate in most colonies in the UK.

34. Fly Orchid
Ophrys insectifera

Botanical Name

Fera, bearing.

Flowering

May/June.

Habitat

In the southern half of England the Fly Orchid is found in beech woods and on woodland margins and in scrubby thickets. In the northern part of England it is a plant of open grassland and moors, but wherever it may be, it is a plant of calcareous soils.

Distribution

Commoner in the south than the north, decreasing as one goes north. It is found in Cumbria and Durham but no further north than this. Not found in Scotland. Recorded from Denbighshire and Anglesey in North Wales and Monmouthshire in South Wales.

Natural History

There are two egg-shaped tubers with a number of shallow roots above them, from which a 15–60cm (10–24in) stem grows. It carries from two to ten flowers, although exceptionally twenty flowers have been observed. Low down on the stem are three long, narrow, glossy leaves with erect sheathing leaves above them.

The flowers really do resemble insects, even to human eyes. The sepals are green, and look like the sepals of a 'normal' flower, except that they are in the vertical plane behind the 'insect', which appears to rest upon that flower. The two upper petals are brown/purple, slender and curved, looking exactly like insect antennae. The labellum is three-lobed, with one long central lobe and two shorter wing-like lobes. The lip colour is a rich red-brown with an iridescent blue band across its centre that shines like insects' wings. There are two nectar-secreting glands, which look like eyes, at the base of the lip.

Male wasps of species *Argogorytes mystaceus* and *A. fargei* attempt to copulate with

the flowers. They are no doubt excited by the scent of the orchid, the chemical composition of which bears a striking resemblance to that of the insect's pheromones, and the fact that they do not know what a female *Arogorytes* looks like, as the males hatch first. In spite of all this frenzied pseudo-sexual activity, seed production is poor, with less than twenty-five per cent of capsules bearing viable seed. Perhaps as a compensation mechanism for low seed production, the development of the plant from seed is rapid in orchid terms, with a tuber formed the year after germination.

35. Lizard Orchid

Himantoglossum hircinum

Botanical Name

Himanto, strap; *glossa*, tongue; *hircinum*, billy-goat (smell).

Flowering

Mid June/early July.

Habitat

Calcareous soils in scrubby areas and among long grass. Found on chalk downs and shell-rich sand dunes. The best UK habitat is on Kentish golf links. In France it is a common roadside verge plant.

Distribution

Although quite common in France, the Lizard Orchid is rare in the UK. Found recently in Kent, Sussex and Cambridgeshire, its regular haunts. It has also been seen flowering in Devon, Wiltshire, Hampshire and Oxfordshire.

RDB Status

For the whole of the twentieth century this species has been fluctuating. At present restricted to the counties named above. It has become extinct in Jersey, and very few permanent colonies survive.

Natural History

The Lizard Orchid is a large plant, one early botanist referring to it as a bush! There are

two elongated oval tubers, above which a rosette of three to six leaves forms in autumn. They are broad and succulent, dark green when fresh, fading to pale greyish-green and withering as the plant flowers. The stem, up to 50cm (20in) high in the UK plants, may grow to 100cm (40in) on the Continent, and bears a number of clasping leaves, reducing in size up the stem. Flowers usually number twenty to fifty in the UK, while continental specimens may have up to one hundred flowers. Although lacking the bright colours of our most showy orchids, the Lizard Orchid's flowers' extravagantly corkscrewing lip and red spotted helmet compensate for their lack of bright colour by their exotic appearance.

The lip's appearance is striking. It is up to 6cm (2.5in) long, dull greenish-brown, with two brown side lobes which are shorter and crinkled like crepe paper. The central lobe is coiled when the flower is newly opened and remains in a spiral after the flower's full opening.

The flowers smell of billy-goat, a deeply unattractive scent, but as flies and other insects are not as fastidious as humans, they visit the flowers, resulting in seed-setting in about thirty-three per cent of capsules.

Sites

The most productive sites at present are in the Sandwich area of Kent. The public footpath which crosses the Royal St George golf links opens every year for orchid viewing. They also flower on the road alongside the links, Princes Drive, to the south of the marker board for Sandwich and Pegwell Bay, usually on the landward side of the road. They even grow on the lawns of conservation-

conscious residents of the area. Go at the right time and you can't miss them. Do not do as I did and go in late July unless you want to see dead flowers!

36. Lady Orchid
Orchis purpurea

Botanical Name

Orchis, testicle (tuber); *purpurea*, purple.

Flowering

Mid-May/early June.

Habitat

Lady Orchid is essentially a woodland plant, beech being its favoured companion, especially on the chalky soils that are so common in Kent. Coppice is favourable as the cycle of cutting regularly opens up any shade in which the plant does not thrive, and in which it may revert to a solely underground existence until the light improves. It likes dappled shade and some shelter and will not do well in open aspects, where wind can scorch the plants.

Distribution

Essentially restricted to Kent at present, although there are recent records from Sussex, Essex and even Hereford.

Natural History

This is one of the most spectacular UK orchids. Like its close relatives the Military and Monkey Orchids, this species has two ovoid tubers with short, fleshy roots. The tuber for the current flowering is plump, while the previous year's withers away. The stem is 20–90cm (8–35in) in length, with a rosette of oval, sheathing leaves at its base; the higher, stem-clasping leaves are less broad. Sometimes the leaves are vertical, and sometimes the rosette leaves spread widely.

The spike is large, from 5–15cm (2–6in) long. It is striking in its appearance, with each flower resembling a lady with spreading skirts and a dark veiled bonnet. The sepals join loosely to form the bonnet, and the petals are hidden beneath it. The sepals are dark red-brown with darker lines, while the lip, the 'lady's' body, is deeply divided into two side lobes (the arms) and a broad, spotted central lobe which is divided centrally to form two 'legs'. The lip is white or pink with darker spots, dots and lines. All these colours vary from lighter to darker in various different flowers, colonies and locations. There is reported to be a faint scent, and small insects are seen to visit the flowers, but seed-setting is very low, less than ten per cent in most plants.

The plants mature very slowly after germination, and are subject to the attentions of rabbits and other herbivores, but at present the species appears secure in its Kent habitats, well looked after by Kent Wildlife Trust.

37. Military Orchid

Orchid militaris

Botanical Name

Militaris, military.

Flowering

Mid-May/mid June.

Habitat

Woodland edges and within light woodland. On rough fields and pasture. At the woods' edges in the site rediscovered by the great amateur botanist J.E. Lousley. Also known from a shaded chalk pit in the only other UK site, where it grows among scrub and moss under privets.

Distribution

Only two revealed sites in UK, a wood near Henley-on-Thames in Buckinghamshire, and the chalk pit in Suffolk. This orchid was thought to be extinct in the UK until J.E. Lousley discovered the Buckinghamshire site in 1947, as recorded in his book *Wild Flowers of Chalk and Limestone*. The Suffolk site was discovered seven years later, and is now a closely guarded nature reserve.

RDB Status

Known only from Buckinghamshire and Suffolk. The Buckingham site has fewer plants than in 1947, possibly due to trampling by visiting naturalists. The reports of

O. militaris in Bolton are either mistaken identity or worse, a misguided planting.

Natural History

This plant has the twin tubers of the other orchid species in this account, and a stem 20–45cm (8–18in) high. There are a few leaves in a rosette at the base of the stem, and one small sheathing leaf clasping the stem.

The flower spike is 2–10cm (1–4in) in height, bearing about twenty-five to thirty-five flowers in the UK; some continental plants have many more. The two upper petals and three sepals form a large, pointed hood; to those endowed with a vivid imagination this resembles a guardsman's bearskin hat. It spreads wide in the fully opened flower, even more than in the Lady Orchid, and on the inside are parallel hoops of dark brown lines. The colour of the 'helmet' ranges from a pinkish off-white to a washed out lilac shade, and the buds look much paler than the open flowers. The lip has four lobes that resemble a human torso with 'arms' and 'legs'. The upper lobes, which make the 'arms', curve forward and the lower 'legs' are broader, with a small 'tail' between them. The lip is pale, often shading to a rich magenta at the extremities of the 'limbs'. There are deeper pink dots and spots on the labellum, formed by papillae, little tufts of coloured hair, as in the Lady Orchid.

The flowers have a faint vanilla scent and are visited by flies and small bees, which feed on the nectar secreted by the spur. Seed is set

in only a small percentage of English plants, and germination to flowering takes seven or eight years. With this in mind, visiting naturalists seeking to photograph the Military Orchid at close range are urged to be very careful when lying down to take close-ups of the flowers, as young seedlings can very easily be destroyed by trampling on the heavily visited sites where access is allowed.

38. Monkey Orchid
Orchis simia

Botanical Name

Simia, monkey.

Flowering

Mid-May/mid-June.

Habitat

Well-drained calcareous soils in light to moderate shade in woods, or open sunny situations on downland.

Distribution

Kent and Oxfordshire. The Yorkshire site, discovered in 1974, was destroyed in 1981.

RDB Status

Now only at two Kent and two Oxfordshire stations. One of the Oxfordshire sites lost a large part of the colony to ploughing in the 1950s. The general cause of decline is picking of flowers.

Natural History

Like its relations in the *Orchis militaris* grouping, the plant has two egg-shaped tubers and a small number of fleshy roots. There are two broad leaves at the base of the 15–30cm (6–12in) stem, with two or three sheathing leaves higher on the stalk. There are fifteen to twenty-five flowers. When the plant is still in bud, the spike is a

cone shape, but uniquely in British orchids the topmost flowers open first, and so the cone becomes cylindrical from the top down as more buds break.

The flowers are very special. The three sepals and two petals form a hood with pointed protrusions resembling ears. The colour is pink to lilac. Inside the hood are darker purple dots, which Alibertis Antonis in his book *The Orchids of Crete and Karpathos* charmingly describes: 'if you look long and hard you will see different expressions on the faces of the apparent apes which range from really serious to very funny.' Deep in the hood the pollinia are dark and look like eyes.

The pink to mauve lip has four lobes, the upper two being the animal's 'arms' and the lower two the 'body' and 'legs'. There is a median tooth between the two lower lobes

that forms the monkey's 'tail'. All the lobes curve outwards, giving an animated appearance to the flowers. The base of the lip is paler than the rest of the structure, with areas of dark-coloured bristles forming spots and dots.

The vanilla scent is detected by insects, especially butterflies. Details of seed-set and germination rates are not available, but it is clear that the plant is only just maintaining its precarious hold in southern England. The open policy of Kent Wildlife Trust should be reciprocated by great care on the part of visitors. For the other Kent site contact Kent Wildlife Trust.

The Chilterns site for *O. simia* is under greater threat. Numbers are fewer and the population is not as stable as at the Kent sites. No doubt when the situation improves significantly the local Wildlife Trust will be more open to requests to view its Monkey Orchid sites.

39. Burnt Orchid

Neotinea ustulata, formerly *Orchis ustulata*

Botanical Name

Neo, new (species); *tinea*, after Vincenzo Tineo, Sicilian botanist (1791–1856); *ustulata*, burnt.

Flowering

Early May/mid-June, southern population; mid-May/end June, northern population.

Habitat

Calcareous soils on undisturbed grassland (the protocorm takes fifteen years to develop to flowering size). The plants usually face south in full sun.

Distribution

An English plant. Southern distribution is Kent, Sussex, Hampshire, Berkshire, Wiltshire and Bedfordshire. The most northerly population is in Derbyshire, Lincolnshire, Cumbria and Durham. Not in Wales, Scotland or Ireland.

Natural History

This diminutive species, which once had the alternative vernacular name of Dwarf Orchid, has two small spherical tubers and a stem 6–9cm (2–3.5in) high. At its base are two to four broad leaves with pronounced veins. They are 2–3cm (.5–1in) long and above them on the stem are smaller, clasping leaves.

The flower spike is only 1–3cm (.5–1in) long, cone-shaped in bud and becoming

cylindrical as the flowers open. The spike is densely packed with as many as eighty sweetly-scented flowers, resembling a tiny Lady Orchid. They have a dark hood, like the Lady Orchid's, and when in bud the dark red-brown top to the inflorescence looks to be scorched, as if a blow lamp had played across the top of the spike. The hood, formed of the five perianth parts apart from the labellum, is red-brown and quickly fades. The lip is three-lobed; the upper two lobes vaguely resemble the arms of *O. militaris* and *O. purpurea* and the central lobe is shallowly divided. It is white or very pale pink, marked with crimson spots and lines.

The flowers are sweetly scented, and attract insects that ensure seed-setting in most capsules. There is no vegetative means of propagation and it takes up to fifteen years for the protocorm formed in the first year after germination to accumulate sufficient energy reserves to start to flower. Only undisturbed pasture and grassland can give this quiescent development to the young Burnt Orchid plants.

40. Green-winged Orchid
Anacamptis morio, formerly *Orchis morio*

Botanical Name

Anacamptis, recurved (pollinia); *morio*, clown
or buffoon. This possibly refers to the stripes
on the lateral sepals, like the crude paint on
the face of a circus performer. Or possibly the
flower parts resemble a fool's cap.

Flowering

Late April/early June.

Habitat

Old meadows and pastures on lime, and on
clay beneath downland. Found in dune
slacks on calcareous sand. It is a plant of
damp ground and open situations, never
found in woodland.

Distribution

Largely an English species, perhaps more
common on the eastern side of the country
although recorded from almost all English
vice-counties. It was not known in Scotland,
apart from a single plant in Banffshire in
1958, until a large colony was found in
Ayrshire in 1981; this remains the only
known Scottish colony at present. In 1951
Victor Summerhayes described the Green-
winged Orchid as one of the most common
orchids in England and Wales. This is no
longer the case; loss of habitat due to drainage

and agricultural improvement is the main cause of the species' decline.

Natural History

The stem, which sometimes has a violet tinge on the upper parts is 6–18cm (2–7in) high and arises from two spherical tubers. There is a basal rosette of blue-green leaves, and up to three sheathing leaves on the stem. The leaves are never spotted, an important distinction from Early Purple Orchid whose leaves are usually blotched and spotted with dark markings.

The flower spike is usually only 2–3cm (.5–1in) long with an average of about twelve flowers that vary greatly in colour, going from pure white and pale lilac through to shades of pink, violet and deep, rich purple.

The hood, formed of the lateral sepals and petals, has distinct veins that show green in the paler flowers but look dark purple in deeper-shaded specimens. The lip is broad and three-lobed with the central lobe slightly longer. The centre is paler than the rest of the lip and is often marked with dark spots. The flowers are scented, white ones especially so, and attract bees which obtain sugar from the spur walls. There is no nectar. A high proportion of flowers set seed and a capsule may contain up to 4,000 fine seeds. In spite of such high seed production (40,000 plus per plant) and the rapid development after germination, with a tuber and a leaf appearing in the second year, the plant continues to decline, and the loss of two more sites has been confirmed during the writing of this book.

41. Early Purple Orchid
Orchis mascula

Botanical Name

Mascula, male.

Flowering

April/mid-June.

Habitat

Prefers calcareous soils, but found on neutral soils also, avoiding very wet or acid environments. Can be found almost anywhere on its favoured soils. In southern England this is chalk downs and roadside banks and verges, also clifftops. In the northern part of the UK, it is found on moorland, hill meadows and by roadsides. In an area of chalk or limestone geology you are likely to see the plant in any open, sunny situation.

Distribution

Found throughout the UK and Ireland. Perhaps the most common orchid of the British Isles, although the Common Spotted Orchid is a close second.

Natural History

Above the two tubers, the shape and size of which give the orchids their botanical name, is a rosette of blunt basal leaves, whose upper, glossy surface is heavily spotted with purple blotches, and out of which the 10–40cm (4–16in) stem rises, with its few sheathing, erect leaves more lightly spotted.

The flower spike is loose in form, with twenty to fifty flowers that are generally deep purple, but can be a paler pink shade. The two lateral sepals spread wide when the flower is newly opened, but recurve with age until they almost touch behind it. The upper sepal and two petals make a loose hood. The lip has three lobes and is longer than it is wide, pale pink or yellowish white in the centre with dark spotting. There is a strong and unpleasant 'tom-cat' scent, although some observers have reported plants with an attractive scent.

Whether or not attractive to humans, the scent attracts bees and the majority of capsules have seeds. Although not quite so quick to develop as *O. morio*, this orchid still has its first tuber by the end of its second year, and can flower after four years. The plant may be monocarpic, usually dying after its flowering if a good seed set has resulted.

Alternative names

Of all our orchid species, the Early Purple is probably the most widespread really attractive plant. There may be more Broad-leaved Helleborines, Twayblades and Spotted Orchids, but they do not catch the eye in the same way. The Early Purple certainly does with its bright colourful display early in the year. This is probably the reason for its multitude of strange, amusing or plain rude local names. These include Rams-horns, Regals, Bollock Grass, Gethsemane, Kettle-cases, Long Purples, and no doubt many other strange and wonderful names, including the superb Granfer Griggles from Dorset!
(Source: Lang, David, *Wild Orchids of Sussex*, Pomegranate Press 2001)

42. Common Spotted Orchid
Dactylorhiza fuchsii

Botanical Name

Dactyl, finger; *rhiza*, root; *fuchsii*, from Fuchs, German botanist (1501–1566).

Flowering

Mid-May/July.

Habitat

Usually found on calcareous soils in widely differing habitats, from open woods of ash, beech or oak, to downland, marshes, railway cuttings, chalk pits and roadsides. Can thrive in dry, damp or wet boggy sites. It is occasionally found on acid bogs. Woodland plants can tolerate heavy shade, persisting in a non-flowering state.

Distribution

All of the UK, perhaps slightly more common in southern and eastern England, but can be found in every vice-county. In Scotland ssp. *hebredensis* is common and very abundant on the machair of the Hebrides and Isles, while ssp. *okellyi* (white-flowered) is common in northern and western Ireland and on the Isle of Man.

Notes on Dactyl Orchids

The spotted and marsh orchid species, which have tubers with finger-like protuberances are difficult to identify in the field. They are new species, and still hybridize promiscuous-

ly, giving rise to swarms of hybrids. The best way to accurate identification is to go with a knowledgeable site warden or botanist with local experience.

Natural History

The tubers of *D. fuchsii* have three to six finger-like lobes and a few fleshy roots. The height of the stem varies greatly, from 6cm (2in) in a poor site to 75cm (30in) in a very favourable situation. There is a cluster of leaves at the base of the stem, with the lowermost leaves being broader than those above, which are more elongated. The leaves

continue up the stem, shortening and becoming less sheathing as they near the inflorescence. The leaves are almost always spotted and blotched with brown or purple markings, which vary from virtually no marks to almost complete obliteration of the leaves' green pigmentation.

The spike resembles a pink bottle-brush, being long, dense and with a slight taper towards the top. The general colour is a pale, anaemic lilac, but ssp. *hebredensis* is a deep purple, while ssp. *okellyi* is white. As a further confusion, there is also an albino form of *D. fuchsii*.

The flowers have the lateral sepals spreading, and the petals and upper sepal forming a hood. The lip is three-lobed, with the long central triangular lobe marked by a double loop pattern, with deep purple 'Morse code' dots and dashes on the paler ground. Albino plants have no such markings, while ssp. *okellyi* has faint marks on the white lip.

A faint scent is reported, and bees and flies visit to enjoy the sugar secreted in the spur. Pollination rates are good and most capsules contain viable seed. A leaf is

produced in the second year after germination, and the leaves develop over a number of years until sufficient energy is available to allow flowering. Vegetative propagation also results in very good stands of flowering stems.

Orchid Ice Cream

In Turkey the roots of wild Dactyl orchids are dug up and dried, then ground to make a flour, which is then mixed with sugar, milk and nuts to make *salepi dondurma*, literally 'fox testicle ice cream'! The mix is so gelatinous and elastic that children can make skipping ropes from it!

43. Heath Spotted Orchid
Dactylorhiza maculata

Botanical Name

Maculata, stained or spotted.

Flowering

Late May (northern)/late July.

Habitat

A plant of open aspect on soils of acid nature, though it can be found on calcareous soils. This predisposes it to moors, heaths and also roadside verges. Seldom found in woodland.

Distribution

Common throughout Britain, but more likely to be found in those areas where limestone and chalk are not, i.e. northern and western England.

Natural History

This dactyl orchid shares a similar rootstock to *D. fuchsii*, but the rest of the plant is fairly easily distinguished.

The stem is 10-30cm (4–12in) tall with a conical or pyramidal flower spike of usually about twenty flowers, a quarter of the number found in a good specimen of *D. fuchsii*.

The leaves are fewer than in *D. fuchsii*, narrower and clasping the stem. The spotted tends to be circular, rather than oblong or rectangular.

The flowers are usually pale pink, the lateral sepals spreading and the upper sepal and petal forming a loose hood. The labellum is broad with two lateral lobes, often longer than the central one, and they are all spotted with darker dots and dashes, but without the distinctive double loop of *D. fuchsii*.

A faint scent is reported and bees and flies are attracted, leading to a good seed-set. Young plants develop in a similar way to *D. fuchsii*, but their mineral-deficient habitat slows growth and restricts somewhat any vegetative means of increase.

44. Early Marsh Orchid
Dactylorhiza incarnata

Because of the division of *D. incarnata* into five sub-species, this chapter differs in style from the rest of the book.

Botanical Name

Incarnata, flesh-coloured.

Botanical Names of Sub-species

Coccinea, scarlet; *pulchella*, beautiful; *cruenta*, blood-red; *ochroleuca*, pale yellowish-white.

Habitats

Sub-species D.i. incarnata
Calcareous-neutral soils on wet grassland, especially wet meadows on floodplains. Dune slacks and old quarries.

Sub-species D.i. coccinea
Dune slacks, Hebridean machair, calcareous fens, old industrial tips with alkaline waste from the Leblanc process of producing soda ash.

Sub-species D.i. pulchella
Acidic environments such as marshes, bogs and heaths.

Sub-species D.i. cruenta
Karst environments in Ireland, neutral or flushed grass in Scotland up to about 450m (1500ft).

Sub-species D.i. ochroleuca
Calcareous fens, in moist but not flooded areas that are slowly drying out, e.g. Norfolk fens over old peat diggings.

Distribution

Sub-species D.i. incarnata
Widespread in England and Wales, less so in Ireland.

Sub-species D.i. coccinea
Random colonies found on the west coast from the south-west peninsula right up to the Shetland Isles. Less frequent on the east coast. South-east Scotland, north-east England and north Norfolk.

Left: D.i. incarnata
Opposite page: D.i. coccinea

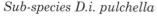
D.i. pulchella

D.i. cruenta

Sub-species D.i. pulchella
A mainly southern ssp. found in Sussex (Ashdown Forest), Hampshire (New Forest), Surrey (on border with Hampshire), Cornwall and Dorset, but also found on Skye and in Sutherland.

Sub-species D.i. cruenta
Western Ireland on the Burren in Co. Clare and in Co. Galway and Co. Mayo. Two small populations in Scotland near Ullapool and another in Assynt, Sutherland.

Sub-species D.i. ochroleuca
Very rare, and only found in East Anglia.

Natural History

Sub-species D.i. incarnata
FLOWERING
May to mid-June. Later in north.
STEM
5–60cm (2–12in), usually hollow, pale green.
LEAVES
Sheathing stem, unspotted and usually hooded.
FLOWERS
Ten to seventy, usually an unearthly flesh pink, sometimes darker. Lip off-white with pink tinge with deeper spots and loops, sides turning downwards.

Sub-species *D.i. coccinea*

FLOWERING

June to early July.

STEM

Short and substantial, to 20cm (8in), giving a squat appearance.

LEAVES

Short, dark green, usually unspotted and tapering sharply from a broad base.

FLOWERS

Deep vermilion-red, with darker, red-brown spots and rings on the lip.

Sub-species *D.i. pulchella*

FLOWERING

June to July.

STEM

Rather slender, to 40cm (16in) sometimes tinged with purple.

LEAVES

Narrower and darker than other ssps.

FLOWERS

Purple-pink, lighter at mouth of spur. Lateral sepals may have loops. Lip has strong double loop and does not curve downwards. A pale, yellowish flowered variety occurs among some normal colonies, ssp *pulchella* var. *ochrantha*.

D.i. ochroleuca

Sub-species *D.i. cruenta*

FLOWERING

Late May-June.

STEM

Slender, up to 40cm (16in), usually purple tinged.

LEAVES

Stiff and erect, spotted or even blotched with purple-brown on upper surface, slightly lighter on lower surface.

FLOWERS

Mid to dark pink lip with loops which have dashes or dots inside. Lip sometimes three-lobed and can also have crinkly edges.

Sub-species *D.i. ochroleuca*

FLOWERING

Late May to early June.

STEM

Broad and up to 70cm (28in).

LEAVES

Large and erect, unspotted.

FLOWERS

Pale cream, darker towards the entrance to the spur. The large lip, 7mm long × 9mm broad (2.5in × 3.5in) is not marked and has three lobes, the outer lobe sometimes being notched.

45. Southern Marsh Orchid
Dactylorhiza praetermissa

Botanical Name

Praetermissa, neglected or overlooked.

Flowering

Mid-June/end July.

Habitat

Fens and limey marshes, damp dune slacks on shell-rich sands. Found in dry places such as chalk hills and old chalk quarries, usually in full sun. In northern England it grows among the limestone ballast of old railway lines and on the alkaline waste tips of long-abandoned chemical works.

Distribution

Mainly south of a line from the Humber estuary to Morecambe Bay, but extending north on the east coast to Co. Durham. It is not found in Scotland or Ireland.

Natural History

The Southern Marsh Orchid has the usual palmate tubers of this group, and a stem, usually hollow, 15–50cm (10–20in) high. Be-tween five and nine yellow-green unspotted leaves surround the stem, becoming more sheathing higher up and resembling bracts. The leaves are not hooded; any plant that follows the description of *D. praetermissa* but has hooded tips to the leaves is probably a hybrid. Such hybrids have been recorded between *D. praetermissa* and *D. fuchsii*, *D. incarnata*, *D. purpurella* and *D. traunsteineri*, as well as with *Gymnadenia conopsea*.

The spike has many flowers and can be up to 20cm (8in) long. The lateral sepals spread wide when the flower is newly opened, but become more erect as the flower ages. The petals and upper sepal form a hood as in other marsh orchids. The lip is broad and lacks the lobes seen in other marsh orchids, but the sides reflex to give a full appearance. The central part is marked by dashes and dots on a paler ground, but without the double loop of *D. incarnata*. The flower colour is usually pink/lilac/mauve but magenta flowers have been recorded in southern and western England.

The insect species that visit are not well-documented, but the high degree of hybridization with other spotted and marsh orchids indicates much cross-pollination. Germination and initial development of the plant is similar to that of *D. incarnata*, with the first leaf in the second year, and a tuber two years after that, flowering being dependent on the energy reserves built up by the green parts of the plant.

46. Northern Marsh Orchid
Dactylorhiza purpurella

Botanical Name

Purpurella, purple.

Flowering

Mid-June/end July.

Habitat

Damp ground, usually on calcareous soils, but found on peaty soils where there are flushes of alkaline water; colonizes old alkaline waste tips in northern England.

Distribution

Northern England, Scotland, Isle of Man and Ireland.

Natural History

This orchid was identified as a separate species in the early 1900s. It has a lobed tuber and a chunky, hollow stem up to 20cm (8in) high. The lower stem has between three and ten dark green glossy leaves, which are spreading rather than erect. They are usually unspotted, although some plants have a light marking of tiny dark spots near the hooded tips of the leaves.

The flower spike is 2–7cm (1–2in) long, with a distinctive squared-off top, almost as if cut across by shears. The colour is a stunning deep rich magenta. The lateral sepals spread wide and then upwards and are spotted. The petals and upper sepal form a loose hood.

The labellum is lozenge-shaped, and not lobed and is marked with dark dashes and spots, which do not form into loops.

The flowers are insect-pollinated and seed-set is high. Hybridization with other spotted and marsh orchids is fairly common, and hybrids with Frog and Fragrant Orchids have been reported.

47. Hebridean Marsh Orchid
Dactylorhiza ebudensis

Botanical Name

Ebudensis, Hebridean.

Flowering

Early/mid-May.

Habitat

Damp or swampy land, dune slacks. Found in UK only in North Uist.

Distribution

Found only on stretches of machair on North Uist in UK and nowhere else in the world.

Natural History

D. ebudensis is a squat plant above its palmate tuber, rarely more than 10cm (4in) high with three broad basal leaves, about 10–14mm (.5in) wide, purple-edged and blotched, so much so that the leaves can appear to be brownish-purple. The flower spike is tight and cylindrical, and of a richness of colour similar to the Northern Marsh Orchid, which is undoubtedly the source of many doubtful sightings of the Hebridean Marsh Orchid. The lateral sepals are upswept behind the hood formed by the upper sepal and petals. The lip is broad, rich purple, three-lobed and with darker purple markings of lines and spots. *D. ebudensis* has developed over time in a remote environment, the Hebrides, and is now considered a separate

species, rather than a ssp. of *D. majalis*. The type species of *D. majalis* does not occur in the UK.

The whole taxonomy of this species and its close relatives is in flux, and it is difficult to identify as it differs in colour and form so greatly and also hybridizes freely.

48. Narrow-leaved Marsh Orchid

(Synonym: Irish Marsh Orchid, formerly Pugsley's Marsh Orchid)

Dactylorhiza traunsteinerioides

Botanical Name

Traunsteiner, from Traunsteiner, Austrian pharmacist (1798–1850); *oides*, similar to (refers to *D. traunsteineri*).

Flowering

May/June.

Habitat

Neutral or alkaline soils in marshes and fens, usually in full sun up to an altitude of 200m (600ft) above sea level.

Distribution

East Anglia and the Fens, Berkshire, Hampshire, North Somerset, western North Wales and Anglesey, Yorkshire and Durham, West Coast of Scotland, Kintyre peninsula, western Invernesshire and Wester Ross. Northern and central/southern Ireland.

Natural History

This many-named orchid grows on wet ground, often in the margins of reed beds. It has the usual lobed tuber of the dactyl orchids and a stem between 10–20cm (4–8in) high, with two or three bright green sheathing leaves, normally unspotted. A non-sheathing leaf, unspotted, but with a purple tinge is sometimes found.

The spike has between ten and twenty lilac/pink flowers and the sepals and petals are arranged as in the previous species, the lateral sepals sweeping upwards wing-like, and the petals and upper sepal forming a hood. The bracts are distinctive, erect and much longer than the flowers. The lip is three-lobed, the central one being long and narrow with a recurved tip, and has a pale centre marked with lines and spots. Seed-set is good, and hybrids with other Dactylorhiza species are not unusual. This species is in decline due to habitat loss and competition from hybrids.

Other sites may be revealed by contacting the Wildlife Trusts in areas where the plant

has flourished in the past. Try Norfolk, Suffolk and Cambridgeshire Wildlife Trusts for the fens of East Anglia. In southern England, the Berkshire, Hampshire and Somerset Trusts may be able to help, as may Yorkshire, Durham and Scottish Wildlife Trusts. It is found in Antrim, so try the Ulster Wildlife Trust.

49. Lapland Marsh Orchid

Dactylorhiza lapponica (now a ssp. of *D. traunsteinerioides*)

Botanical Name

Lapponica, from Lapland.

Flowering

Late May/July but very variable depending upon local climatic conditions.

Habitat

Soils with a pH hovering around the seven mark – just either side of neutral. This generally means alkaline flushes over acidic soils, and always in full sun. In Scotland it is never at any great altitude, but in Switzerland and Austria it is found up to 1000m (3300ft) above sea level.

Distribution

Western Scotland, where it was discovered in the 1980s by A.G. Kenneth, M.R. Lowe and D.U. Tennant after a painstaking study of the Marsh Orchid populations of western Scottish areas revealed a species which could not be fitted into any known British taxon.

Natural History

Described in 1988 as a species new to the British Isles, *D. lapponica* has so far only been identified in Scottish locations, although base-rich hill flushes over peaty soil are not uncommon in the north of the UK. The plants are slim, with a 5–20cm (2–8in) stem, sometimes shading purple near to the top. There are two or three sheathing leaves, and sometimes one or two non-sheathing. The leaves are pale green with purple blotches, spots and bars.

The flower spike is loose with only three to ten flowers, which are usually magenta, but sometimes more purplish and sometimes more toward the crimson end of the spectrum. The lateral sepals stand erect with rounded tips and the other sepal and petals form a hood. The labellum is strongly marked with deep purple lines, rings and dots, and has a longer central lobe, sometimes reflexed at the tip. No certain records of hybrids have yet been made, but there have been odd plants found with characteristics between *D. lapponica* and *D. traunsteinerioides* where the two plants occur together.

Sites

No precise details revealed, but contact Scottish Wildlife Trust. The plant occurs on Rhum, South Harris, the Kintyre Peninsula, Ardnamurchan and Morvern, and in Invernesshire.

50. Man Orchid

Aceras anthropophorum

Botanical Name

A, lacking; *kera*, spur; *anthropos*, man; *phorum*, carrier.

Flowering

Early May/July.

Habitat

Chalk and limestone pasture in undisturbed situations. Disused limestone and chalk quarries such as Barnack, where the stone for Cambridge Colleges and Ely Cathedral was won.

Distribution

Largely confined to eastern and southern counties in England, from south Lincoln-shire to Kent. Its western limit is around Hampshire and the Isle of Wight, but it is recorded from north Somerset.

Natural History

Unlike the previous dactyl orchids, this plant grows from two egg-shaped tubers, as do the Orchis species. The tuber supporting the current year's growth is shrivelled, while the new tuber for the following year is plump, storing energy as this year's tuber is

depleted. The stem is 10–20cm (4–8in) in length, but can reach 40cm (16in) when in competition with long grasses. There are four leaves, about 5–10cm (2–4in) long. The lower leaves have pronounced venation and are blunter than the narrow, pointed upper leaves.

The spike is compact with as many as one hundred dull yellow manikin-shaped flowers, which sometimes have a red ochre shading to their edges. All three sepals and two petals form a hood, the 'man's head', while the long dangling labellum has two side lobes (the 'arms') and the long central lobe is split to form two 'legs'. There is no spur to carry nectar, but it is secreted at the base of the labellum and this attracts ants and hoverflies, seemingly a successful stratagem as seed is set in a high proportion of capsules. A hybrid with the Monkey Orchid has been reported.

51. Pyramidal Orchid
Anacamptis pyramidalis

Botanical Name

Anacamptis, recurved (pollinia); *pyramidalis*, pyramid-shaped.

Flowering

Mid-June/mid August.

Habitat

An early colonizer of waste ground on calcareous soils, in a dry and sunny situation. Found on chalk downs, hawthorn and blackthorn scrubland, shell-rich dune slacks, old quarries, and old alkali waste tips in the industrial areas of the north.

Distribution

All of southern England and the Midlands, northern England, eastern Scotland to the Firth of Forth. Western Scotland, the Western Isles, Isle of Man and Ireland.

Natural History

There are two round tubers from which grow a small number of succulent roots, and a stem that grows up to 55–60cm (22–24in) high. The basal leaves are dull green, pointed and three or four in number; they develop in autumn and over the winter. As the stem grows, it throws out five or six narrow, erect sheathing leaves.

The flower spike is conical (but despite the name, it does not have straight sides and

angles like a pyramid!), the lower flowers opening wide while the buds at the top of the plant remain tight shut and pointing upwards. The flowers are usually bright pink, an attractive shade, but white and deep red variants can be found. The tightly-packed flowers are usually thirty to forty in number. The lateral sepals spread wide, curving forward at their tips, and a loose hood is formed from the other sepal and two petals. The lip is deeply divided into three lobes, at the base of which are two ridges that guide visiting insects towards the nectar-bearing spur. The flowers have a scent, which I have seen

described variously as 'unpleasant', 'foxy' and 'faintly sweet'. Form your own judgement!

Butterflies, moths and small insects visit, and seed is set in a high percentage of cap- sules. It takes five years for the first leaf to appear and several more to store sufficient energy to permit flowering.

Glossary

Acid
Having a pH of less than seven, usually an indication of peaty ground or industrial contamination.

Alkaline
Having a pH greater than seven. An indication of the presence of chalk or lime in the soil, or waste dumps from lime-using industries.

Anther
The part of the stamen that produces pollen.

Base Rich
Soils rich in alkaline materials with a pH above 7.

Bog
Damp or wet, acidic ground underlain by peat, the product of the decay of plant material in wet conditions where no oxygen is present.

Bract
A small leaf at the base of a flower or on a stem.

Bulbil(s)
Small bulbs, as in the Bog Orchid, that form on the leaf tips and can separate and grow on to form a new plant.

Calcareous
Soils containing limestone or chalk (calcium carbonate), which may be derived from rock or seashells.

Campanulate
Describing flowers in which the petals are fused together to form a tube.

Capsule
A dry fruit containing seeds, which splits to release them.

Caudicle
The stalk which carries the pollinia (q.v.).

Chlorophyll
Green plant pigments containing magnesium, which convert the energy of light into sugars by photosynthesis (q.v.).

Cleistogamous
Self-fertilization, before a flower opens.

Column
A specialized organ in orchids, comprised of the style stigma and stamens fused together.

Dense
Descriptive of spikes where the individual flowers are tightly packed.

Dicotyledon
One of the two main divisions of flowering plants usually distinguished by having two seed leaves, net-veined leaves and flower parts in multiples of two.

Dune Slack
The hollow areas between the hills of old established sand dune systems, often with a covering of dwarf willow (*Salix repens*).

They are usually just above the impervious bed rock and so remain damp.

Epichile
That part of the lip of an orchid furthest away from its base, the ovary. *See* Hypochile below.

Fen
Similar to a bog, but where the peaty substrate is submerged in water with a neutral to alkaline pH.

Glandular
Describing groups of cells (usually hairs in orchids) exuding liquids, which can vary from water to sticky, sugary solutions.

Hybrid
A plant resulting from the cross-fertilization of two different species or sub-species.

Hypochile
The part of the labellum (lip) nearest to the ovary in those orchids such as Epipactis where the organ is divided into two distinct sections by a hinge mechanism.

Inflorescence
Strictly a shoot with flowers and without leaves. Used here to describe the flowering top of a shoot, which may bear leaves.

Karst
Geological term to describe surface limestone features which have been shaped by the carbonic acid formed by rainwater reaction with soil, into pavements, clints, grikes, swallow holes, caves and potholes. Named for the region in Yugoslavia where these features are spectacular.

Keeled
Description of leaves with an acute angle about their mid-rib to give a folded effect.

Labellum
The third petal of an orchid flower, usually highly modified in its appearance from the two upper petals. It is naturally the upper petal of the three, and would stand at the top of the flower except that in most orchids the stalk/ovary twists through 180 degrees to bring the labellum to the lowest part of the flower. The Ghost Orchid does not have this twisting, so the labellum is uppermost, while the Bog Orchid has a 360 degrees twist, giving the same uppermost lip.

Lateral Sepals
The two sepals (q.v.) of an orchid flower which spread out at the sides, and from behind the base of the labellum.

Lax
Of inflorescences where the flowers are not closely spaced.

Lip
The English name for the Latin 'labellum'.

Machair
An environment unique to northwest Scotland and the Western Isles in the UK, a lime-rich, grazed coastal pasture growing on calcareous shell sands; a home to many orchids and chalk-loving plants.

Median
Central, middle. In orchid species usually used to describe a small tooth, or extra lobe in the middle of the central lobe of the lip.

Monocarpic
Describes a plant, not a biennial or annual, which develops over several years, flowers once and dies after flowering.

Monocotyledon
The second major division of the angiosperms, seed-bearing plants, where the seeds are contained in closed organs. They are distinguished from dicotyledons (q.v.) by leaves with parallel veins, seedlings with only one seed leaf (cotyledon) and flower parts in multiples of three (orchids having three sepals and three petals, one of which is modified to form the labellum).

Mycorrhiza
A fungus that inhabits the roots of many orchids and other photosynthesizing plants. Fungi can provide the leafy plant with the products of decomposing organic material (especially nitrogen compounds), while the green leaves of the flowering plant produce sugars, which can sustain the fungus.

Nectar
A liquid secreted by the orchid and other flowers containing sugars and complex organic chemicals attractive to insects.

Neutral
Neither acidic nor alkaline.

Node
A point on a stem, or rhizome, from which leaves or shoots can grow.

Orchid
A monocotyledonous plant of the family *Orchidaceae*, perhaps the largest family of plants with about 20,000 different species worldwide, but only fifty-one in the UK. Apart from the florist trade, the main commercial use of orchids is the production of vanilla.

Ovary
That part of the reproductive system of the flower containing the ovules, which become the seeds after fertilization.

Palmate
Describing a leaf or root shaped like a hand with outstretched fingers and a flat palm.

Papillae
Tiny projections, usually hairy. In orchids they are usually on the labellum.

Pavement
Exposed slabs of bedded limestone which have been divided into blocks (called clints) and which are separated from their neighbours by grikes, cracks formed by the downward percolation of acids dissolved from the surface vegetation by rain water. The individual slab may also be undermined by the same action along its bedding planes and may rock when trodden on. It can be a dangerous environment when wet.

Perennial
A plant that lives for more than two years (cf. annual and biennial). Most perennials flower for several years, but monocarpic (q.v.) perennials do not.

Perianth
The showy parts of a flower, in orchids the petals, sepals and lip.

Petal
In an orchid part of the inner ring of the perianth and including the lip. The sepals are the outer ring.

Pheromone
A scented chemical produced by insects and other creatures, which can be detected by

other individuals and which affects their behaviour, often in a sexual way.

Phloem

A series of vessels within a plant which translocate (q.v.) the products of photosynthesis (q.v.) from the leaves to other parts of the organism.

Photosynthesis

The most important chemical reaction of all and the source of almost all life on earth. The chlorophyll pigments in plants use the energy of sunlight to produce carbohydrate foods such as sugar by taking carbon dioxide and water and chemically converting them to starches and oxygen. The starches are converted to sugars and the oxygen is 'breathed out' by the plant, maintaining the delicate balance of our atmosphere. The chemical reactions may not be perfectly understood, but their importance can hardly be overstated. Their formula is: $6CO_2 + 6H_2O$ (+ sunlight energy) $C_6 H_{12}O + 6O_2$.

Pollinia

Plural of pollinium. In most plants the pollen grains (the male element of fertilization) are distinct and separate, but in all UK orchids except Lady's Slipper the individual grains of pollen fuse together at the top of the caudicle to form pollinia. These are often removed by visiting insects as they stick on to the animals' heads and then fertilize the next flower to be visited. (Read Charles Darwin for a far superior account.)

Protocorm

The minute tuber that first develops after an orchid seed germinates. It is the organism usually infected by mycorrhizal fungus, and the symbiosis of the two different organisms is the key to the orchid

plants' successful growth; most orchid seeds contain almost no energy resources and initially rely on the mycorrhiza to sustain them.

Pseuodobulb

A stem that swells, usually just above ground level, to produce a bulb-like organ in which energy is stored (cf. tuber).

Pseudocopulation

Describes the attempts of newly hatched male insects to mate with a flower that gives off visual and pheromone signals to which the insect responds. Usually occurs before any females of the particular insect species have hatched.

Reflex(ed)

Folded back upon itself.

Resupinate

Turned upside down by the twisting of a stalk, etc. Many orchid flowers are resupinate, having the lip at the lower part of the flowers because the ovary has twisted through 180°.

Rhizome

A stem that is adapted to grow underground. It usually grows horizontally, just below the soil surface, and new growth can arise from its tip, or less frequently its nodes.

Rostellum

The part of the female structure of the orchid flower between the stamens and stigma. It is actually a sterile third stigma, and carries the viscous discs (*see* viscidia) of the pollinia.

Runner

A stem that grows along the ground and can

produce new plants at intervals at the nodes. The Garden Strawberry and Creeping Buttercup *Ranunculus repens* are examples probably familiar to most people.

Saprophyte

A plant which, while not parasitic on other vascular plants, is unable to photosynthesize and so depends on mycorrhiza in its root system to break down dead organic matter in the surrounding humus to provide energy. There may be green leaves or other chlorophyll-bearing tissue to supplement the fungus-derived sources of food.

Sepal

The outer whorl of a flower. In orchids there are three sepals, two lateral, often spreading, and an upper sepal, usually in a vertical position opposite the labellum.

Sheathing

Describing a leaf or bract whose base completely encircles the stem upon which it grows.

Spur

A tube or pouch at the base of the lip which usually contains nectar.

Stamen

The male part of a flower. In orchids it is part of the column, where the style, stigma and stamens are fused together.

Stigma

The female part of a flower; in orchids a sticky area to which the pollinia adhere when brought in by insects, or when self-pollination occurs as the pollinia fall forwards on to the stigma.

Stolon

A creeping above-ground, stem similar to a runner (q.v.) but producing new growth only at the nodes.

Style

That part of the column connecting the ovary and stigma in orchids.

Symbiosis

A situation in which two different types of organism (plants and fungi in orchids; algae and fungi in lichens), exist together in the same living being and both contribute and receive some benefit. Sometimes the benefits are hard to evaluate.

Taxonomy

The science of classification of all living systems by assigning them to various taxons. A difficult task in the case of orchids, and the practitioners are not envied their task.

Theca (plural Thecae)

The two halves of the stamen containing pollinia at the top of the column. In the Ophrys species they often contain nectar and glisten, resembling shiny insect eyes.

Translocation

The movement of fluids and energy-containing liquids, such as the products of photosynthesis, from the productive part of the plant to where it is needed, e.g. sugars from leaves to roots and flowers.

Tuber

Swollen parts of roots in which energy is stored. A potato or a dahlia tuber are familiar examples.

Vascular System

The tissues that move liquids and food from one part of a plant to another. The adjective 'vascular' describes all plants with such systems.

Vegetative

Descriptive of a method of multiplication that is not sexual. In wild plants this obviously excludes cuttings and other manipulative processes, and refers to processes such as increase by runners, bulbils, stolons, bulbs, rhizomes and tubers that are not involved in seed production.

Venation

The pattern of the veins in a leaf. In monocotyledons, such as orchids, the venation is usually, although not invariably, parallel. In dicotyledonous plants venation is usually reticulate, or netted.

Viscidium (plural Viscidia)

The sticky disc at the base of a pollinium by which it attaches itself to the probosces of visiting insects (and the pencils of probing botanists such as Charles Darwin!).

Site locations

County	Site	Location	NGR	Contact
2. White Helleborine				
Avon	Brown's Folly	Bath	ST7966	Avon WT
Cambridgeshire	Beechwood	Cambridge	TL4854	Beds, Cambs & Northants WT
Dorset	Badbury Rings	Wimborne Minster	ST9603	National Trust
Hampshire	Wealden Edge Hangers	Petersfield	SU7228	Hants CC
			SU7966	
Hereford	Leeping Stocks	Monmouth	SO5416	Hereford WT
Hereford	Great Doward Reserves	Monmouth	SO5415	Hereford WT
Hertfordshire	Telegraph Hill	Hitchin	TL1128	Herts & Middx WT
Kent	Queendown Warren	Maidstone	TR8262	Kent WT
Kent	Yocklett's Bank	Ashford	TR1247	Kent WT
Northants	Fox Covert	Royston	TL3339	Northants WT
Oxfordshire	Aston Rowant	Thame	SU7397	English Nature
Oxfordshire	Lewknor Copse	Stokenchurch	SU7197	Bucks, Beds & Oxon WT
Surrey	Boxhill CP	Dorking	TQ1751	National Trust
3. Narrow-leaved Helleborine				
Gloucestershire	Coopers Hill	Painswick	SO8814	Glos. CC
Gloucestershire	Cotswold Common	Painswick	SO8913	Glos. CC
Oxfordshire	Warburg Reserve	Henley-on-Thames	SU7288	Berks, Bucks & Oxford WT
Oxfordshire	Lewknor Copse	Stokenchurch	SU7197	Berks, Bucks & Oxford WT
Worcestershire	Wyre Forest	Kidderminster	SO7576	Nature Conservancy Council
5. Marsh Helleborine				
Ceredigion	Dyfi	Aberdovey	SN6697	Countryside Council for Wales
Cumbria	Sandscale Haws	Barrow-in-Furness	SD1975	National Trust
Glamorgan	Kenfig Dunes	Port Talbot	SS8081	Countryside Council for Wales
Gwynedd	Cors Goch	Bangor	SH4632	North Wales WT
Kent	Sandwich Bay	Sandwich	TR3559	Kent WT, RSPB, National Trust
Lancashire	Ainsdale & Birkdale	Southport	SD2912	English Nature
Lancashire	Lytham St Annes	Blackpool	SD3030	Lancs WT
Lancashire	Mere Sands	Southport	SD4415	Lancs WT
Norfolk	Braunton Burrows	Braunton	SS4632	English Nature
Norfolk	Holkham Dunes	Wells-next-the-Sea	TF8944	English Nature
Norfolk	Strumpshaw	Norwich	TG3406	RSPB
Norfolk	Upton Fen	S. Walsham	TG3713	Norfolk WT
Northumberland	Druridge Bay	Ashington	NZ2994	English Nature
Northumberland	Lindisfarne	Berwick-upon-Tweed	NU0943	English Nature
Oxfordshire	Cothill Fen	Abingdon	SU4599	Bucks, Beds & Oxon WT
Somerset	Berrow Dunes	Burnham-on-Sea	ST2954	Sedgemoor DC
N Yorkshire	Farndale	Kirkbymoorside	SE6697	N Yorks Nat. Park Committee
6. Broad-leaved Helleborine				
Avon	Brown's Folly	Bath	ST7966	Avon WT
Cornwall	Sylvia's Meadow	Tavistock	SX4170	Cornwall WT

County	Site	Location	NGR	Contact
Cumbria	Smardale Line	Kirkby Stephen	NY7308	English Nature
Devon	Andrew's Wood	Plymouth	SX7051	Devon WT
Essex	Danbury	Chelmsford	TL7804	English Nature
Essex	Hatfield Forest	Bishops Stortford	TL5419	National Trust
Gloucestershire	Frith Wood	Stroud	SJ9948	Glos WT
Kent	Yocklett's Bank	Ashford	TR1247	Kent WT
Lancashire	Gait Barrows	Carnforth	SD4877	English Nature
Northumberland	Briarwood Banks	Haydon Bridge	NY7962	Northumberland WT
Nottinghamshire	Dyscarr Wood	Worksop	SK5886	Nottinghamshire WT
Staffordshire	Churnet Valley Woods	Stoke-on-Trent	SJ9948	RSPB
Strathclyde	Lochwinnoch	Paisley	NS3558	RSPB Scotland
Surrey	Graeme Hendry Reserve	Godstone	TQ3450	Surrey WT
Surrey	Walliswood	Horsham	TQ1238	Surrey WT
Warwickshire	Snitterfield Bushes	Stratford-upon-Avon	SP2060	Warwicks WT
Worcestershire	The Knapp & Watermill	Worcester	SO7452	Worcs WT

7. Violet Helleborine

County	Site	Location	NGR	Contact
Essex	Chalkney Wood	Braintree	TL8727	Essex CC
Gloucestershire	Wetmoor	Wotton-under- Edge	ST7487	Gloucester WT
Leicestershire	Cloud Wood	Ashby-de-la-Zouche	TBA	Leics & Rutland WT
Leicestershire	Prior's Coppice	Oakham	SK8305	Leics & Rutland WT
Oxfordshire	Aston Rowant	Thame	SU7397	English Nature
Oxfordshire	Warburg Reserve	Henley-on-Thames	SU7288	Bucks, Beds & Oxon WT
Suffolk	Grotton Wood	Sudbury	TL9743	Suffolk WT
Suffolk	Wolves Wood	Ipswich	TM0536	RSPB
Surrey	Walliswood	Horsham	TQ1238	Suffolk WT
Worcestershire	Nunnery Wood	Worcester	SO8754	Worcester WT
Worcestershire	The Knapp & Papermill	Worcester	SO7452	Worcester WT

8. Slender-lipped Helleborine

County	Site	Location	NGR	Contact
Gloucestershire	Frith Wood	Stroud	SO8708	Glos WT

9. Dune Helleborine

County	Site	Location	NGR	Contact
Cumbria	Sandscale Haws	Barrow-in-Furness	SD1975	National Trust
Gwynedd	Aberffraw Dunes	Holyhead	SH3568	N Wales WT
Gwynedd	Newborough Warren	SE Anglesey	SH4063	Countryside Council for Wales
Lancashire	Ainsdale & Birkdale	Southport	SD2912	English Nature
Northumberland	Lindisfarne	Berwick-upon-Tweed	NU0943	English Nature

10. Young's Helleborine

County	Site	Location	NGR	Contact
Northumberland	Killingworth	Not disclosed	None available	
Northumberland	Gosforth Park*	Newcastle-upon-Tyne	Not disclosed	Natural History Society of Northumberland Members only
Northumberland	Settlingstones	Hexham	On private land	

*This site is open to members of the Natural History Society of Northumbria only. It is wardened, and the plants are difficult to find without the warden's assistance. Contact the Northumbria Society to gain access.

County	Site	Location	NGR	Contact
11. Green-flowered Helleborine				
Cumbria	North Walney	Barrow-in-Furness	SD1769	English Nature
Gloucestershire	Buckholt Wood	Gloucester	SO8913	English Nature/Glos. WT
Gloucestershire	Frith Wood	Stroud	SO8708	Glos. WT
Hampshire	Winnall Moors	Winchester	SU4930	Hants & IoW WT
Gwynnedd	Morfa Dyffryn	Harlech	SH5527	Countryside Council for Wales
Lancashire	Ainsdale & Birkdale	Southport	SD2912	English Nature
Lancashire	Gait Barrows	Carnforth	SD4877	English Nature
Northumberland	Lindisfarne	Berwick-upon-Tweed	NU0943	English Nature
12. Dark Red Helleborine				
Conwy	Bryn Pydew	Colwyn Bay	SH8179	North Wales WT
Cumbria	Clawthorpe Fell	Kirkby Lonsdale	SD5378	English Nature
Durham	Bishop Middleton Quarry	Newton Aycliffe	NZ3322	Durham WT
Durham	Raisby Quarry	Durham	NZ3337	Durham WT
Highland	Ben Suardal	Skye	NG6362	Scottish Natural Heritage
Highland	Inchnadamph	Knockan Visitor Centre	NC2719	Scottish Natural Heritage
Highland	Invernaver	Bettyhill	NC6961	Scottish Natural Heritage
Lancashire	Arnside Knott	Arnside	SD4577	National Trust
Lancashire	Gait Barrows	Carnforth	SD4877	English Nature
14. Autumn Lady's Tresses				
Devon	Dawlish Warren	Exmouth	SX9878	Devon WT
Dorset	Fontmell Down	Shaftesbury	ST8817	Dorset WT
Gloucestershire	Plump Hill Dolomite Quarry	Gloucester	SU6617	Glos WT
Hampshire	Catherington Down	Portsmouth	SU6814	Hants & IOW WT
Kent	Lydden Temple Ewell	Dover	TR2745	Kent WT
Kent	Queendown Warren	Gillingham	TQ8262	Kent WT
Lancashire	The Lots	Silverdale	SD4575	National Trust
Shropshire	Llanymynech Rocks	Oswestry	SJ2622	Both Salop and Montgomery WTs
Somerset	Dolebury Warren	Shipham	ST4559	Avon WT
Somerset	Goblin Combe	Bristol Airport	ST4765	Avon WT
Somerset	Ham Hill Country Park	Yeovil	ST4716	Yeovil DC
Somerset	Walborough	Weston-super-Mare	ST3158	Avon WT
Surrey	Box Hill CP	Dorking	TQ1751	National Trust
Surrey	Hackhurst Down	Dorking	TQ0948	National Trust
Sussex	Kingley Vale	Chichester	SU8208	English Nature
Wiltshire	Middleton Down	Salisbury	SU0423	Wilts WT
16. Irish Lady's Tresses				
Argyll & Bute	No specific sites identified for this species	Colonsay		
Argyll & Bute		Argyll		
Devon		Tavistock		

County	Site	Location	NGR	Contact
Hebrides		Barra, Benbecula,		
		Vatersay, Islay,		
		Mull & Tiree		
Highland		Coll		
Highland		Inverness		
Highland		Shiel Bridge		
Highland		Ardnamurchan		
Highland		Moidart		
Highland		Morvern		

17. Common Twayblade

County	Site	Location	NGR	Contact
Avon	Folly Farm	Bristol	ST6160	Avon WT
Ayrshire	Auchalton Meadows	Maybole	NS3303	Scottish WT
Bedfordshire	Bramingham Wood	Luton	TL0625	Woodland Trust
Berkshire	Thatchham Reedbeds	Newbury	SU5067	Newbury DC
Berwickshire	Duns Castle	Duns	NT7755	Scottish WT
Cumbria	Sizergh Castle	Kendal	SD4987	National Trust
Dorset	Badbury Rings	Wimborne Minster	ST9603	National Trust
Devon	Braunton Burrows	Barnstaple	SS4632	English Nature
Durham	Wingate Quarry	Durham	NZ3737	Durham CC
Highland	Loch Fleet	Dornoch	NH7996	Scottish WT
Kent	Burham Down	Chatham	TQ7262	Kent WT
Kent	Fore Wood	Hastings	TQ7512	Kent WT
Kent	Kiln Wood	Lenham	TQ8851	Kent WT
Kent	Yocklett's Bank	Ashford	TR1247	Kent WT
Lancashire	Gait Barrows	Carnforth	SD4877	English Nature
Leicestershire	Ambion Wood	Market Bosworth	SP4099	Bosworth Field Visitor Centre
Northamptonshire	Newbottle Spinney	Banbury	SP5136	Northants WT
Nottinghamshire	Dyscarr Wood	Workshop	SK5886	Notts WT
Nottinghamshire	Attenborough	Long Eaton	SK5234	Notts WT
Orkney	Birsay	Finstown	HY3719	RSPB Scotland
Orkney	Cottascarth	Finstown	HY3719	RSPB Scotland
Perth & Kinross	Keltneyburn	Aberfeldy	NN7650	Scottish WT
Shropshire	Llynclys Hill	Oswestry	SJ2723	Salop WT
Staffordshire	Rod Wood	Leek	SJ9952	Staffs WT
Suffolk	Groton Wood	Suffolk	TL9743	Suffolk WT
Surrey	Box Hill CP	Dorking	TQ1751	Surrey WT
Worcestershire	Tyddesley Wood	Pershore	SO9246	Worcester WT
Wiltshire	Morgan's Hill	Calne	SU0167	Wilts WT
Yorkshire	Brockadale	Doncaster	SE5117	Yorks WT

18. Lesser Twayblade

County	Site	Location	NGR	Contact
Denbighshire	Lake Vyrnwy	Welshpool	SH9821	RSPB
Glamorgan	South Gower Coast	Oxwich	SS5086	RSPB
Grampian	Loch Fleet	Dornoch	NH7796	Scottish WT
Grampian	Glen Tanar	Ballater	NO4891	Scottish Natural History Heritage
Highland	Cairngorms	Aviemore	NJ0101	Scottish WT
Highland	Culbin Sands	Nairn	NJ9362	RSPB Scotland

County	Site	Location	NGR	Contact
Highland	Glenmore Forest Park	Aviemore	NH9810	Forestry Commission
Highland	Lochfleet	Aviemore	NH7796	Scottish WT
Highland	Loch Garten	Aviemore	NH9718	RSPB Scotland
Highland	Rothiemurchus	Aviemore	NH9110	Rothiemurchus Estate
Highland	Strathfarrar	Inverness	NH2737	Scottish Natural Heritage
Northumberland	Holystone	Rothbury	NT9402	Northumberland WT
Orkney	Birsay Moors	Finstown	HY3426	RSPB Scotland
Orkney	Cottasgarth	Finstown	HY3719	RSPB Scotland
Shetland	Fair Isle	Lerwick	HZ2172	National Trust for Scotland
Skye	Clan Donald Centre	Armadale	NG6105	Clan Donald Lands Trust
Tayside	Black Wood of Rannoch	Pitlochry	NN5755	Forestry Commission

19. Bird's Nest Orchid

County	Site	Location	NGR	Contact
Argyll & Bute	Glen Nant	Taynuilt	NN1020	Scottish Natural Heritage
Avon	Avon Gorge	Bristol	ST5396	Avon WT
Avon	Weston Big Wood	Portishead	ST4575	Avon WT
Buckinghamshire	Grangelands & Pulpit Hill	Princes Risborough	SP8302	Bucks, Beds & Oxon WT
Borders	Whitlaw Wood	Hawick	NT5013	Scottish WT
Cleveland	Castle Eden Dene	Peterlee	NZ4339	English Nature
Cumbria	Roudsea Wood	Ulverston	SD3382	English Nature
Denbighshire	Cilgroeslwyd	Ruthin	SJ1255	N Wales WT
Derbyshire	Lathkill Dale	Bakewell	SK2066	English Nature
Cornwall	Sylvia's Meadow	Tavistock	SX4170	Cornwall WT
Dorset	Badbury Rings	Wimborne Minster	ST9603	National Trust
Gloucestershire	Buckholt Wood	Gloucester	SO8913	English Nature
Gloucestershire	Dean Heritage Centre	Cinderford	SO6610	Glos. WT
Gloucestershire	Forest of Dean	Cinderford	SO6610	Forestry Commisssion
Gloucestershire	Lancault	Bristol	ST5396	Glos. WT
Gloucestershire	Wetmoor	Wotton under Edge	ST7488	Glos. WT
Gwynnedd	Cwm Clydach	Brynmawr	SO2112	Countryside Council for Wales
Hampshire	Crab Wood	Winchester	SU4329	Hants & IoW WT
Hampshire	Wealden Edge Hangers	Petersfield	SU7427	Hants CC
Leicestershire	Cloud Wood	Ashby-de-la-Zouch	SK4121	Leics WT
Northumberland	Briarwood Banks	Haltwhistle	NY7962	Northumberland WT
Perth & Kinross	Glen Nant	Taynuilt	NN1020	Scottish National Heritage
Renfrewshire	Lochwinnoch	Paisley	NS3558	RSPB Scotland
Suffolk	Reydon Wood	Wangford	TM4778	Suffolk WT
Suffolk	Wolves Wood	Ipswich	TM0543	RSPB
Worcestershire	Pipers Hill	Bromsgrove	SO9664	Worcs WT
Worcestershire	Tyddesley Wood	Pershore	SO9245	Worcs WT
Yorkshire	Farndale	Kirkby Moorside	SE7089	N Yorks Moors Nat. Park Committee

20. Creeping Lady's Tresses

County	Site	Location	NGR	Contact
Grampian	Culbin Forest	Nairn	NH9861	Forestry Commission
Grampian	Glen Tanar	Ballater	NO4891	Nature Conservancy Council
Grampian	Sands of Forvie	Peterhead	NK0227	Scottish Natural Heritage
Highland	Benn Eighe	Kinlochewe	NG9862	Scottish Natural Heritage

County	Site	Location	NGR	Contact
Highland	Glenmore Forest	Aviemore	NH9810	Forestry Commission
Highland	Loch Fleet	Dornoch	NH7796	Scottish WT
Highland	Loch Garten	Boat of Garten	NH9718	RSPB Scotland
Highland	Rothiemurchus Forest	Aviemore	NH9810	Rothiemurchus Estate
Highland	Stratharrar	Inverness	N2737	Scottish Natural Heritage
Norfolk	Wells Wood	Wells-next-the-Sea	NK0227	Norfolk WT

21. Bog Orchid

County	Site	Location	NGR	Contact
Argyll & Bute	Rahoy Hills	Mull	NM6553	Scottish WT
Cumbria	Lake District National Park	Various, enquire locally	N/A	Lake District Nat. Park Centre
Dorset	Isle of Purbeck	Various, enquire locally	N/A	Dorset WT
Hampshire	New Forest	Various, enquire locally	N/A	Forestry Commission
Highland	Eigg	Various	N/A	Scottish WT

22. Fen Orchid

County	Site	Location	NGR	Contact
Glamorgan	Kenfig Dunes	Bridgend	SS8081	Countryside Council for Wales

23. Coralroot Orchid

County	Site	Location	NGR	Contact
Borders	Gordon Moss	Gordon	NT6342	Scottish WT
Cumbria	Sandscale Haws	Barrow-in-Furness	SD1975	National Trust
Fife	Tentsmuir Point	Newport-on-Tay		Scots Natural Heritage
Grampian	Culbin Sands	Nairn	NH9057	RSPB Scotland
Highland	Loch Garten	Boat of Garten	NH9718	RSPB Scotland
Northumberland	Lindisfarne	Berwick-upon-Tweed	NJ0943	National Trust

24. Musk Orchid

County	Site	Location	NGR	Contact
Dorset	Badbury Rings	Wimborne Minster	ST9603	National Trust
Hampshire	St Catherine's Hill	Winchester	SU4827	Hants & IOW WT
Hertfordshire	Ivinghoe Beacon	Dunstable	SP9616	National Trust
Kent	Park Gate Downs	Ashford	TQ1645	Kent WT
Kent	Wye Downs	Ashford	TR0745	Kent WT
Sussex	Linch Down	Didling	SU8417	Sussex WT

25. Frog Orchid

County	Site	Location	NGR	Contact
Ayrshire	Auchalton Meadow	Maybole	NS3303	Scottish WT
Ayrshire	Feoch Meadows	Barrhill	NX2682	Scottish WT
Buckinghamshire	Chinnor Hill	Princes Risborough	SP7600	Bucks, Beds & Oxon WT
Derbyshire	Rose End Meadows	Matlock	SK2956	Derbys WT
Dorset	Badbury Rings	Wimborne Minster	ST9603	National Trust
Dorset	Fontmell Down	Shaftesbury	ST8817	Dorset WT
Hampshire	Old Winchester Hill	Petersfield	SU6421	English Nature
Hampshire	St Catherine's Hill	Winchester	SU4827	Hants & IOW WT
Hebrides	Rhum		NM3798	Scottish Natural Heritage
Shetland	Fair Isle		HZ2172	National Trust for Scotland
Sussex	Kingley Vale	Chichester	SU8211	English Nature

County	Site	Location	NGR	Contact
Wiltshire	Martin Down	Salisbury	SU0519	English Nature
Wiltshire	Middleton Down	Salisbury	SU0423	Wilts WT
Wiltshire	Morgans Hill	Avebury	SU0267	Wiltshire WT
Yorkshire	Farndale	Kirkby Moorside	SE7089	North York Moor National Park Committee

26. Chalk Fragrant Orchid

County	Site	Location	NGR	Contact
Ayrshire	Auchalton Meadow	Maybole	NS3303	Scottish WT
Ayrshire	Keltneyburn	Aberfeldy	NN7650	Scottish WT
Buckinghamshire	Aston Rowant	Stokenchurch	SU7496	English Nature
Cheshire	Plumley Lime Beds	Northwich	SJ7075	Cheshire WT
Cornwall	Sylvia's Meadow	Tavistock	SX4176	Cornwall WT
Cumbria	Asby Scar	Kirkby Stephen	NY6410	English Nature
Cumbria	Smardale Gill	Kirkby Stephen	NY7308	Cumbria WT
Derbyshire	Millers Dale	Bakewell	SK1473	Peak Park Planning Board
Dorset	Badbury Rings	Wimborne Minster	ST9603	National Trust
Dorset	Chudleigh Knighton Heath	Bovey Tracey	SX8377	Devon WT
Durham	Wingate Quarry	Peterlee	NZ3737	Durham CC
Gwynnedd	Cors Goch	Bangor	SH4632	N Wales WT
Hampshire	Old Winchester Hill	Petersfield	SU6421	English Nature
Hertfordshire	Ivinghoe Beacon	Hemel Hempstead	SP9616	National Trust
Hertfordshire	Therfield Heath	Royston	TL6421	English Nature
Hebrides	Rhum		NM3798	Scottish Natural Heritage
Kent	Wye Downs	Ashford	TR0745	English Nature
Lancashire	Gait Barrows	Carnforth	SD4877	English Nature
Leicestershire	Ulverscroft	Coalville	SK4912	Leics & Rutland WT
Perth & Kinross	Keltneyburn	Aberfeldy	NN7650	Scottish WT
Shropshire	Lynclys Hill	Oswestry	SJ2723	Salop WT
Surrey	Box Hill	Dorking	TQ1751	National Trust
Sussex	Kingley Vale	Chichester	SU8211	English Nature
Sutherland	Kintail	Sheilbridge	NH0019	National Trust for Scotland
Wiltshire	Cockey Down	Salisbury	SU1732	Wilts WT
Wiltshire	Devenish Reserve	Salisbury		Wilts WT
Wiltshire	Martin Down	Salisbury	SU0519	English Nature
Wiltshire	Middleton Down	Salisbury	SU0423	Wilts WT
Wiltshire	Morgans Hill	Avebury	SU0267	Wilts WT
Yorkshire	Levisham Moor	Pickering	SE8392	N Yorks National Park Committee

27. Small White Orchid

County	Site	Location	NGR	Contact
Argyll & Bute	Morrone Birkwood	Braemar	NO1390	Scottish Natural Heritage
Ayrshire	Feoch Meadows	Barrhill	NX2682	Scottish WT
Perth & Kinross	Keltneyburn	Aberfeldy	NN7650	Scottish WT
Yorkshire	Farndale	Kirkby Moorside	SE7089	North Yorks Moors National Park Committee

28. Greater Butterfly Orchid

County	Site	Location	NGR	Contact
Aberdeenshire	Loch of Strathbeg	Fraserburgh	NK0557	RSPB Scotland

County	Site	Location	NGR	Contact
Ayrshire	Auchalton Meadow	Maybole	NS3303	Scottish WT
Ayrshire	Feoch Meadows	Barrhill	NX2682	Scottish WT
Carmarthen	Caeau Tan y Bwlch	Penygroes	SH4348	N Wales WT
Cornwall	Sylvia's Meadow	Tavistock	SX4176	Cornwall WT
Cumbria	Sizergh Castle	Kendal	SD4988	National Trust
Denbighshire	Cilgroeslwyd Wood	Ruthin	SJ12551	N Wales WT
Derbyshire	Manifold Valley	Ashbourne	SK1054	National Trust
Dorset	Badbury Rings	Wimborne Minster	ST9607	National Trust
Dorset	Powerstock Common	Bridport	SY5497	Dorset WT
Essex	Danbury Common	Chelmsford	TL7804	Dorset WT
Hampshire	Old Winchester Hill	Petersfield	SU4827	English Nature
Hereford	Queenswood CP	Leominster	SO5051	Hereford & Worcester CC
Highlands	Culbin Sands	Nairn	NH9057	RSPB Scotland
Highlands	Kintail	Shiel Bridge	NH0019	National Trust for Scotland
Kent	Yockletts Bank	Canterbury	TR1247	Kent WT
Leicestershire	Cloud Wood	Ashby-de-la-Zouch	SK4121	Leicester & Rutland WT
Leicestershire	Priors Coppice	Oakham	SK8305	Leicester & Rutland WT
Northamptonshire	Salcey Forest	Northampton	SP8151	Forestry Commission
Nottinghamshire	Kirton Wood	Tuxford	SK7068	Notts WT
Perth & Kinross	Keltneyburn	Aberfeldy	NN7650	Scottish WT
Shropshire	Llynclys Hill	Oswestry	SJ2723	Salop WT
Staffordshire	Coombes Valley	Leek	SK0053	English Nature
Strathclyde	Lochwinnoch	Paisley	NS3558	RSPB Scotland
Suffolk	Reydon Wood	Wangford	TM4778	Suffolk WT
Warwickshire	Snitterfield Bushes	Henley-in-Arden	SP2060	Warks WT
Wiltshire	Blackmoor Copse	Salisbury	SU2328	Wilts WT
Wiltshire	Green Lane Wood	Trowbridge	ST8857	Wilts WT
Wiltshire	Ravensroost Wood	Malmesbury	SU0287	Wilts WT
Worcestershire	Tyddesley Wood	Pershore	SO9245	Worcs WT

29. Lesser Butterfly Orchid

County	Site	Location	NGR	Contact
Avon & Somerset	Street Heath	Glastonbury	ST4639	Avon WT
Ayrshire	Auchalton Meadow	Maybole	NS3306	Scottish WT
Ayrshire	Feoch Meadows	Barrhill	NX2682	Scottish WT
Borders	Gordon Moss	Gordon	NT6342	Scottish WT
Cornwall	The Lizard	Mullion	SW7014	Cornwall WT
Cornwall	Sylvia's Meadow	Tavistock	SX4170	Cornwall WT
Cumbria	Helsington Barrows	Kendal	SD4990	Cumbria WT
Glamorgan	Lavernock Point	Barry	ST1868	Glamorgan WT
Gwynedd	Cors Goch	Bangor	SH5081	N Wales WT
Ross & Cromarty	Talich	Tain	NH8578	Scottish WT
Sutherland	Kintail	Shiel Bridge	NH0019	National Trust for Scotland
Strathclyde	Lochwinnoch	Paisley	NS3558	RSPB Scotland
Wiltshire	Morgans Hill	Calne	SU0167	Wilts WT

31. Bee Orchid

County	Site	Location	NGR	Contact
Avon	Walborough	Weston-super-Mare	ST3157	Avon WT
Bedfordshire	Felmersham	Bedford	SP9958	Beds WT

County	Site	Location	NGR	Contact
Cambridgeshire	Devils Dyke	Newmarket	TL5266 linear	Cambridge WT
Cambridgeshire	Fleam Dyke	Cambridge	TL5454 linear	Various Owners
Ceredigion	Dyfi	Aberdovey	SN6094	Countryside Council for Wales
Cumbria	Sandscale Haws	Barrow-in-Furness	SD1975	National Trust
Derbyshire	Millers Dale	Bakewell	SK1473	Derbys WT
Derbyshire	Rose End Meadows	Matlock	SK2956	Derbys WT
Dorset	Badbury Rings	Wimborne Minster	ST9603	National Trust
Dorset	Fontmell Down	Shaftesbury	ST8817	Dorset WT
Essex	Fingringhoe Wick	Colchester	TM0419	Essex WT for Wales
Glamorgan	Parc Slip	Bridgend	SS8884	Glamorgan WT
Gloucestershire	Rodborough Common	Stroud	SO8503	National Trust
Gwynnedd	Aberffraw Dunes	Holyhead	SH3568	N Wales WT
Hampshire	Kingley Vale	Havant	SU8208	English Nature
Hampshire	Martin Down	Fordingbridge	SU0519	English Nature
Hereford	Doward Reserves	Monmouth	SO5415	Hereford WT
Hereford	Leeping Stocks	Monmouth	SO5416	Hereford WT
Hertfordshire	Therfield Heath	Royston	TL3440	Herts CC
Isle of Wight	Compton Down	Freshwater	SZ3685	Hants & IOW WT
Isle of Wight	Martin Down	Fordingbridge	SU0519	English Nature
Kent	Park Gate Down	Ashford	TR1645	Kent WT
Kent	Queendown Warren	Sittingbourne	TQ8262	Kent WT
Kent	Yocklett's Bank	Ashford	TR1247	Kent WT
Lancashire	Crosshill Quarry	Clitheroe	SD7443	Lancs WT
Lancashire	Salthill Quarry	Clitheroe	SD7504	Lancs WT
Lincolnshire	Red Hill	Louth	TF2680	Lincs WT
Lincolnshire	Saltfleetby Dunes	Mablethorpe	TF4790	English Nature
Leicestershire	Cloudwood	Ashby-de-la-Zouch	SK4121	Leics & Rutland WT
Merseyside	Mere Sands Wood	Ormskirk	SD4415	Lancs WT
Norfolk	Holkham	Wells-next-the-Sea	TF8944	English Nature
Norfolk	Holmes Dunes	Hunstanton	TF7044	Norfolk WT
Oxfordshire	Chinnor Hill	Thame	SP7600	Bucks, Beds & Oxon WT
Oxfordshire	Warburg Reserves	Henley-on-Thames	SU7285	Bucks, Beds & Oxon WT
Pembrokeshire	West Williamston	Pembroke	SN0206	National Trust/ W Wales WT
Powys	Bailey Einon	Llandindrod Wells	SO0861	Radnor WT
Surrey	Box Hill	Dorking	TQ1751	National Trust
Sussex	Ditchling Beacon	Lewes	TQ3313	National Trust
Warwickshire	Ufton Field	Leamington Spa	SP3761	Warwicks WT
Wiltshire	Middleton Down	Salisbury	SU0423	Wilts WT
Yorkshire	Burton Riggs	Scarborough	TA0383	Yorks WT

32. Late Spider Orchid

County	Site	Location	NGR	Contact
Kent	Park Gate Down	Ashford	TQ1645	Kent WT
Kent	Wye Downs	Ashford	TR0745	English Nature

33. Early Spider Orchid

County	Site	Location	NGR	Contact
Dorset	Isle of Purbeck	Corfe Castle	SY9582	English Nature & Others
Kent	Lydden Temple Ewell	Dover	TR2745	Kent WT

County	Site	Location	NGR	Contact
Kent	Queendown Warren	Chatham	TQ8262	Kent WT
Kent	Wye Downs	Ashford	TR0745	English Nature
Sussex	South Downs	Petersfield	SU7619-TU6097	Sussex WT

34. Fly Orchid

Avon	Brown's Folly	Bath	ST7966	Avon WT
Bedfordshire	Waresley Wood	Sandy	TL2654	Beds, Cambs, Northants & Peterborough WT
Cleveland	Castle Eden Dene	Peterlee	NZ4349	English Nature
Cumbria	Gait Barrows	Carnforth	SD4877	English Nature
Cumbria	Helsington Barrows	Kendal	SD4990	Cumbria WT
Cumbria	Sizergh Castle	Kendal	SD4988	National Trust
Gloucestershire	Snows Farm	Stroud	SO8808	Glos WT
Hampshire	Martin Down	Fordingbridge	SU0519	English Nature
Hampshire	Old Burghclere	Newbury	SU4757	Hants & IOW WT
Hampshire	Seale Chalk Pit	Aldershot	SU8948	Surrey WT
Kent	Kemsing Downs	Sevenoaks	TQ5559	Kent WT
Kent	Park Gate Down	Ashford	TQ1645	Kent WT
Kent	Queendown Warren	Chatham	TQ8262	Kent WT
Kent	Stockbury Hill	Sittingbourne	TQ8360	Kent WT
Kent	Wye Down	Ashford	TR0745	English Nature
Kent	Yocklett's Bank	Canterbury	TR1247	Kent WT
Lancashire	Gait Barrows	Carnforth	SD4877	English Nature
Oxfordshire	Warburg Reserves	Henley-on-Thames	SU7288	Bucks, Beds & Oxon WT
Sussex	Kingley Vale	Chichester	SU8210	English Nature

36. Lady Orchid

Kent	Park Gate Down	Ashford	TQ16451	Kent WT
Kent	Spong Wood	Ashford/Folkestone	TR1245	Kent WT
Kent	Stockbury Hill Wood	Sittingbourne	TQ8360	Kent WT
Kent	Yocklett's Bank	Canterbury	TR1247	Kent WT

37. Military Orchid

Oxfordshire	Homefield Wood*	Henley-on-Thames	SU8186	Bucks, Beds & Oxon WT
Suffolk	Rex Graham Reserve**	Mildenhall	TL7374	Suffolk WT

* Wardened Site
** Site open one day a year for viewings. Date can vary so contact the Suffolk WT well in advance. There may be a small charge for photography.

38. Monkey Orchid

Kent	Park Gate Down	Ashford	TQ1645	Kent WT
Oxfordshire	Hartslock Reserve	Pangbourne	SU6179	Bucks, Beds & Oxon WT

39. Burnt Orchid

Kent	Lydden Temple Ewell	Dover	TR2745	Kent WT
Kent	Queendown Warren	Chatham	TQ8262	Kent WT
Kent	Wye Downs	Ashford	TR0745	Kent WT

County	Site	Location	NGR	Contact
Sussex	Beachy Head	Eastbourne	TV5896	Eastbourne BC
Sussex	Cuckmere Haven	Seaford	TV5199	East Sussex CC
Sussex	Mount Caburn	Lewes	TQ4409	English Nature
Wiltshire	Coombe Bissett Down	Salisbury	SU1125	Wilts WT
Wiltshire	Great Cheverell Hill*	Salisbury Plain	ST9852	Wilts WT Conversation/ Office of Defence Estates
Wiltshire	Pewsey Down	Devizes	SU1163	English Nature
Yorkshire	Farndale	Kirkby Moorside	SE6697	N Yorks Moors National Park Committee
Yorkshire	Leyburn Old Glebe	Leyburn	SE1084	Yorks WT

* On MOD land, watch out for tanks!

40. Green-Winged Orchid

County	Site	Location	NGR	Contact
Avon	Chew Valley Lake**	Bristol Airport	ST5761	Bristol Waterworks Company
Avon	Hellenge Hill	Weston-super-Mare	ST3497	Avon WT
Avon	Walborough	Weston-super-Mare	ST3158	Avon WT
Bedfordshire	Upwood Meadows	Huntingdon	TL2582	English Nature
Cambridgeshire	Houghton Meadows	St Ives	TL2971	Beds, Cambs, Northants & Peterborough WT
Cambridgeshire	Upwood Meadows	Huntingdon	TL2582	Beds & Hunts Naturalists Trust
Dorset	Badbury Rings	Wimborne Minster	ST9603	National Trust
Derbyshire	Manifold Valley	Ashbourne	SK1054	National Trust
Essex	Langdon	Basildon	TQ6587	Essex WT
Glamorgan	Kenfig Dunes	Bridgend	SS8801	Countryside Council for Wales
Glamorgan	Lavernock Point	Barry	ST1868	Glamorgan WT
Glamorgan	Oxwich Bay	Swansea	SS5086	Countryside Council for Wales
Gloucestershire	Rodborough Common	Stroud	SO8503	National Trust
Gwynnedd	Cors Goch	Bangor	SH5081	N Wales WT
Hampshire	Lower Test Marshes	Southampton	SU3613	Hants & IOW WT
Herefordshire	Doward Group	Monmouth	SU5415	Hereford & Radnor WT
Isle of Wight	Compton Down	Yarmouth	SZ3685	National Trust
Leicestershire	Herberts Meadow	Coalville	SK4912	Leics & Rutland WT
Lincolnshire	Axholme Line	Gainsborough	SE7700	Lincs WT
Leicestershire	Cribbs Meadow	Melton Mowbray	SK8918	National Trust
Lincolnshire	Little Scrubbs Meadow	Wragby	TF1474	
Lincolnshire	Rush Furlong	Epworth	SE7800	Lincs WT
Lincolnshire	Sotby Meadow	Wragby	TF2077	Lincs WT
Norfolk	Hoe Rough	East Dereham	TF9716	Norfolk WT
Norfolk	Buckenham Common	Attleborough	TM0990	Norfolk WT
Sussex	Rye Harbour	Rye	TQ9418	East Sussex CC
Warwickshire	Draycote Meadows	Rugby	SP4470	Warwicks WT
Worcestershire	Wyre Forest	Bewdley	SO7070	Worcs WT
Wiltshire	Clattinger Farm	Cirencester	SU0193	Wilts WT
Wiltshire	Distillery Meadows	Wootton Bassett	SU0384	Wilts WT
Wiltshire	Pewsey Downs	Marlborough	SU1163	English Nature

**Permit required from Bristol Waterworks Co.

County	Site	Location	NGR	Contact
41. Early Purple Orchid				
Avon	Folly Farm	Midsomer Norton	ST6160	Avon WT
Avon	Hellenge Hill	Weston-super-Mare	ST3457	Avon WT
Avon	Walborough	Weston-super-Mare	ST3157	Avon WT
Ayrshire	Auchalton Meadow	Maybole	NS3303	Scottish WT
Ayrshire	Feoch Meadows	Barrhill	NX2682	Scottish WT
Cumbria	St Bees Head	Whitehaven	NX9511	RSPB
Devon	Lower East Lounston	Newton Abbot	SX7975	Devon WT
Dorset	Badbury Rings	Wimborne Minster	ST9603	National Trust
Essex	Danbury Group	Chelmsford	TL7804	Essex WT
Gloucestershire	Rodborough Common	Stroud	SO8503	National Trust
Glamorgan	Cwm Ivy Wood	Swansea	SS4493	Glamorgan WT
Gwynnedd	Cwm Idwal	Bethesda	SH6459	Countryside for Wales
Hampshire	Crab Wood	Winchester	SU4329	Hants & IoW WT
Isle of Wight	Compton Down	Yarmouth	SZ3685	National Trust
Isle of Wight	Tennyson Down	Freshwater	SZ3684	National Trust
Kent	Park Gate Down	Ashford	TQ1645	Kent WT
Kent	Yocklett's Bank	Ashford	TR1349	Kent WT
Lincolnshire	Rigsby Wood	Spilsby	TF4276	Lincs WT
Northamptonshire	King's Wood	Corby	SP8687	Northants WT
Northumberland	East Cramlington Pond	Morpeth	NZ2975	Northumbria WT
Northumberland	Tony's Patch	Haydon Bridge	NY8265	Northumbria WT
Staffordshire	Coombes Valley	Leek	SK0053	RSPB
Suffolk	Bradfield Woods	Bury St Edmonds	TL9358	Suffolk WT
Suffolk	Bulls Wood	Stowmarket	TL9254	Suffolk WT
Suffolk	Groton Wood	Sudbury	TL9743	Suffolk WT
Suffolk	Wolves Wood	Ipswich	TM0544	RSPB
Surrey	Selsdon Wood	Croydon	TQ3661	National Trust
Sussex	Cuckmere Haven	Seaford	TV5199	E Sussex DC
Sussex	Fore Wood	Hastings	TQ7512	RSPB
Sussex	Kiln Wood	Uckfield	TQ5220	Woodland Trust
Tayside	Keltneyburn	Aberfeldy	NN7650	Scottish WT
Wiltshire	Middleton Down	Salisbury	SU0425	Wilts WT
Wiltshire	Ravensroost Wood & Meadows	Malmersbury	SU0287	Wilts WT
Worcestershire	The Knapp and Papermill	Worcester	SO7452	Worcs WT
Yorkshire	Forge Valley Wood	Scarborough	SE9886	English Nature
42. Common Spotted Orchid				
Ayrshire	Culzean Country Park	Ayr	NS2310	National Trust for Scotland
Bedfordshire	Ivinghoe Beacon	Dunstable	SP9512	National Trust
Berkshire	Church Wood	Slough	SU9787	RSPB
Berkshire	Inkpen Common	Newbury	SU3864	BBOWT
Cambridgeshire	Castor Hanglands	Peterborough	TF1102	English Nature
Derbyshire	Manifold Valley	Ashbourne	SK1054	National Trust
Derbyshire	Millers Dale	Buxton	SK1473	Derbys WT
Derbyshire	Rose End Meadows	Matlock	SK2956	Derbys WT
Devon	Little Bradley Ponds	Bovey Tracey	SX8277	Devon WT

County	Site	Location	NGR	Contact
Dorset	Badbury Rings	Wimborne Minster	ST9603	National Trust
Dorset	Powerstock Common	Bridport	SY5496	Dorset WT
Durham	Rosa Shafto	Durham	NZ2435	Durham WT
Durham	Wingate Quarry	Peterlee	NZ3737	Durham CC
Durham	Wilton-le-Wear	Bishop Auckland	NZ1631	Durham WT
Essex	Hatfield Forest	Bishops Stortford	TL5419	National Trust
Gloucestershire	Rodborough Common	Stroud	SO8503	National Trust
Gwynnedd	Caeau Tan y Bwlch	Caernarfon	SH4348	N Wales WT
Hampshire	Crab Wood	Winchester	SU4329	Hants & IOW WT
Herefordshire	Queenswood Country Park	Leominster	SO5151	Hereford & Worcs WT
Kent	Kiln Wood	Ashford	TQ8851	Kent WT
Kent	Yocklett's Bank	Canterbury	TR1247	Kent WT
Lancashire	Crosshill Quarry	Clitheroe	SD4743	Ribble Valley BC
Lancashire	Cuerden Valley Park	Preston	SD5623	Lancs WT
Lancashire	Gait Barrows	Carnforth	SD4877	English Nature
Lancashire	Healey Dell	Rochdale	SD8815	Rochdale MBC
Lancashire	Leighton Moss	Carnforth	SD4775	RSPB
Leicestershire	Ambion Wood	Market Bosworth	SP4099	Bosworth Battlefield Visitor Centre
Leicestershire	Swithlands Woods	Loughborough	SK5312	Leics & Rutland WT
Lincolnshire	Bradley Woods	Grimsby	TA2405	Grimsby BC
Lincolnshire	Snipe Dales	Horncastle	RF3286	Lincs WT
Merseyside	Red Rocks Marsh	Birkenhead	SJ2084	Cheshire WT
Merseyside	Sankey Valley	St Helens	SJ5396	St Helens MBC
Norfolk	Hickling Broad	Stalham	TG4222	Norfolk WT
Northamptonshire	King's Wood	Corby	SP8687	Northants WT
Northamptonshire	Newbottle Spinney	Banbury	SP5136	Northants Trust for Nature Conservancy
Northamptonshire	Salcey Forest	Northampton	SP8151	Northants WT
Northumberland	Beltingham & Williamston	Haltwhistle	NY78-64 NY68-52	Northumbria WT
Northumberland	Lindisfarne	Berwick-upon-Tweed	NU0943	English Nature
Nottinghamshire	Attenborough	Long Eaton	SK5234	Notts WT
Oxfordshire	Aston Rowant	Thame	SP7496	English Nature
Oxfordshire	Dry Sandford Pit	Abingdon	SU4699	Bucks, Beds & Oxon WT
Rutland	Prior's Coppice	Oakham	SK8305	Leics & Rutland WT
Shropshire	Corbet Wood Trail	Shrewsbury	TU5199	Salop WT
Shropshire	Llanymynech Rocks	Oswestry	SJ2621	Montgomery WT
Somerset	Brackett's Coppice	Yeovil	ST5107	Dorset WT
Somerset	Cheddar Gorge	Cheddar	ST4854	Somerset WT
Staffordshire	Cannock Chase	Stafford	SJ9784	Staffs CC
Staffordshire	Coombes Valley	Leek	SK0053	RSPB
Strathclyde	Lochwinnoch	Paisley	NS3538	RSPB Scotland
Suffolk	Minsmere	Aldeburgh	TM4767	RSPB
Suffolk	Wolves Wood	Ipswich	TM0544	RSPB
Sussex	Fore Wood	Hastings	TQ7512	RSPB
Sussex	Mallydam's Wood	Hastings	TQ8512	RSPCA

County	Site	Location	NGR	Contact
Sussex	Wood's Mill	Hove	TQ2113	Sussex WT
Wiltshire	Distillery Meadows	Malmesbury	SU0389	Wilts WT
Wiltshire	Jones Mill	Pewsey	SU1761	Wilts WT
Wiltshire	Middleton Down	Salisbury	SU0423	Wilts WT
Wiltshire	Ravenscroft	Malmesbury	SU0287	Wilts WT
Wiltshire	Red Lodge Pond	Swindon	SU0588	Wilts WT
Worcestershire	The Knapp & Papermill	Worcester	SO7452	Worcs WT

43. Heath Spotted Orchid

County	Site	Location	NGR	Contact
Anglesey	Penrhosfeilw Common	Holyhead	SH2280	RSPB
Avon	Folly Farm	Bristol	ST6160	Avon WT
Ayrshire	Auchalton Meadow	Maybole	NS3303	Scottish WT
Ayrshire	Feoch Meadows	Barrhill	NX2682	Scottish WT
Ceredigion	Dyfi	Aberdovey	SN6094	Countryside Council for Wales
Devon	Meshaw Moss	Tiverton	SS7618	Devon WT
Devon	Rackenford & Knowstone Moors	Tiverton	SS8521	Devon WT
Devon	The Rough	Honiton	ST1704	Devon WT
Devon	Vealand Farm	Bude	SS2806	Devon WT
Devon	Volehouse Moor	Clovelly	SS3417	Devon WT
Gwynnedd	Caeau Tan y Bwlch	Caernarfon	SH4348	N Wales WT
Gwynnedd	South Stack	Holyhead	SH2082	RSPB
Kent	Hothfield Common	Ashford	TQ9645	Kent WT
Leicestershire	Lea Meadows	Leicester	SK5011	Leics & Rutland WT
Leicestershire	Ulverscroft	Coalville	SK4912	Leics & Rutland WT
Powys	Burfa Bog	Presteigne	SO2761	Radnor WT
Perth & Kinross	Keltneyburn	Aberfeldy	NN7656	Scottish WT
Wiltshire	Disillery Meadows	Malmesbury	SU0389	Wilts WT

44. Early Marsh Orchid

County	Site	Location	NGR	Contact
Borders	Lindean Reservoir	Selkirk	NT5128	Borders Regional Council
Buckinghamshire	Tring Reservoir	Aylesbury	SP9114	English Nature
Cambridgeshire	Castor Hanglands	Peterborough	TF1102	English Nature
Ceredigion	Dyfi	Aberdovey	SN6094	Countryside Council for Wales
Cumbria	Sandscale Haws	Barrow-in-Furness	SD2075	National Trust
Dorset	Higher Hyde Heath	Dorchester	SY8590	Dorset WT
Huntingdonshire	St Neots Common	St Neots	TL1861	Various bodies
Lancashire	Ainsdale Dunes	Southport	SD2910	English Nature
Lancashire	Lytham St Annes Dunes	Blackpool	SD3030	Lytham BC
Lincolnshire	Saltfleetby Dunes	Mablethorpe	TF4692	English Nature
Lothian	Aberlady Bay	North Berwick	NT4680	East Lothian DC
Norfolk	Thompson Common	Thetford	TL9496	Norfolk WT
Northumberland	Lindisfarne	Berwick-upon-Tweed	NU0943	National Trust
Oxfordshire	Dry Sandford Pit	Abingdon	SU4699	BBOWT
Powys	Llyn Mawr	Newtown	SO0197	Montgomery WT
Suffolk	Lakenheath Poors Fen	Mildenhall	TL7383	Suffolk WT

County	Site	Location	NGR	Contact
45. Southern Marsh Orchid				
Avon	Netcotts Meadow	Nailsea	ST4769	Avon WT
Buckinghamshire	Tring Reservoirs	Tring	SP9114	English Nature
Cornwall	Redmoor	Bodmin	SX0762	Cornwall WT
Derbyshire	Hilton Reserve	Derby	SK2431	Derbys WT
Devonshire	Little Bradley Ponds	Bovey Tracey	SX8277	Devon WT
Devonshire	Meshaw Moor	Tiverton	SS7618	Devon WT
Devonshire	New Cross Pond	Kingteignton	SX8673	Devon WT
Devonshire	Swanpool Marsh	Braunton	SS4736	Devon WT
Gower	Oxwich	Swansea	SS5086	Countryside Council for Wales
Hampshire	Winnan Moors	Winchester	SU4930	Hants & IOW WT
Huntingdonshire	St Neots Common	Huntingdon	TL1861	Various Bodies
Kent	Sandwich Bay	Ramsgate	TR3562	Kent WT
Lancashire	Healey Dell	Rochdale	SD8715	Rochdale MBC
Lancashire	Leighton Moss	Carnforth	SD4775	RSPB
Lancashire	Mere Sands Woods	Ormskirk	SD4418	Lancs WT
Lancashire	Ribble Marshes	Southport	SD3020	English Nature
Lincolnshire	Whisby Nature Park	Lincoln	SK9166	Lincs WT
Lincolnshire	Saltfleetby Dunes	Mablethorpe	TF4790	English Nature
Merseyside	Red Rocks Marsh	West Kirby	SJ2088	Cheshire WT
Norfolk	Chedgrave Common	Loddon	TM3799	English Nature
Norfolk	East Winch Common	Kings Lynn	TF6916	Norfolk WT
Norfolk	Strumpshaw Fen	Norwich	TG3406	RSPB
Norfolk	Thompson Common	Walton	TL9496	Norfolk WT
Nottinghamshire	Daneshill Lakes	East Retford	SK6686	Notts WT
Northumberland	Thornley Wood	Newcastle-upon-Tyne	NZ1760	Gateshead MBC
Somerset	Catcott Heath & Lows	Bridgwater	ST3914	Somerset WT
Staffordshire	Cannock Chase	Rugeley	SK0117	Staffs CC
Suffolk	Lakenheath Poors Fen	Mildenhall	TL7383	Suffolk WT
Suffolk	Minsmere	Aldeburgh	TM4767	RSPB
Surrey	Thursley	Godalming	SU9040	English Nature
Warwickshire	Alvecote Pools	Tamworth	SK2603	Warwicks WT
Wiltshire	Jones Mill	Pewsey	SU1661	Wilts WT
Wiltshire	North Meadow	Cricklade	SU0994	English Nature
Wiltshire	Smallbrook Meadow	Warminster	ST8844	Wilts WT
Yorkshire	Carlton Marsh	Cudworth	SE3709	Barnsley MBC
46. Northern Marsh Orchid				
Angus	Seaton Cliffs	Arbroath	NO6641	Scottish WT
Argyll & Bute	Taynish	Lochgilphead	NR7384	Scottish Natural Heritage
Ayrshire	Auchalton Meadow	Maybole	NS3303	Scottish WT
Ayrshire	Feoch Meadows	Barrhill	NX2682	Scottish WT
Ceredigion	Dyfi	Aberdovey	SN6094	Countryside Council for Wales
Durham	Witton-le-Wear	Bishop Auckland	NZ1631	Durham WT
East Lothian	Aberlady Bay	North Berwick	NT4681	East Lothian DC
Gwynnedd	Aberffraw Dunes	Anglesey	SH3568	Countryside Council for Wales
Gwynnedd	Cors Goch	Anglesey	SH5081	N Wales WT

County	Site	Location	NGR	Contact
Highlands & Island	Handa Island (boat access)	Scourie	NC1348	RSPB Scotland
Lancashire	Gait Barrow	Carnforth	SD4877	English Nature
Lancashire	Healey Dell	Rochdale	SD8715	Rochdale MBC
Northumberland	Arnold	Craster	NU2519	Northumbria WT
Northumberland	Beltingham & Williamston	Haltwhistle	NY7864	Northumbria WT
Northumberland	Lindisfarne	Berwick-upon-Tweed	NU0943	English Nature
Perth & Kinross	Keltneyburn	Aberfeldy	NN7650	Scottish WT
Powys	Llyn Mawr	Newtown	SO0097	N Wales WT

47. Hebridean Marsh Orchid

Outer Hebrides	Balranald *(s.s p. scotia)*	N. Uist	NF7070	RSPB Scotland

48. Narrow- leaved Marsh Orchid

Gwynnedd	Cors Erddreiniog	SH4782	Benllech	Countryside Council for Wales

50. Man Orchid

Cambridgeshire	Barnack Hills & Holes	Stamford	TF0704	English Nature
Kent	Queendown Warren	Sittingbourne	TQ8262	Kent WT
Kent	Wye Downs	Ashford	TR0745	English Nature
Surrey	Box Hill	Dorking	TQ1751	Surrey WT
Surrey	Headley Warren	Leatherhead	TQ1953	Surrey WT
Warwickshire	Ufton Fields	Leamington Spa	SP3761	Warwicks WT

51. Pyramidal Orchid

Ceredigion	Dyfi	Aberdovey	SS5086	Countryside Council for Wales
Wiltshire	Pepperbox Hill	Salisbury	SU2124	National Trust
Wiltshire	Pewsey Down	Devizes	SU1163	English Nature
Yorkshire	Spurn Peninsula	Hull	TA4115	Yorks WT

Appendix 1
Contact details for the UK Wildlife Trusts

As a courtesy, permission should be requested to visit any site.

Avon Wildlife Trust
The Wildlife Centre, 32 Jacob's Wells Road,
Bristol, BS8 1DR.
Tel: 0117 9 268018.
Email: avonwt@cix.compulink.co.uk

The Wildlife Trust for Bedfordshire, Cambridgeshire, Northamptonshire & Peterborough
3B Langford Arch, London Road, Sawston, Cambridge, CB2 4EE.
Tel: 01223 712400.
Email: cambswt@cix.co.uk

Berkshire, Buckinghamshire & Oxfordshire Wildlife Trust
The Lodge, 1 Armstrong Road, Littlemore,
Oxford OX4 4XT.
Tel: 01865775476.
Email: bbowt@cix.co.uk

The Wildlife Trust for Birmingham & the Black Country
Unit 310, Jubilee Trade Centre, 130 Pershore St,
Birmingham, B5 6ND.
Tel: 0121 666 7474.
Email: urbanwt@cix.co.uk

Brecknock Wildlife Trust
Lion House, Bethel Square, Brecon, Powys, LD3 7AY.
Tel: 01874 625708.
Email: brecknockwt@cix.co.uk

Cheshire Wildlife Trust
Grebe House, Reaseheath, Nantwich,
Cheshire, CW5 6DG.
Tel: 01270 610180.
Email: cheshirewt@cix.co.uk

Cornwall Wildlife Trust
Five Acres, Allet, Truro, Cornwall, TR4 9DJ.
Tel: 01872 273939.
Email: cornwt@cix.co.uk

Cumbria Wildlife Trust
Brockhole, Windermere, Cumbria, LA23 1LJ.
Tel: 015394 48280.
Email: cumbriawt@cix.co.uk

Derbyshire Wildlife Trust
Elvaston Castle, Derby, DE72 3EP.
Tel: 01332 756610.
Email:derbywt@cix.co.uk

Devon Wildlife Trust
Shirehampton House, 35-37 St David's Hill, Exeter,
Devon EX4 4DA.
Tel: 01392 279244.
Email: devonwt:cix.co.uk

Dorset Wildlife Trust
Brooklands Farm, Forston, Dorchester, DT2 7AA.
Tel: 01305 264620.
Email: dorsetwt@cix.co.uk

Durham Wildlife Trust
Rainton Meadows, Chilton Moor, Houghton-le-Spring,
Tyne & Wear, DH4 6PU.
Tel: 0191 584 3112.
Email: durhamwt@cix.co.uk

Essex Wildlife Trust
Fingringhoe Wick Nature Reserve, Fingringhoe,
Colchester, Essex, CO5 7DN.
Tel: 01206 729678.
Email: admin@essexwt.org.uk

Glamorgan Wildlife Trust
Nature Centre, Fountain Road, Tondu, Mid-Glamorgan,
CF32 OEH.
Tel: 01656 724100.
Email: glamorganwt@cix.co.uk

Gloucestershire Wildlife Trust
Dulverton Building, Robinswood Hill Country Park,
Reservoir Road, Gloucester, GL4 6SX.
Tel: 01452 383333.
Email: gmcg@cix.co.uk

Gwent Wildlife Trust
16 White Swan Court, Church Street, Monmouth,
Gwent, NP25 3NY.
Tel: 01600 715501.
Email: gwentwildlife@cix.co.uk

Hampshire & Isle of Wight Wildlife Trust
8 Romsey Road, Eastleigh, Hampshire, SO50 9AL.
Tel: 01703 613636/613737.
Email: hampswt@cix.co.uk

Herefordshire Nature Trust
Lower House Farm, Ledbury Road,
Tupsley, Hereford, HR1 1UT.
Tel: 01432 356872.
Email: herefordwt@cix.co.uk

Hertfordshire & Middlesex Wildlife Trust
Grebe House, St Michael's Street, St Albans,
Herts, AL3 4SN.
Tel: 01727 858901.
Email: hertswt@cix.co.uk

Kent Wildlife Trust
Tyland Barn, Sandling, Maidstone, Kent, ME14 3BD.
Tel: 01622 662012.
Email: kentwildlife@cix.co.uk

Lancashire Wildlife Trust
Cuerden Park Wildlife Centre, Shady Lane, Bamber
Bridge, Preston, Lancs. PR5 6AU.
Tel: 01772 324129.
Email: lancswt@cix.compulink.co.uk

Leicestershire & Rutland Wildlife Trust
1 West Street, Leicester, LE1 6UU.
Tel: 01162 553904.
Email: leicswt@cix.compulink.co.uk

The Lincolnshire Trust
Vanovallum House, Manor House Street, Horncastle,
Lincolnshire LN 5HF.
Tel: 01507 526667.
Email: lincstrust@cix.compulink.co.uk

London Wildlife Trust
Harling House, 47-51 Great Suffolk Street,
London, SE1 0BS. Tel: 0207 261 0447.
Email: londonwt@cix.compulink.co.uk

Manx Wildlife Trust
Conservation Centre, The Courtyard, Tynwald Mills,
St Johns, Isle of Man.
Tel: 01624 801985.
Email: manxwt@cix.co.uk

Montgomeryshire Wildlife Trust
Collott House, 20 Severn Street, Welshpool,
Powys, SY21 7AD.
Tel: 01938 555654.
Email: montwt@cix.compulink.co.uk

Norfolk Wildlife Trust
72 Cathedral Close, Norwich, Norfolk, NR1 4DF.
Tel: 01603 625540.
Email: nwt@cix.compulink.co.uk

Northumberland Wildlife Trust
The Garden House, St Nicholas Park, Jubilee Road,
Newcastle upon Tyne, NE3 3XT.
Tel: 0191 284 6884.
Email: northwildlife@cix.compulink.co.uk

North Wales Wildlife Trust
376 High Street, Bangor, Gwynedd, LL57 1YE.
Tel: 01248 351541.
Email: nwwt@cix.compulink.co.uk

Nottinghamshire Wildlife Trust
The Old Ragged School, Brook Street,
Nottingham, NG1 1EA.
Tel: 0115 958 8242.
Email: nottswt@cix.compulink.co.uk

Radnorshire Wildlife Trust
Warwick House, High Street, Llandrindod Wells,
Powys, LD1 6AG.
Tel: 01597 823298.
Email: radnorshirewt@cix.compulink.co.uk

Scottish Wildlife Trust
Cramond House, Kirk Cramond, Cramond Glebe Rd,
Edinburgh, EH4 6NS.
Tel: 0131 312 7765.
Email: scottishwt@cix.compulink.co.uk

Sheffield Wildlife Trust
Wood Lane House, 52 Wood Lane, Sheffield, S6 5HF.
Tel: 0114231 0120.
Email: sheffieldwt@cix.co.uk

Shropshire Wildlife Trust
167 Frankwell, Shrewsbury, Shropshire, SY3 8LG.
Tel: 01743 241691.
Email: shropshirewt@ cix.co.uk

Somerset Wildlife Trust
Fyne Court, Broomfield, Bridgwater,
Somerset, TA5 2EQ.
Tel: 01823 451587.
Email: somwt@cix.co.uk

Staffordshire Wildlife Trust
Coutts House, Sandon, Staffordshire, ST18 ODN.
Tel: 01889 508534/509800.
Email: staffswt@cix.co.uk

Suffolk Wildlife Trust
Brooke House, The Green, Ashbocking, Nr Ipswich,
Suffolk, IP6 9JY.
Tel: 01473 890089.
Email: suffolkwt@cix.co.uk

Surrey Wildlife Trust
School Lane, Pirbright, Woking, Surrey, GU24 OJN.
Tel: 01483 488055.
Email: surreywt@cix.co.uk

Sussex Wildlife Trust
Woods Mill, Shoreham Road, Henfield,
West Sussex, BN5 9SD.
Tel: 01273 492630.
Email: sussexwt@cix.co.uk

Tees Valley Wildlife Trust
Bellamy Pavilion, Kirkleatham Old Hall, Kirkleatham,
Redcar, Cleveland, TS10 5NW.
Tel: 01642 759900.
Email: clevelandwt@cix.co.uk

Ulster Wildlife Trust
3 New Line, Crossgar, Co. Down, BT30 9EP.
Tel: 01396 830282.
Email: ulsterwt@cix.co.uk

Warwickshire Wildlife Trust
Brandon Marsh Nature Centre, Brandon Lane,
Coventry, CV3 3GW.
Tel: 01203 302912.
Email: warkswt@cix.co.uk

The Wildlife Trust: West Wales
7 Market Street, Haverfordwest, Dyfed, SA61 1NF.
Tel: 01437 765462.
Email: wildlife@wildlife-wales.org.uk

Wiltshire Wildlife Trust
Elm Tree Court, Long Street, Devizes,
Wiltshire, SN10 1NJ.
Tel: 01380 725670.
Email: wiltwt@cix.co.uk

Worcestershire Wildlife Trust
Lower Smite Farm, Smite Hill, Hindlip,
Worcester, WR3 8SZ.
Tel: 01905 754919.
Email: worcswt@cix.co.uk

Yorkshire Wildlife Trust
10 Toft Green, York, YO1 6JT.
Tel: 01904 659570.
Email: yorkshirewt@cix.co.uk

Appendix 2
Contact details for English Nature

Head Office
English Nature, Northminster House,
Peterborough PE1 1UA.
Tel: 01733 455100.
Email: enquiries @ english-nature.org.uk

Northumbria Team
Tel: 01661 845500.
Email: northumbria@english-nature.org.uk

Cumbria Team
Tel: 01539 792800.
Email: cumbria@english-nature.org.uk

North-West Team
Tel: 01942 820342.
Email: northwest@english-nature.org.uk

N & E Yorkshire Team
Tel: 01904 435500.
Email: york@english-nature.org.uk

Humber/Pennines Team
Tel: 01924 387010.
Email: humber.pennines@english-nature.org.uk

East Midlands Team
Tel: 01476 568431.
Email: ingrid.green@english-nature.org.uk

Peak District & Derbyshire Team
Tel: 01629 815095.
Email: julie.green@english-nature.org.uk

West Midlands Team
Tel: 01743 709611.
Email: wmt.en.ap@gtnet.gor.uk

Three Counties Team (Glos, Hereford, Worcs)
Tel: 01531 638500.
Email: three.counties@english-nature.org.uk

Bedfordshire, Cambs & Northants Team
Tel: 01733 405850.
Email: beds.cambs.nhants@english-nature.org.uk

Norfolk Team
Tel: 01603 620558.
Email: norfolk@english-nature.org.uk

Suffolk Team
Tel: 01284 762218.
Email: suffolk@english-nature.org.uk

Essex, Herts & London Team
Tel: 01206 796666.
Email: essex.herts@english-nature.org.uk

Kent Team
Tel: 01233 812525.
Email: donna.hills@english-nature.org.uk

Sussex & Surrey Team
Tel: 01273 476595.
Email: sussex.surrey@english-nature.org.uk

Thames & Chilterns Team
Tel: 01635 268881.
Email: thames.chilterns@english-nature.org.uk

Hampshire & Isle of Wight Team
Tel: 02380 283944.
Email: hants.iwight@english-nature.org.uk

Wiltshire Team
Tel: 01380 726344.
Email: wiltshire@english-nature.org.uk

Dorset Team
Tel: 01929 556688.
Email: dorset@english-nature.org.uk

Somerset Team
Tel: 01823 283211.
Email: linda.kingston@english-nature.org.uk

Devon Team
Tel: 01837 55045.
Email: devon@english-nature.org.uk

Cornwall & Scilly Isles Team
Tel: 01872 262550.
Email: cornwall@english-nature.org.uk

Appendix 3
Contact details for the National Trust

Head Office
The National Trust, 36 Queen Anne's Gate,
London SW1H 9AS.
Tel: 020 8315 1111.
Email: enquiries@ntrust.org.uk.
Website: www.nationaltrust.org.uk

English Regional Offices:

Cornwall
Tel: 01208 74281

Devon
Tel: 01392 881691

East Anglia
Tel: 01263 733471

East Midlands
Tel: 01909 486411

Kent & East Sussex
Tel: 01892 890651

Mercia
Tel: 01743 708100

North-West
Tel: 015394 35599

Northumbria
Tel: 01670 774691

Severn
Tel: 01684 850051

Southern
Tel: 01372 453401

Thames & Chilterns
Tel: 01494 528051

Wessex
Tel: 01985 843600

Yorkshire
Tel: 01904 702021

National Trust for Scotland
28 Charlotte Square, Edinburgh EH2 4ET.
Tel: 0131 226 5922

National Trust, Wales Office
Trinity Square, Llandudno, Gwynedd LL30 2DE.
Tel: 01492 860123

National Trust, Northern Ireland Office
Rowallane House, Saintfield, Ballynahinch,
Co. Down BT24 7LH.
Tel: 01238 510721

Appendix 4
Contact details for councils and other organizations

Barnsley Metropolitan Borough Council, Town Hall, Barnsley, S. Yorks S70 2TA

Borders Regional Council, Planning Department, Newton Boswells, Roxburghshire TD6 OSA

Bristol Waterworks Company, Recreations Department, Woodford Lodge, Chew Stoke, Bristol BS18 8XH

Clan Donald Lands Trust, Visitor Centre, Armadale Castle, Sleat, Isle of Skye

Countryside Council for Wales, Plas Penrhos, Ffordd Penrhos, Bangor, Gwynedd LL57 2LQ

Defence Estates Organisation, Conservation Department, St George's House, Blakemore Drive, Sutton Coldfield, W. Midlands B95 7RL

Dorset County Council, County Hall, Colliton Park, Dorchester DT1 1X

Durham County Council, County Hall, Durham DH1 5UF

Eastbourne Borough Council, Town Hall, Eastbourne, Sussex BN21 4UG

East Lothian District Council, Tourism Department, Brunton Hall, Musselburgh EH21 6AF

East Sussex County Council, Pelham House, St Andrew's Lane, Lewes, BN7 1UN

The Environment & Heritage Service, Commonwealth House, Castle Street, Belfast BT1 1GU

Essex County Council, Conservation Department, Chelmsford, Essex CM1 1LF

Forestry Commission, 231 Corstophine Road, Edinburgh EH12 7AT

Gateshead Metropolitan Borough Council, Civic Centre, Regent Street, Gateshead NE8 1HH

Gloucestershire County Council, Shire Hall, Gloucester GL1 2TG

Grimsby Borough Council/N.E. Lincs Council, Town Hall Square, Great Grimsby, Lincs DN31 1HU

Hampshire County Council, The Castle, Winchester SO23 8UJ

Hereford & Worcester County Council, New County Office, Farrier Street, Worcester WR1 3BH

Hertfordshire County Council, Peg's Lane, Hertford SG13 8DE

Lake District National Park Centre, Brockhole, Windermere, Cumbria

Lytham/Fylde Borough Council, Town Hall, Lytham St Annes, Fylde, FY8 1LW

Newbury/W. Berkshire District Council, Council Offices, Market Street, Newbury RG14 5LD

Northumbria Natural History Society, The Hancock Museum, Newcastle-upon-Tyne NE2 4PT

North Yorks Moors National Park Committee, The Old Vicarage, Bondgate, Helmsley, York YO6 5B

Peak Park Joint Planning Board, Aldern House, Baslow Road, Bakewell, Derbyshire DE4 1AE

Ribble Valley Borough Council, Council Offices, Church Walk, Clitheroe, Lancashire BB7 2RA

Rochdale Metropolitan Borough Council, Town Hall, Rochdale, Greater Manchester OL16 1AB

Rothiemurchus Estate, By Aviemore, Invernesshire PH22 1QH

RSPB, The Lodge, Sandy, Bedfordshire SG19 2DL

RSPB for Scotland, 17 Regent Terrace, Edinburgh EH7 5BN

Scottish Natural Heritage, 12 Hope Terrace, Edinburgh EH9 2AS

Sedgemoor District Council, Bridgwater House, King Square, Bridgwater, Somerset TA6 3AR

Snowdonia National Park Committee, Penrhyndeudraeth, Gwynedd LL48 6LS

St Helens Metropolitan Borough Council, Town Hall, Victoria Square, St Helens, Merseyside WA10 1HP

Staffordshire County Council, County Building, Stafford ST16 2LH

The Woodland Trust, Westgate, Grantham, Lincs NG31 6LL